Developing a Professional Teaching Portfolio

Developing a Professional Teaching Portfolio

A Guide for Success

THIRD EDITION

Patricia M. Costantino
University of Maryland

Marie N. De Lorenzo
University of Maryland

with

Christy Tirrell-Corbin
University of Maryland

Upper Saddle River, New Jersey
Columbus, Ohio

Library of Congress Cataloging-in-Publication Data

Costantino, Patricia M.
Developing a professional teaching portfolio : a guide for success /
Patricia M. Costantino, Marie N. De Lorenzo with Christy Tirrell-Corbin. — 3rd ed.
p. cm.
Includes bibliographical references and index.
ISBN-13: 978-0-205-60857-7 (alk. paper)
ISBN-10: 0-205-60857-4 (alk. paper)
1. Teachers—Rating of—United States. 2. Teachers—Training of—United States. 3. Portfolios in education—United States. I. De Lorenzo, Marie N. II. Tirrell-Corbin, Christy. III. Title.

LB1728.C67 2009
371.14'4—dc22 2008026134

Executive Editor and Publisher: *Stephen D. Dragin*
Series Editorial Assistant: *Anne Whittaker*
Marketing Manager: *Erica DeLuca*
Production Editor: *Gregory Erb*
Editorial Production Service: *Publishers' Design and Production Services, Inc.*
Composition Buyer: *Linda Cox*
Manufacturing Buyer: *Megan Cochran*
Cover Designer: *Linda Knowles*

This book was set in Palatino by Publishers' Design & Production Services, Inc. It was printed and bound by Bind-Rite Graphics. The cover was printed by Phoenix Color Corporation/Hagerstown.

Pearson Education Ltd., London
Pearson Education Singapore Pte. Ltd
Pearson Education Canada, Ltd.
Pearson Education—Japan
Pearson Education Australia PTY. Limited
Pearson Education North Asia Ltd.
Pearson Educación de Mexico, S.A. de C.V.
Pearson Education Malaysia Pte. Ltd.

10 9 8 7 6 5 4 3 2 1

Merrill
is an imprint of

www.pearsonhighered.com

ISBN-13: 978-0-205-60857-7
ISBN-10: 0-205-60857-4

This book is dedicated to our families
for their love and support.

About the Authors

Patricia Costantino received her B.A. and M.Ed. from the University of Maryland at College Park. She taught in the Montgomery County and Prince George's County, Maryland school systems for six years prior to her appointment as the Coordinator for the University of Maryland/Prince George's County Elementary Professional Development Schools. During this time, Ms. Costantino served as a statewide consultant on Mastery Teaching, Supervision, Peer Coaching, and Portfolio Development. She has been recognized by the Maryland Association of Teacher Educators (MATE) for the Most Innovative Staff Development Program and also received an award, with her team of colleagues, from the National Association of Teacher Educators (ATE) for the Most Distinguished Program in Teacher Education, "The Teaching Effectiveness Network." Ms. Costantino has served on the Professional Standards and Teacher Education Board for the State of Maryland and was the President of MATE for several years. After leaving her position as a Professional Development School Coordinator, she became the Director of the Office of Laboratory Experiences for the College of Education at the University of Maryland, overseeing the Professional Development School partnerships between local school systems and the college and the placement of student teachers for the early childhood, elementary, secondary, and special education certification programs. Ms. Costantino is currently the Director of Alumni Relations for the College of Education at the University of Maryland.

Marie De Lorenzo received her B.A. from Montclair State College, now University, and M.Ed. in Educational Communication from the University of Maryland at College Park. She served as the early childhood/elementary education placement coordinator in the Office of Laboratory Experiences at the University of Maryland for twenty-five years, where she worked closely with the local school systems to arrange early field experiences and student teaching placements. During the latter part of her career, Ms. De Lorenzo became interested in portfolio development for pre-service and in-service teachers and conducted several workshops and seminars with students and teachers on the process of developing a professional teaching portfolio as well as the development of e-portfolios. She and Ms. Costantino presented numerous workshops on the development of professional teaching portfolios throughout the state of Maryland. In addition, she presented several papers at various International Society for Teacher Education seminars in England, Germany, the Netherlands, South Africa, and Taiwan on the topics of Integrating Computer Technology into the Pre-service Field Experience; Developing a Professional Portfolio: A Model for Pre-service and In-service Teachers; Portfolio Development: Phases and Assessment; Developing a Professional Portfolio: A Focus on the Teacher Candidate; and the Beginning Teacher. Ms. De Lorenzo retired from the University in 2002.

Christy Tirrell-Corbin received her B.A. from Connecticut College and Ph.D. from the University of Maryland at College Park. Dr. Tirrell-Corbin has worked in the field of teacher education for more than twenty-five years, having served as a University Supervisor and Professional Development Schools Coordinator. She currently serves as the Director of Early Childhood Teacher Education and the College of Education Honors Program at the University of Maryland. In addition to teaching undergraduate and graduate courses, she facilitates inquiry groups in professional development schools in partnership with the Early Childhood Education program and serves on a School Leadership Team. Dr. Tirrell-Corbin's areas of expertise include parent-teacher relationships, student achievement in professional development schools, No Child Left Behind, and the sociocultural world of the child. She has received a number of awards, but most recently received the College of Education Excellence in Teaching Award and was named as a Phillip Merrill Distinguished Faculty Mentor. Dr. Tirrell-Corbin is a member of the American Educational Research Association, Society for Research in Child Development, and the National Association for the Education of Young Children.

Contents

Preface

The field of teacher education and the K–12 sector have changed considerably since the first edition of this book in 2002 and even more so since the publication of the second edition in 2006. Technology has infiltrated all aspects of our society, which has resulted in the majority of teacher candidates growing up with computers as the tool through which most, if not all, is accomplished. Moreover, the focus on high-stakes accountability has increased the emphasis on standards as the framework for the planning, delivery, and assessment of instruction.

However, the advances in digital technology and emphasis on accountability have not changed the fundamental importance of becoming a skilled and reflective teacher, which was the objective in the first edition. Good teaching is and will always be a matter of sound planning and preparation, able classroom management, attention to quality instruction, and taking responsibility for continuous professional growth. Documenting these qualities in a professional portfolio, whether paper or electronic, continues to be the objective of this book. This edition emphasizes a strong relationship between INTASC (Interstate New Teacher Assessment and Support Consortium) standards, as well as specialized program area standards and portfolio evidence.

In response to the most significant educational change of our time, the implementation of the No Child Left Behind (NCLB) legislation of 2002, this edition reflects the major impact of NCLB on K–12 education, teacher education, and the continued professional development of practicing teachers. For example, Chapter 2 discusses the pillars of NCLB as important elements of portfolio development as well as the cycle of data-driven instruction expected in public schools across the country. Chapter 3 reflects increased attention to e-portfolio development, independently and through the use of Web-based software programs frequently purchased by school systems and higher education institutions.

Chapters 4, 5, and 6 guide the reader through the phases of portfolio development. The appendixes provide worksheets to facilitate the process of selecting artifacts, writing reflections, and evaluating the portfolio. Chapter 7 is a collection of examples taken from pre-service and in-service teacher portfolios to stimulate your thinking about how to represent your artifacts in support of professional standards. We believe this book to be a comprehensive manual for the development of a portfolio whether you are a student immersed in a teacher education program or a practicing teacher with years of experience.

The authors express their deep gratitude to Dr. Christy Tirrell-Corbin, University of Maryland, College Park, for her contributions to the revision of this book. Dr. Corbin's knowledge of teacher education, the impact of NCLB, the use of data-driven instruction, and e-portfolio development has been an invaluable asset. We also want to thank Ms. Deborah L. Davis, Technology Liaison, Martin Luther King, Jr., Middle School, Prince George's County, Maryland, for her review of the information related to e-portfolio development and Steve Pragel, University of Maryland, for his suggestions. In addition, we appreciate the willingness of teachers who gave permission to use their portfolio documents in the examples section of this book. The names of these individuals are cited with their document. We would also like to thank the following reviewers for their time and input: Amity Currie, Marist College; Kelly Moore Dunn, New Hampshire Technical Institute; Cynthia G. Kruger, University of Massachusetts, Dartmouth; and Teresa Sychterz, Kutztown University.

We remain convinced that the process and product of portfolio development comprise one of the most meaningful activities that teachers can pursue for their own professional growth. Portfolio development is one of the most effective vehicles for capturing the essence of a teacher's work and performance. We hope that this revised edition will be a valued resource in your professional library.

Patricia M. Costantino
Marie N. De Lorenzo

Developing a Professional Teaching Portfolio

CHAPTER 1

Understanding the Concept

Introduction

The use of a professional teaching portfolio has become increasingly valued in the field of education. School systems and teacher education institutions consider portfolio development a worthwhile process for documenting teaching performance, fostering professional growth, and facilitating reflective thinking. A paper or electronic portfolio, often referred to as an *e-portfolio*[1] is one of the many approaches that may be considered to determine the effectiveness of a teacher. When a portfolio is used in conjunction with other forms of assessment, it can provide a broader perspective of a teacher's full range of professional competencies.

Because of the widespread expectation inherent in portfolios, we have developed this handbook to help you understand the concept of a professional teaching portfolio and to assist you in the process of developing a paper or electronic portfolio. This set of practical guidelines includes information and materials to help prospective and practicing teachers communicate their teaching effectiveness and professional accomplishments through a portfolio. It provides information for creating a meaningful and useful portfolio relevant to your purpose. These guidelines may be adapted to many types of educational personnel; however, the focus of this handbook is primarily on the use of portfolios for:

Pre-service Teacher Candidates Who

- are required to develop a portfolio to document their professional growth and learning
- are seeking initial employment and choose to use a portfolio to enhance the job search and interview process

[1]The terms *electronic portfolio* and *e-portfolio* are used interchangeably throughout this book.

In-service Teachers Who

- are documenting their teaching performance as a component of the teacher evaluation process
- are fulfilling recertification or continuing professional development requirements
- are seeking career advancement, making lateral moves within the school system, or relocating and choosing to use a portfolio to enhance this process

The information, worksheets, and examples in this handbook are designed to increase your understanding of:

- the concept of a professional teaching portfolio
- the importance of using performance standards as a framework for portfolio documentation
- the electronic portfolio
- the phases of portfolio development
- the variety of documents that can be included in a paper or electronic portfolio

What Is a Professional Teaching Portfolio?

A professional teaching portfolio is an organized, goal-driven set of documents[2] that provide evidence of a teacher's knowledge, dispositions, and skills. It is an evolving collection of carefully selected or created documents that are accompanied by reflection and self-assessment. In general, the teaching portfolio provides authentic evidence of a teacher's work and is a vehicle for fostering reflection on the art and practice of teaching.

Types of Portfolios

There are many kinds of portfolios developed by teacher education candidates and practicing teachers. The types of portfolios described in this handbook are parallel in definition to portfolios discussed throughout the literature. Although different terms may be used, the intent is similar. The following information will clarify several types of portfolios that are typically used by pre-service and in-service teachers.[3]

Pre-service Teacher Portfolios

The ongoing nature of the portfolio development process provides the opportunity for teacher candidates, college faculty, mentor teachers, and

[2]The terms *documents, artifacts, assets, entries, evidence, examples, items,* and *materials* are used interchangeably when referring to the contents of a portfolio.
[3]For the purpose of this handbook, the terms *pre-service teacher candidate* and *in-service teacher* will be referred to as "teacher," except in cases where the specific term is more appropriate.

field supervisors to dialogue and reflect on a teacher candidate's growth and learning throughout the entire program. Four types of *pre-service* teacher portfolios are described here.

Entrance Portfolio—This type of portfolio may be required by teacher education programs as a component of their admission screening process. The materials in an entrance portfolio are intended to provide information about individuals' prior knowledge, skills, dispositions, and experiences that support their potential to be successful in a teacher education program. Items that might be included in an entrance portfolio are: transcripts; letters of recommendation; prior job experience; and a personal letter describing strengths, skills, and special qualities that would be valued by the college or university.

Working Portfolio—A working portfolio is a vehicle for documenting growth and development toward performance standards and teacher education program requirements. The intent of this type of portfolio is to integrate academic coursework and field experiences so that there is a meaningful connection between theory, practice, and the documentation presented in the portfolio. The materials included in this portfolio provide evidence of a teacher candidate's accomplishments at various benchmarks throughout the program. They reflect *work in progress* and growth over time and are not intended to be polished documents. The teacher candidate meets with college faculty, field supervisors, and mentor teachers using portfolio documentation as a basis for discussing teaching performance and areas for continued growth. Some examples of items that may be included in this type of portfolio are: course assignments, lesson plans, unit plans, case studies, observation data and analysis, and reflective journal entries.

Exit Portfolio—Exit portfolios are a final selection of materials that provide substantial evidence of a teacher candidate's level of mastery related to performance standards and the goals of the program. Items included in this type of portfolio are similar to the examples for the working portfolio. However, they need to be in a polished format appropriate to this final stage of the program. These portfolios are usually evaluated by individuals affiliated with the teacher education program and are rated using scoring rubrics. Some colleges of education require teacher candidates to formally present their portfolio as a part of the requirements for successful completion of their teacher education program.

Interview Portfolio—The artifacts in this portfolio are a subset of the best work from the working and exit portfolios. The intent of this type of portfolio is to limit the documentation in order to create a presentation of exemplary items representative of a teacher candidate's *best work* and accomplishments for the purpose of gaining employment. Chapter 7 provides many examples of portfolio entries from exit and interview portfolios ranging from sample lesson plans to research projects.

In-service Teacher Portfolios

While some school districts are not yet requiring that teachers develop professional portfolios, many are using portfolios to support national and state initiatives toward performance-based assessment and continued professional development. Furthermore, a substantial number of teachers are applying for national certification, which includes the submission of a teaching portfolio as part of the review process. In addition, portfolios are being developed by teachers to support their career enhancement efforts. The working and showcase portfolios are two of the most often used by in-service teachers who produce portfolios.

Working Portfolio—A working portfolio for the in-service teacher is similar to that of a teacher candidate in that it is a vehicle for documenting teaching performance and accomplishments. The major difference is that the in-service teacher works collaboratively with a school administrator to identify goals for continued professional growth related to the total school improvement plan. The portfolio becomes a vehicle for documenting accomplishments toward those goals. A working portfolio may be used in conjunction with the ongoing teacher observation and evaluation process and the performance standards established by the school system or state. Items included in this portfolio are artifacts specific to the practicing teacher and may include a professional development plan, examples of data-driven instruction, sample assessment instruments, results of parent-teacher conferences, evidence of involvement in professional organizations, and staff development activities.

Showcase Portfolio—The showcase portfolio parallels the teacher candidate interview portfolio. It is a *polished* collection of exemplary evidence that highlights a teacher's best work and accomplishments. Teachers may use this type of portfolio for informally sharing information about themselves with colleagues, administrators, parents, and community members. It may also be used for more goal-oriented purposes such as obtaining leadership roles, seeking job advancement, making lateral moves, fulfilling requirements for recertification, or making a career change.

Benefits of Portfolio Development

There are many benefits of portfolio development. These benefits range from personal to professional and are explained here.

Fosters Self-Assessment and Reflection

The process of portfolio development requires teachers to identify episodes of teaching, analyze what occurred, and assess the effectiveness of their teaching performance and the outcomes of student learning. Wolf and Dietz

(1998) indicate that depending on the purpose, portfolios have the potential to "stimulate and strengthen teacher reflection and practice" and "provide a comprehensive and authentic evaluation of a teacher's performance" (p. 6). In short, portfolios are an improvement in assessing strengths and weaknesses because the thinking of the learner is visible (Delandshere & Arens, 2003).

Provides Personal Satisfaction and Renewal

The act of collecting, reviewing, and reflecting on portfolio artifacts is consistently viewed as satisfying and renewing by teacher candidates and in-service teachers alike. Whether learning to be a teacher or having been in the profession for a number of years, it is easy to lose sight of the big picture and one's accomplishments. The sheer act of completing a portfolio, however, forces teachers to focus on the planning, delivery, assessment, and reflection of their instruction. Consequently, novices and veterans are able to identify their strengths, which are personally satisfying, and areas of growth, which facilitate a sense of renewal, as they move foward in the teaching profession.

Provides Tools for Empowerment

Portfolios can be tools for empowerment. They encourage teachers to assume more responsibility and ownership for their own learning and professional growth. In-service teachers can become self-directed to identify their goals and plans for continued professional growth instead of depending on an administrator to determine their teaching effectiveness through one or two yearly evaluations.

Pre-service teachers who use portfolios gain an understanding that learning is an ongoing process. Portfolio development facilitates self-assessment, and teacher candidates often gain confidence by reflecting on their own learning. Learning to teach is influenced by coursework and multiple experiences, such as clinical internships, research, seminars, and other educational activities that contribute to their professional growth. The process of developing a portfolio requires that teacher candidates become more responsible for integrating and documenting the knowledge, dispositions, and skills they learned through their courses and experiences. The process of reflecting and documenting what they learned is highly empowering and contributes to their self-confidence as novice teachers.

Promotes Collaboration

Using the portfolio process as a method of evaluating teaching performance provides the opportunity for a teacher to engage in a collaborative discussion with the reviewer and to receive formative feedback and guidance on a regular basis. This collaborative event is highly personalized with the intent to promote self-reflection and the improvement of teaching skills. It can lead to a mutual identification of goals for ongoing professional growth.

Provides a Holistic Approach to Assessment

Portfolios provide multiple sources of evidence that are not apparent in traditional assessments. A portfolio is a more authentic tool for evaluating teacher growth and learning. Many individuals do not perform well on standardized tests. Items included in a portfolio, such as original lesson plans, evidence of student learning, written feedback from observations and evaluations, digital video and audio clips, and reflective journal entries, present a holistic view of one's performance—as opposed to a resume, transcripts, or test results, which only document or measure achievement. Portfolios are an important assessment option because they add the breadth and depth of performance that may not be present in more traditional evaluation methods.

Portfolio Development Issues

It is not enough to cite the benefits of portfolio development without recognizing that there are dilemmas inherent in this process.

Labor-Intensive and Time-Consuming Preparation

One issue in creating a portfolio is that the process is labor intensive and time-consuming. Many pre-service teachers feel overwhelmed at the thought of having to develop a portfolio. Unfortunately, many teacher candidates do not begin their collection of evidence until they enter their student teaching semester. The demands and expectations of student teaching compound the stress associated with the development of a portfolio. A remedy to this dilemma is for teacher candidates to start collecting potential documents early in their teacher education program. In addition, a reflective journal helps teacher candidates remember how these documents contributed to their professional growth and learning. Collecting and reflecting then becomes a routine element of professional practice. The earlier time is invested in the collection and reflection process, the easier it will be to prepare an *exit* or *interview* portfolio. This helps eliminate the stress associated with beginning the process during student teaching.

Many in-service and pre-service teachers may feel that they need to document everything they have accomplished. This is an unreasonable, self-imposed expectation. Identification of a realistic set of professional goals or standards with a small number of artifacts that best support the goals or standards will make the task more manageable.

If your teacher education program or school system requires that you develop an electronic portfolio, it is essential that you master the technical skills necessary for this process. This already demanding process, magnified by your lack of technical skills, may make the experience even more labor intensive and stressful. Increasing your technical skills early in your teacher preparation program or teaching career will reduce the complexity of developing an portfolio.

Quality of Document Presentation

Teachers who are very artistic or have access to superior technical resources are able to easily assemble a visually pleasing and impressive product. This places the teacher without the talent or resources at a disadvantage and may affect the scoring process when the portfolio is used for interview or evaluation purposes. The key is to make sure that you have a neat and well-organized portfolio with evidence of substance and insightful reflections.

Evaluation of Portfolio Evidence

Another major concern is the identification of an acceptable method of assessing portfolios. The selection of portfolio artifacts is usually left to the discretion of the portfolio developer. This is a highly individualized process and unique to each person. While this is one of the most beneficial aspects for the use of portfolios, it may present a problem when portfolios are used in the evaluation process. The more diverse the documentation, the more difficult it becomes to compare and evaluate the portfolio. Evaluation depends on the professional judgment of the reviewer and is highly subjective (Martin-Kniep, 1999). A solution to this problem that is often chosen is the use of a rubric or Likert-type evaluation scale that includes the aspects of performance to be measured and the criteria for rating those aspects. It is in the best interest of teachers to become familiar with the instruments used to rate portfolio documentation by their teacher education program or school system. Becoming familiar with the specific rating criteria and scoring instruments helps the teacher select appropriate documentation that meets the standards determined by their program or school system. Chapter 6 discusses the criteria for portfolio evaluation.

Conclusion

It is obvious that there are many issues associated with portfolio development. Despite this, the literature shows that the benefits of portfolio development outweigh the drawbacks. Portfolios are one of the most authentic ways to represent the knowledge, dispositions, and skills of a teacher. As stated earlier, when used with other methods of evaluating teacher performance, portfolios can provide a broader perspective of a teacher's full range of professional competencies.

Chapter 1 ACTIVITIES

The information presented in this chapter was intended to provide you with an understanding of the concept of a professional teaching portfolio. Use these questions as a review for yourself and as an opportunity to meaningfully link the information to your individual situation or portfolio purpose.

How would the development of professional teaching portfolio benefit you?

At this time, what type of portfolio best suits your purpose?

Which portfolio development issue is most troublesome to you, and how will you deal with it?

CHAPTER 2

Performance Standards, Accountability, and Portfolio Development

Introduction

National standards for beginning and experienced teachers provide the foundation for a unifying vision needed to ensure consistency and compatibility with the many approaches to teacher education and professional development. The criteria imbedded in the standards dictate the specific knowledge, dispositions, and skills essential for assessing the growth and effectiveness of pre-service and in-service teachers. The ultimate intent of standards is to improve the quality of teaching and increase student achievement. Consequently, standards provide a comprehensive framework for portfolio development, as articulated throughout this chapter.

Performance Standards as a Determinant of Teacher Competency

The national focus on student achievement and high-level accountability has not only had a profound impact on K–12 curriculum, but also on teacher education and determinants of teacher quality. Performance standards for teachers are grounded in the proposition that high standards for student achievement can best be reached if teachers have the in-depth knowledge and skills necessary to prepare all students to meet these standards, and demonstrate continual progress regardless of ethnicity, native language, or special needs. In 1987 the National Board for Professional Teaching Standards (NBPTS) was created to establish high and rigorous standards for what accomplished teachers should know and be able to do in their classrooms. In the same year, the Interstate New Teacher Assessment and Support Consortium (INTASC) was established to restructure teacher assessment for initial licensure as well as for preparation and induction into the profession. INTASC developed performance standards that articulated the knowledge and skills expected of novice teachers as they embark on their careers.

In 1997 and 2004, the National Commission on Teaching issued reports that challenged the nation and its teacher education institutions to become more rigorous in the utilization of performance standards throughout teacher preparation. Responding to the National Commission's recommendation regarding standards, teacher performance standards were not only developed by national organizations such as INTASC, but were also developed by specialized program associations (SPA); organizations such as The Council for Exceptional Children, Association of Childhood Education International, National Association for the Education of Young Children (NAEYC), The National Council for Teachers of Mathematics, and other domain-specific associations represented in U.S. classrooms. In addition, the International Society for Technology in Education (ISTE) developed the National Educational Technology Standards for Teachers (NETS) in an effort to ensure teacher competency in the utilization and teaching of technology across domains. Moreover, colleges of education, state departments of education, and local education agencies also developed their own standards for the purpose of teacher preparation, initial licensure, and continuing professional development. What is clear is the consensus of NBPTS, INTASC, ISTE, National Education Association (NEA), National Council for the Accreditation of Teacher Education (NCATE), and SPAs that the complex art of teaching requires performance-based standards to assess competency.

The Importance of Performance Standards to Teaching and Professional Portfolios

All performance standards, whether national, state, or local, are based on shared views within the educational community of what constitutes professional teaching. Each set of standards captures the knowledge, dispositions, and skills related to effective teaching in general or relative to a specific domain. More than a decade ago, Linda Darling-Hammond (Darling-Hammond, Wise, & Klein, 1995) defined these attributes as follows: *Professional knowledge* includes a grounding in the many areas that provide an understanding of students and their learning (p. 38); *teaching dispositions* are the orientations teachers develop to think and behave in professionally responsive ways (p. 39); *teaching skills* include the abilities to transform knowledge into actions needed for effective teaching (p. 39). It is clear that the standards movement significantly influenced all aspects of the teaching profession, from teacher education to initial licensure to national certification.

Having a basic understanding of performance standards is important. Just as critical is the understanding of how these standards are meaningfully linked to the practice of teaching and portfolio development. The following information provides a rationale supporting the importance of performance standards and their relationship to teaching and professional portfolios.

Teaching Standards Correlate with Student Standards

There is a direct correlation between performance standards for student learning and performance standards for teachers. What teachers know and are able to do is the most important influence on what students learn (National Commission on Teaching and America's Future, 1997, 2004). Teachers need to demonstrate their own competency in order to validate their ability to promote student achievement.

Standards Target Outcomes for Teachers

Standards provide teachers with targeted outcomes in the knowledge, dispositions, and skills related to effective teaching. Targeted outcomes allow teacher candidates to monitor their own growth toward program requirements and help experienced teachers to identify goals for professional growth based on accepted standards of the profession.

Standards Establish Credibility

Using national or state standards when developing a portfolio provides credibility to the documentation. Portfolio artifacts should be selected or created to directly support and validate a teacher's competency toward a performance standard as opposed to the arbitrary selection and display of evidence. Furthermore, INTASC standards for beginning teachers are currently being used across the nation for initial certification of teachers. Teacher candidates will be responsible for collecting appropriate documentation for initial certification related to performance standards. In addition, the NBPTS for accomplished teachers requires the use of standards in portfolio development for national certification. In-service teachers who consider performance standards when developing their portfolio will be in step with the current national and state reform initiatives for high standards for teaching performance.

Standards Provide a Common Language

Using standards provides a common language that is understood by most portfolio reviewers. Regardless of which set of standards is considered, there is a common core of teaching knowledge, dispositions, and skills that have similar outcomes but are stated differently. Therefore, a standards-based portfolio can be appropriate and acceptable in many situations. A standards-based portfolio can be especially beneficial when applying for employment or licensure in different geographic areas.

Standards Demonstrate a Commitment to Professional Accountability

Utilizing INTASC or another set of respected, professional standards demonstrates a willingness and ability to hold oneself accountable for the multiple facets of effective teaching. Standards in the field of education not only focus on content knowledge and pedagogy, but also include a strong focus on formative and summative assessment (in aggregate and disaggregate form), as well as relationships and professionalism. Student achievement is dependent on teachers who have strong content knowledge and a multitude of skills that continue to evolve throughout their careers. Adherence to standards conveys a commitment to professional growth as a teacher candidate or an accomplished teacher.

Standards Provide a Framework for Teaching Assessment and Evaluation

Many performance-based teacher education programs are designed around national or state standards. Performance assessment instruments have been developed by colleges of education to evaluate teacher candidate competency in meeting those standards. In addition, school systems are using performance standards to evaluate teacher growth and ongoing professional development. Such standards provide a natural alignment with standards-based assessment and evaluation.

Several examples of national standards can be found in Appendix A of this handbook. They are *representative* of the many sets of standards established by national, state, and local organizations. These examples provide an overview of the standards and do not include the full range of knowledge, dispositions, and skills inherent in the complete set. The overviews presented are the INTASC standards for beginning teachers and NBPTS standards for accomplished teachers. Also included is an example of standards developed by the Council for Exceptional Children (CEC). Other sets of standards may be selected to meet individual content or specialty area requirements. Appendix B includes a list of professional organizations and their websites that have developed content or specialty area performance standards.

Using Standards and Universal Themes as a Framework for Portfolio Development

As indicated earlier, standards are shared views within the educational community of what constitutes professional teaching. Although the standards may be stated differently by various national, state, or local agencies or organizations, the performance outcomes are similar. In fact, when comparing the standards of various organizations, we have identified six universally understood themes:

- Knowledge of subject matter and educational theory
- Knowledge of development and learning
- Planning, delivery and assessment of instruction
- Classroom management and organization
- Human relationships
- Professionalism

The NBPTS has a prescribed set of standards around which teachers must develop their portfolios. In contrast, colleges and schools of education require a variety of approaches in the development of standards-based portfolios. While some institutions require portfolio development around the college's conceptual framework, others require portfolio frameworks based on INTASC or specialized program area (e.g., NAEYC, NCTM, CEC) standards.

Regardless of the required framework, each of the categories articulated within a set of standards is correlated with the INTASC standards and provides a credible organizational foundation for the development of a professional teaching portfolio. This handbook uses the terms *standards, principles,* and *themes* interchangeably when discussing the relationship of portfolio evidence to performance standards. Figure 2.1 shows the alignment between the universally understood themes, INTASC Standards, and selected performance standards.

Many teachers prefer using these or other terms to guide the selection of documents for their portfolio. Terms help to simplify the complexity inherent in each standard, thus making it easier to create or collect artifacts that relate to the standards. For this book, we are using the six universally understood themes as a framework for portfolio documentation based on standards for both pre-service and in-service teachers.

Linking Coursework to Performance Standards

Individual teacher education programs identify specific performance standards for teacher candidates. As previously mentioned, these standards range from the INTASC Standards for beginning teachers to specific content area standards developed by professional organizations to standards for licensure mandated by the state. Knowing the expected performance standards of their teacher education program enables teacher candidates to make connections between required coursework and field experiences.

Each course that is taken should meaningfully relate to one or more of the performance standards. The assignments, readings, research papers, and special projects identified in the course syllabus should all contribute to the

INTASC Standards	*Universal Themes*	*NBPTS Standards*	*Pillars of NCLB*	*NAEYC Standards*	*CEC Standards*
1. Subject Matter	■ Knowledge of Subject Matter and Educational Theory	2. Teachers know the subjects they teach and how to teach those subjects to their students	■ Proven Educational Methods ■ Stronger Accountability for Results	4b. Using Developmentally Effective Approaches 4c. Understanding Content Knowledge 4d. Building Meaningful Curriculum	1. Foundations 2. Development and Characteristics of Learners 3. Individual Learning Differences
2. Child Development	■ Knowledge of Development and Learning	1. Teachers are committed to students and their learning	■ Stronger Accountability for Results ■ Proven Educational Methods ■ More Choices for Parents	1. Promoting Child Development and Learning 4b. Using Developmentally Effective Approaches 4c. Understanding Content Knowledge 4d. Building Meaningful Curriculum	2. Development and Characteristics of Learners 3. Individual Learning Differences
3. Diverse Learners	■ Planning, Delivery, and Assessment of Instruction	1. Teachers are committed to students and their learning 3. Teachers are responsible for managing and monitoring student learning	■ Stronger Accountability for Results	1. Promoting Child Development and Learning 2. Building Family and Community Relationships Content Knowledge 4c. Understanding Content Knowledge 4d. Building Meaningful Curriculum	2. Development and Characteristics of Learners 3. Individual Learning Differences 4. Instructional Strategies 5. Learning Environments and Social Interactions

FIGURE 2.1 Alignment of INTASC standards, universal themes, NBPTS, and selected performance standards.

INTASC Standards	*Universal Themes*	*NBPTS Standards*	*Pillars of NCLB*	*NAEYC Standards*	*CEC Standards*
4. Instructional Strategies	■ Planning, Delivery, and Assessment of Instruction	1. Teachers are committed to students and their learning 2. Teachers know the subjects they teach and how to teach those subjects to their students 3. Teachers are responsible for managing and monitoring student learning	■ Proven Educational Methods	4b. Using Developmentally Effective Approaches 4d. Building Meaningful Curriculum	2. Development and Characteristics of Learners 3. Individual Learning Differences 5. Learning Environments and Social Interactions 7. Instructional Planning 10. Collaboration
5. Learning Environment	■ Classroom Management and Organization	1. Teachers are committed to students and their learning 3. Teachers are responsible for managing and monitoring student learning	■ Proven Educational Methods	1. Promoting Child Development and Learning 3. Observing, Documenting, and Assessing 4b. Using Developmentally Effective Approaches 4d. Building Meaningful Curriculum	2. Development and Characteristics of Learners 3. Individual Learning Differences 4. Instructional Strategies 5. Learning Environments and Social Interactions 6. Language 9. Professional and Ethical Practice

FIGURE 2.1 Continued

INTASC Standards	*Universal Themes*	*NBPTS Standards*	*Pillars of NCLB*	*NAEYC Standards*	*CEC Standards*
6. Communication	Human Relationships	1. Engaging and supporting students in learning 2. Creating and maintaining effective environments for student learning 3. Understanding and organizing subject matter for student learning	■ More Choices for Parents ■ More Freedom for States and Communities	4a. Connecting with Children and Families 4b. Using Developmentally Effective Approaches 4d. Building Meaningful Curriculum	3. Individual Learning Differences 4. Instructional Strategies 5. Learning Environments and Social Interactions 6. Language
7. Planning Instruction	Planning, Delivery, and Assessment of Instruction	4. Planning and designing learning experiences for all students	■ Proven Educational Methods	1. Promoting Child Development and Learning 2. Building Family and Community Relationships 3. Observing, Documenting, and Assessing 4a. Connecting with Children and Families 4b. Using Developmentally Effective Approaches 4d. Building Meaningful Curriculum	2. Development and Characteristics of Learners 3. Individual Learning Differences 4. Instructional Strategies 5. Learning Environments and Social Interactions 6 Language 8. Assessment 9. Professional and Ethical Practice 10. Collaboration
8. Assessment	Planning, Delivery, and Assessment of Instruction	5. Assessing student learning	■ Proven Educational Methods ■ Stronger Accountability for Results	3. Observing, Documenting, and Assessing	7. Instructional Planning 8. Assessment 9. Professional and Ethical Practice

FIGURE 2.1 Continued

INTASC Standards	*Universal Themes*	*NBPTS Standards*	*Pillars of NCLB*	*NAEYC Standards*	*CEC Standards*
9. Reflection and Professional Development	Professionalism	6. Developing as a professional educator	■ Stronger Accountability for Results	5. Becoming a Professional	2. Development and Characteristics of Learners 3. Individual Learning Differences 8. Assessment 9. Professional and Ethical Practice
10. Collaboration, Ethics, and Relationships	Human Relationships	1. Engaging and supporting students in learning 4. Planning and designing learning experiences for all students 6. Developing as a professional educator	■ More Choices for Parents ■ More Freedom for States and Communities	2. Building Family and Community Relationships 4a. Connecting with Children and Families 5. Becoming a Professional	8. Assessment 9. Professional and Ethical Practice

FIGURE 2.1 Continued

acquisition of the knowledge, dispositions, and skills described in the standards. Similarly, field experiences will also need to be meaningfully linked to performance standards. Therefore, teacher candidates need to give considerable thought to how ongoing teaching responsibilities (such as designing lessons, delivering instruction, assessing student learning, managing the classroom, attending professional activities, communicating with colleagues, and working with diversity) fit into supporting their growth toward a performance standard. The more familiar one becomes with the standards, the easier it will be to see the connections between coursework, clinical field experiences, and the standards. By routinely analyzing how coursework and field experiences contribute to meeting the performance standards, teacher candidates can become highly reflective while creating an ongoing record of their growth and development throughout their entire program.

Figure 2.2 illustrates how a teacher candidate might systematically envision the connection between coursework, clinical field experiences, and growth toward a performance standard. This type of chart can be used throughout the entire teacher education program. The teacher candidates begin by identifying the course and assignments that significantly contribute to their knowledge, dispositions, and skills related to the standard. They then reflect on what occurred, what was learned, and what evidence should be included in the portfolio, thereby linking theory and practice. Appendix C provides a blank worksheet for you to use.

Linking a Professional Development Plan to Performance Standards

A professional development plan delineates a teacher's goals for short- and long-term professional growth. These goals should be aligned with the performance standards identified by the school system or teacher preparation program. The in-service teacher's professional development plan is focused on continued professional growth related to performance evaluations and individual career objectives. The teacher candidate's professional development plan is related to coursework, field experiences, and the required performance outcomes of the teacher education program.

Figure 2.3 describes a process for creating a professional development plan related to performance standards and the practice of teaching. The intent of this process is to facilitate reflection and to improve teaching effectiveness. This chart is an example of a professional development plan that focuses on a goal related to cooperative learning strategies.

This seven-step approach can be invaluable at the in-service and preservice levels. It requires collaborative planning, focused dialogue, and ongoing communication between the teacher and those individuals who guide and support the development of professional portfolios. It can provide the

Directions:

- Identify the course.
- List the assignments.
- Determine how the assignment contributed to your knowledge, disposition, and skills.
- Identify the appropriate performance standard or theme.
- Reflect in writing what you learned.
- Consider what could be placed in your portfolio to capture this experience.

Course	*Assignment*	*Knowledge*	*Dispositions*	*Skills*	*Standard(s)*
Human Development and Learning	Case Study ■ Third-grade child	Vygotsky's Theory of Sociocultural Development ■ Scaffolding	I believe that learning occurs when children are supported in their efforts to increase knowledge. Scaffolding requires teachers to provide appropriate materials, guidance, and questioning to bring the individual learner to a higher or new level (example: science—exploration of primary and secondary colors provides a wealth of learning opportunities when a child is prompted toward discovery through opportunity and questioning)	■ Observation of student behavior ■ Assessment of prior knowledge on the part of individual learners ■ Individualizing instruction	INTASC Standards 4, 7, 8 Planning, delivery, and assessment of instruction

Reflection: Observation of case study subject helped me realize the effectiveness of teacher scaffolding on the learning process. Children are more likely to attain new knowledge when they are questioned and supported while exploring new concepts/mediums.
Possible Portfolio Artifacts: Written observation of a teacher using the scaffolding process.

Course	*Assignment*	*Knowledge*	*Dispositions*	*Skills*	*Standard(s)*
Assessment, Instruction, and Curriculum for Students with Severe Disabilities	To write a functional domestic living program on a student's morning grooming routine	Life skills instruction relevant to independent community, personal living, and employment	Special educators should provide learning opportunities in a variety of environments including the home, the school, and the community	Select, adapt, and use instruction strategies and materials according to characteristics of the learner	CEC Common Core: K6; S8 Planning and delivery of instruction

Reflection: This domestic living program was based on documented patterns of behavior and data from informal assessment tools. Insight was gained into the importance of assessing skills prior to designing supports and adaptations. I realized the need to solicit feedback from the parents and siblings of the student to facilitate instructional delivery.
Possible Portfolio Artifacts: Interview format and results of interview with parents and siblings; task analysis of morning grooming routine.

See Appendix C for a blank chart for your personal use.

FIGURE 2.2 Linking coursework to standards and portfolio artifacts.

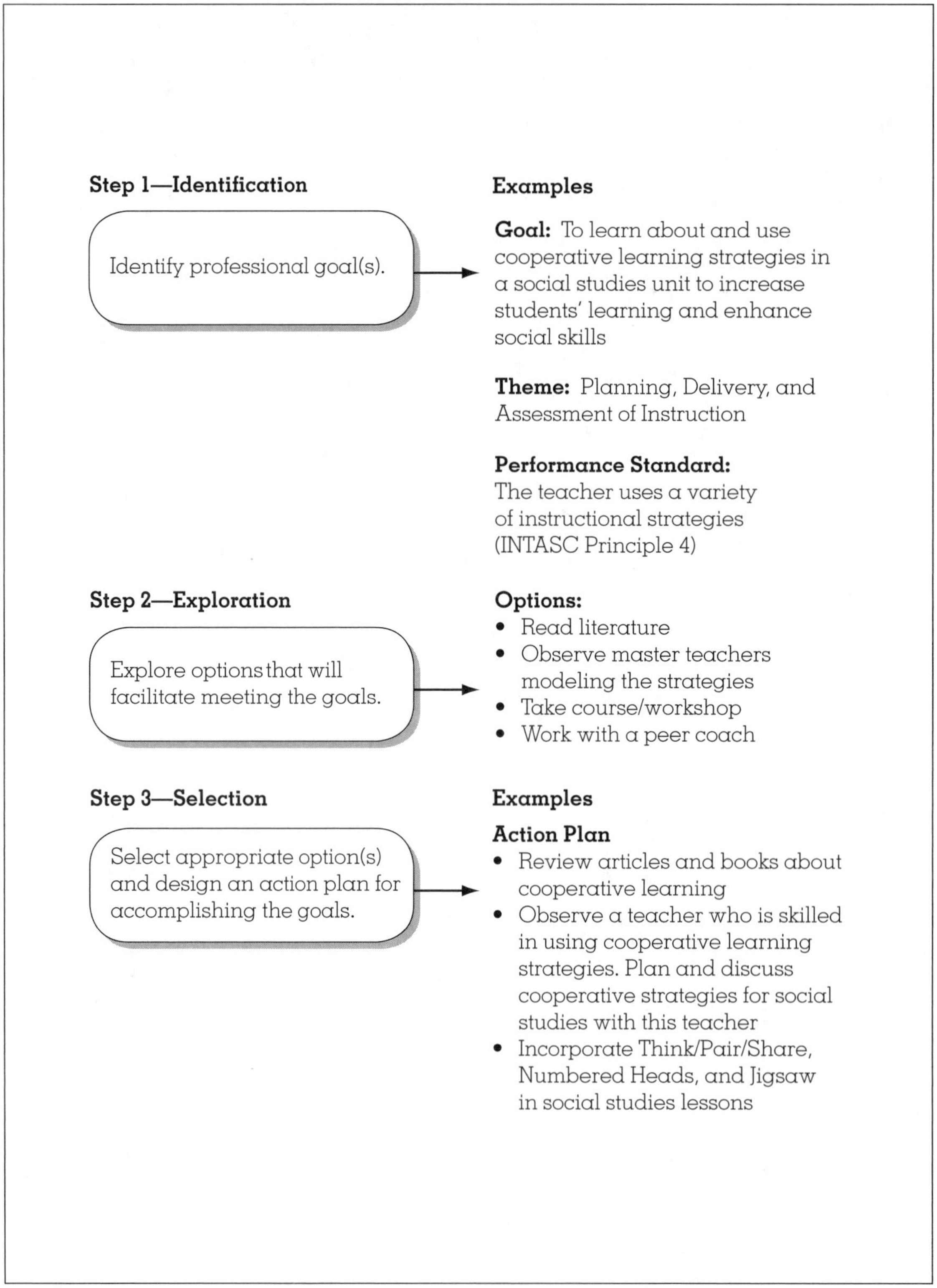

Step 1—Identification

Identify professional goal(s).

Examples

Goal: To learn about and use cooperative learning strategies in a social studies unit to increase students' learning and enhance social skills

Theme: Planning, Delivery, and Assessment of Instruction

Performance Standard:
The teacher uses a variety of instructional strategies (INTASC Principle 4)

Step 2—Exploration

Explore options that will facilitate meeting the goals.

Options:
- Read literature
- Observe master teachers modeling the strategies
- Take course/workshop
- Work with a peer coach

Step 3—Selection

Select appropriate option(s) and design an action plan for accomplishing the goals.

Examples

Action Plan
- Review articles and books about cooperative learning
- Observe a teacher who is skilled in using cooperative learning strategies. Plan and discuss cooperative strategies for social studies with this teacher
- Incorporate Think/Pair/Share, Numbered Heads, and Jigsaw in social studies lessons

FIGURE 2.3 Process for creating a professional development plan related to performance standards and the practice of teaching.

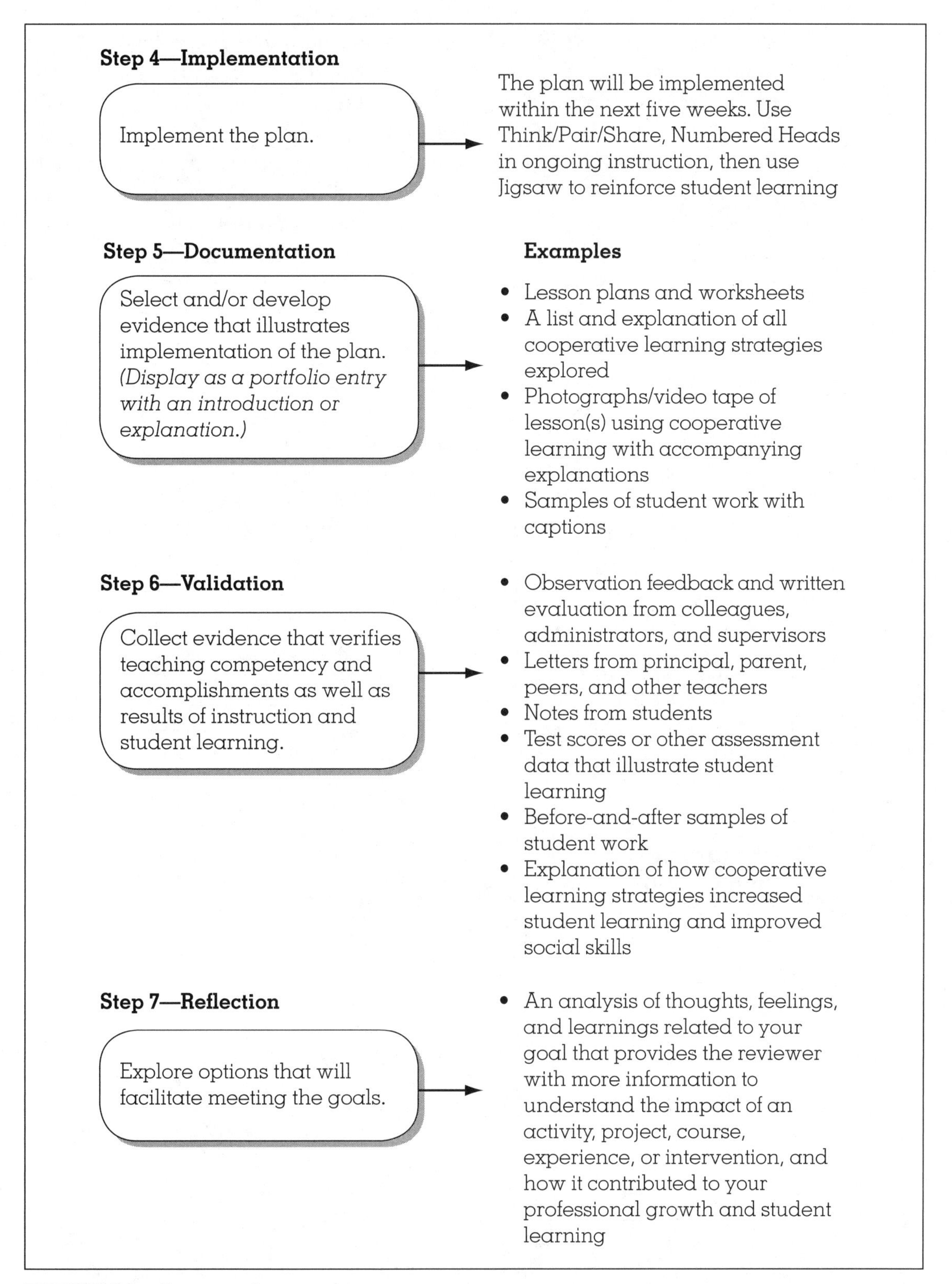

Step 4—Implementation
Implement the plan.
The plan will be implemented within the next five weeks. Use Think/Pair/Share, Numbered Heads in ongoing instruction, then use Jigsaw to reinforce student learning
Step 5—Documentation
Select and/or develop evidence that illustrates implementation of the plan. (Display as a portfolio entry with an introduction or explanation.)
Examples
• Lesson plans and worksheets
• A list and explanation of all cooperative learning strategies explored
• Photographs/video tape of lesson(s) using cooperative learning with accompanying explanations
• Samples of student work with captions
Step 6—Validation
Collect evidence that verifies teaching competency and accomplishments as well as results of instruction and student learning.
• Observation feedback and written evaluation from colleagues, administrators, and supervisors
• Letters from principal, parent, peers, and other teachers
• Notes from students
• Test scores or other assessment data that illustrate student learning
• Before-and-after samples of student work
• Explanation of how cooperative learning strategies increased student learning and improved social skills
Step 7—Reflection
Explore options that will facilitate meeting the goals.
• An analysis of thoughts, feelings, and learnings related to your goal that provides the reviewer with more information to understand the impact of an activity, project, course, experience, or intervention, and how it contributed to your professional growth and student learning

FIGURE 2.3 Continued

structure for conversations between a teacher and an administrator or a university faculty member during an evaluation conference. It can be the tool for empowering teachers to identify their professional goals, or it could provide the structure for collaborative decision making, which sets the direction for a teacher's ongoing professional development. In this approach, teaching becomes a collaborative event with discussion based on the identification of teaching goals and the design of purposeful plans for continued professional development. Appendix D provides a worksheet for documenting your professional development plan.

Figure 2.4 illustrates how the seven-step process could be represented in a portfolio. This professional development plan example consolidates the

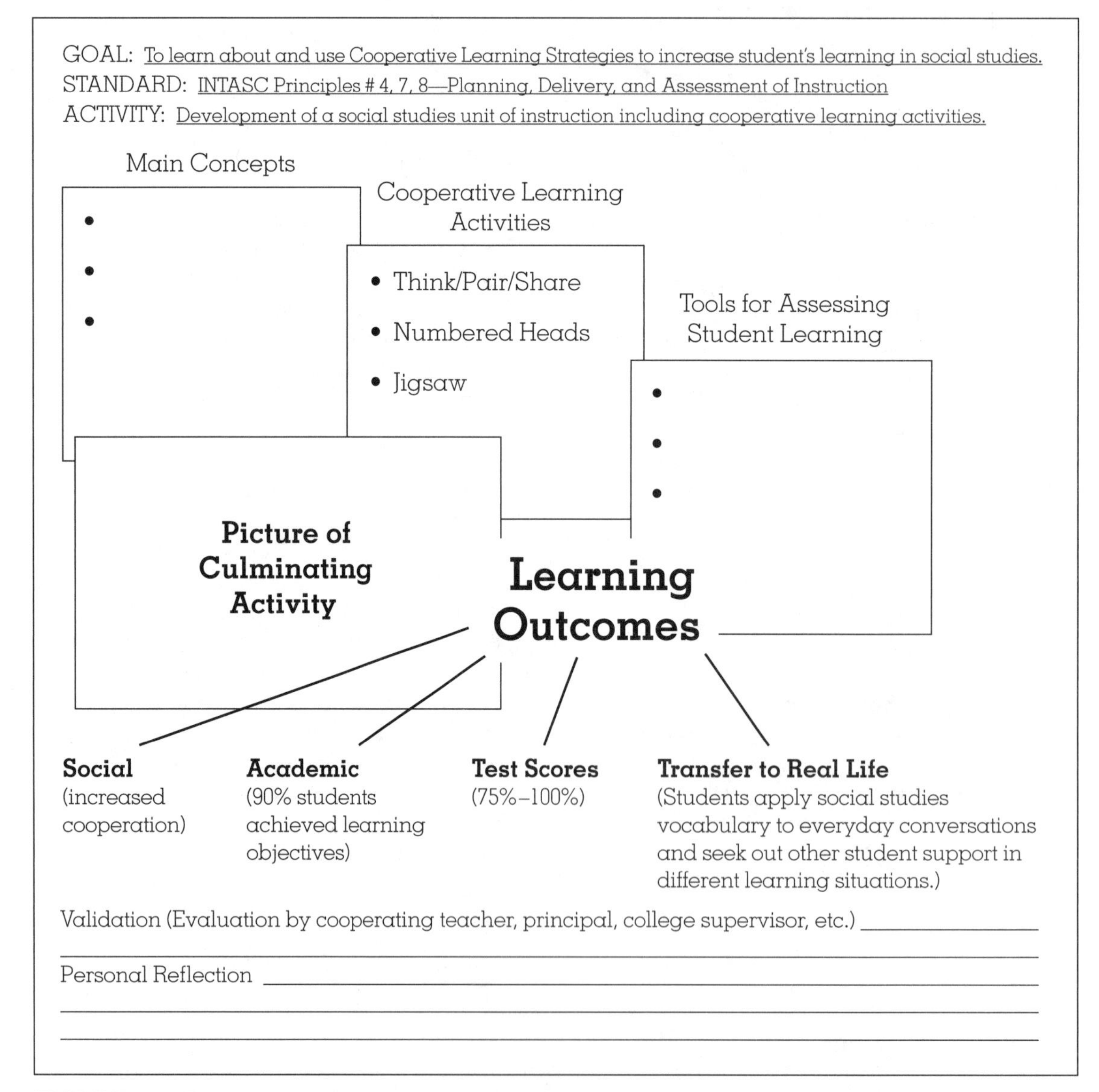

FIGURE 2.4 Representing your professional development plan as a portfolio entry.

evidence of how a goal was accomplished by highlighting the essentials of a social studies unit that incorporates cooperative learning strategies. In reality, this type of entry may require more than one page to fully capture the richness of this unit of instruction. See Chapter 7 for other examples of how to represent your professional development plan as a document in your paper or e-portfolio.

No Child Left Behind—The Era of Widespread Accountability

The No Child Left Behind (NCLB) legislation of 2002 had a marked influence on all aspects and levels of education in the United States. Although modifications in the NCLB legislation and policy were necessary, the overarching goal of eliminating the achievement gap between minority and majority populations will remain in the forefront of the policy agenda for years to come. In an effort to attain that goal, NCLB was designed around "Four Pillars": Stronger Accountability for Results, More Freedom for States and Communities, Proven Educational Methods, and More Choice for Parents (U.S. Department of Education).

The pillars with the most direct impact on teacher preparation and the teaching profession are Stronger Accountability for Results and Proven Educational Methods. The passage of NCLB affirmed the work of INTASC and NBPTS, but raised the stakes to include the impact of teacher competence on the academic achievement of students through:

- The development of an accountability system requiring teacher certification in all areas of instruction;
- Teacher certification dependent on demonstrated content knowledge as determined through exams such as the PRAXIS; and
- Penalties for schools whose students fail to meet adequate yearly progress (AYP), as determined through aggregated and disaggregated (by race, English language learners, special education, poverty/free and reduced price meals [FARMs] and gender) standardized test scores.

Given the significant impact NCLB had on public (K–12) and teacher education, it is advisable to demonstrate a working knowledge of NCLB policy and competence throughout your portfolio.

Data-Driven Instruction

As previously mentioned, NCLB had a profound impact on education in both public and teacher education. Accountability and Proven Education Methods are the two pillars most critical to portfolio development followed by Parental Choice and Freedom for States and Communities. *Parental Choice* allows parents the option of transferring their children to another school if their home school is deemed to perform poorly. *Freedom for States and Communities* affords states expanded flexibility in the use of federal funds to educational programs. Hence, ensure that your portfolio provides clear evidence of your credentials, documentation of your planning and instructional delivery skills, involvement of parents in your classroom, and evidence of your awareness of state- and system-level policies.

As a result of NCLB, public school principals and systems are particularly interested in (and impressed by) a teacher's ability to analyze both student, classroom, and standardized data disaggregated by English language learners (ELLs), special education designation, ethnicity, and poverty status, as determined by FARMs.

The Cycle of Data-Driven Instruction (Figure 2.5) provides a model appropriate to all classrooms and schools focused on eliminating the achievement gap for all learners. The process is always driven by curricular goals and objectives, but the instructional planning and delivery are determined or influenced by the students in the classroom.

In the Differentiated Planning stage, the teacher prepares plans to meet the needs of the learners in the classroom; of particular note will be delivery to ELLs or students with different foundational skills. In the Instructional Delivery stage teachers utilize one instructional delivery strategy differentiated for the varied ability levels of the students or utilize two or more approaches (e.g., whole-group instruction with small-group instruc-

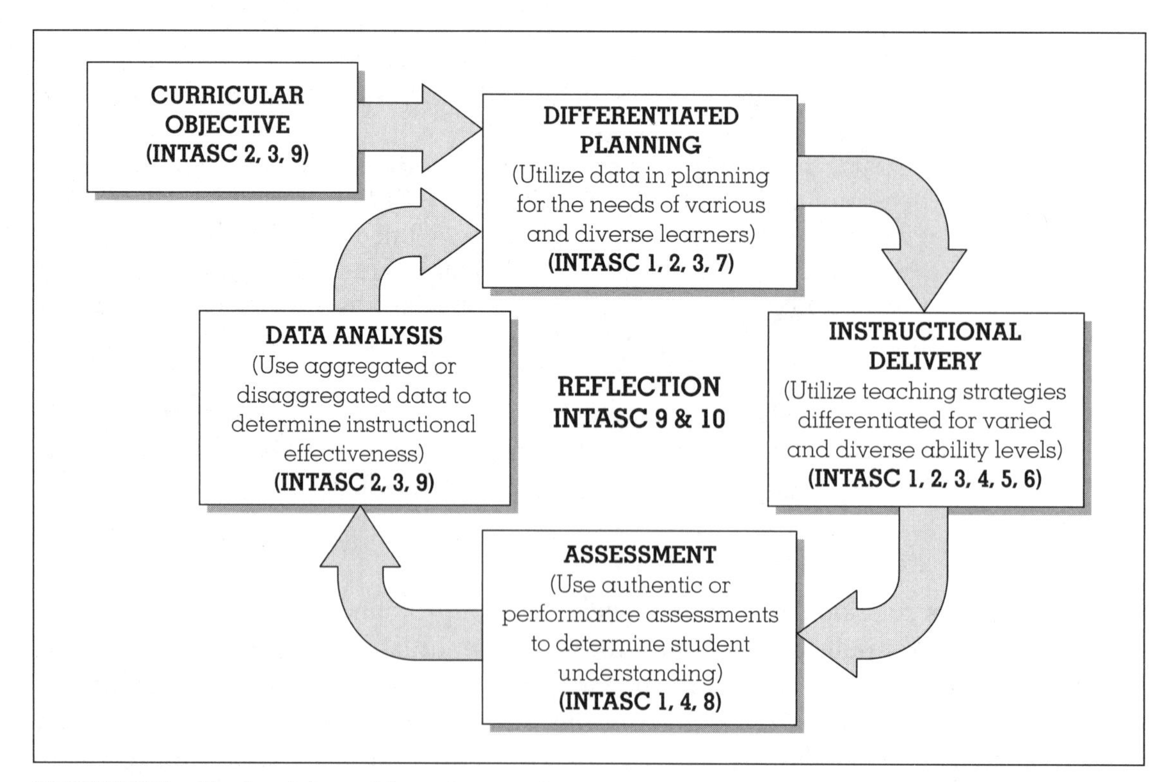

FIGURE 2.5 Cycle of data-driven instruction.

tion for ELLs) to ensure student understanding. In the Assessment stage, a critical component of the Accountability Pillar of NCLB, teachers use authentic (work sampling, etc.) and standards-based assessment strategies to determine comprehension by individual students. The Data Analysis stage, which is also a critical component of the Accountability Pillar, allows teachers to determine the effectiveness of their instruction through aggregate and disaggregate classroom and student data. Through the use of programs such as Excel, a teacher can code students into different categories, thereby making it very simple to disaggregate according to subgroups on a single or series of assessments. See Figure 2.6 for an example of an Excel spreadsheet showing student test data and disaggregated variables.

Disaggregated data allows teachers to determine if their instruction is effective for all learners or if there is a pattern of lower performance for a particular subgroup. See Figure 2.7 for an example of bar graphs illustrating disaggregated data.

Such information not only informs the planning stage but also gives teachers insight into their strengths and areas of growth in the planning and delivery of differentiated instruction. If data indicate the need for further instruction, the cycle is repeated with the whole class or the group of students in need of reteaching. If the data indicate successful delivery, the cycle continues with instruction based on a new curricular goal or objective.

Although particularly important for schools that have not made adequate yearly progress (AYP) or schools at risk of not making AYP, all public schools engage in data analysis by classroom, grade level, and disaggregated subgroups. School leadership teams or teachers grouped by grade-level teams review aggregate and disaggregate data in order to identify schoolwide, grade level, instructional specialty (e.g., reading, math, special education, ELLs) trends, and subsequent strategies for improvement.

Figure 2.8 depicts a variation of the cycle of data-driven instruction, with a graphic depicting the use of data to plan and facilitate a parent-teacher conference.

The essential first step in the process will always be the planning stage where a teacher gathers and reviews formative and summative student data to provide parents with tangible examples of their child's performance and ability. The ultimate goal of the Parent Conference is for the teacher and parents to "work together" in support of the student through the development of an action plan (e.g., strategies undertaken by the teacher and by the parents in the home). In the next stage, the teacher implements the action plan (which may have an instructional, behavioral, or other focus) followed by an appropriate assessment of effectiveness. If the goal(s) for the student are attained, the process is complete. If, however, the assessment data show little improvement or continued challenges, the teacher and parents may hold another conference to modify the existing action plan or develop a new plan based on new data.

Name	Gender	Ethnicity	ESOL	FARMS	SPED	Spell 1	Spell 2	Spell 3	Spell 4	Write 1	Write 2	Unit 1	Unit 2	Unit 3
Amira M	F	Hispanic	no	no	no	65	66	64	60	72	78	96	87	85
Caroline P	F	African Am	no	no	no	98	82	81	83	93	97	76	85	78
Charles T	M	Caucasian	no	yes	yes	93	85	84	79	83	85	86	80	74
Christopher M	M	African Am	no	yes	no	85	83	82	80	78	82	90	69	58
Danielle C	F	Caucasian	no	no	no	84	83	86	90	79	90	92	85	76
Decarlo W	M	Hispanic	no	yes	no	80	78	85	75	88	95	80	94	83
Jane P	F	Caucasian	no	no	no	88	90	90	89	93	95	93	90	83
John W	M	African	yes	yes	no	89	82	75	79	89	94	84	94	80
Juan P	M	Hispanic	yes	yes	yes	78	74	75	75	80	84	81	75	55
Kathleen C	F	Asian	no	no	no	85	86	84	85	92	97	99	89	85
Kim Y	F	African Am	no	yes	no	70	72	75	74	72	81	97	86	80
Li W	M	Asian	yes	yes	no	91	85	75	70	94	97	86	75	55
Louis K	M	Asian	yes	yes	no	69	65	65	68	75	81	98	88	85
Lyndsey L	F	Caucasian	no	yes	no	100	97	94	98	92	94	99	90	85
Maria L	F	Hispanic	no	yes	no	80	74	76	73	88	90	76	74	66
Matthew Z	M	African	yes	yes	no	74	76	69	68	88	98	100	93	85
Nikolina R	F	Hispanic	no	yes	no	65	62	65	64	75	80	85	83	66
Ramon H	M	Hispanic	yes	yes	no	80	74	73	70	90	97	100	94	88
Robin K	M	African	yes	yes	no	97	92	92	88	88	98	87	88	85
Sharamin M	F	African Am	no	yes	no	88	85	93	92	90	95	85	88	72

FIGURE 2.6 Sample Excel spreadsheet of student test data and disaggregated variables.

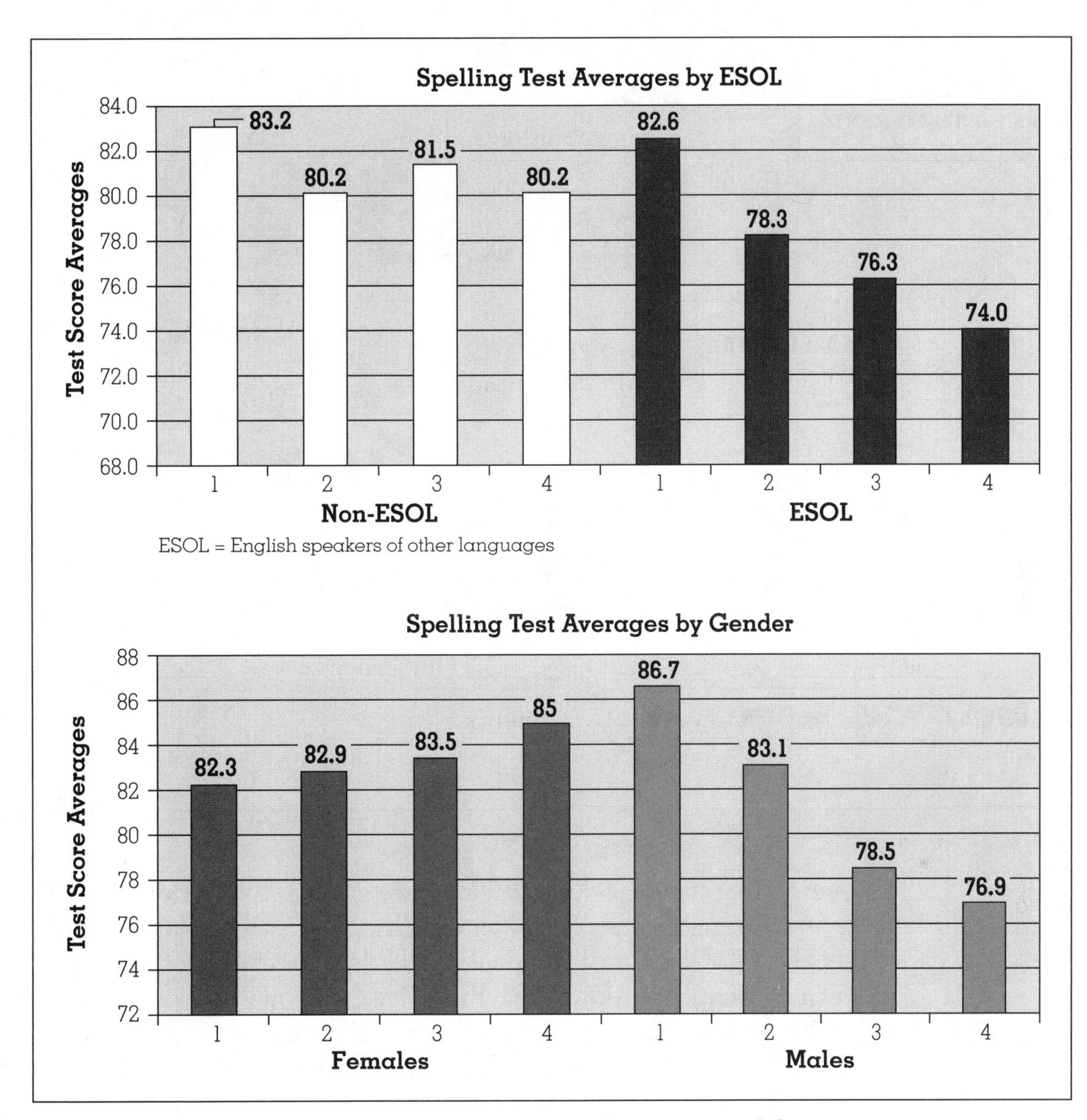

FIGURE 2.7 Examples of bar graphs illustrating disaggregated data.

Both data-driven instruction models depict the teacher's reliance on data to plan, deliver, and assess instruction. The relevance of this model extends beyond the scope of NCLB by demonstrating a teacher's commitment to accountability and a desire to meet the needs (e.g., differentiate) of the students in the classroom. Without disaggregated data, teachers and schools will not be able to determine if they are making progress in eliminating the minority achievement gap in the United States.

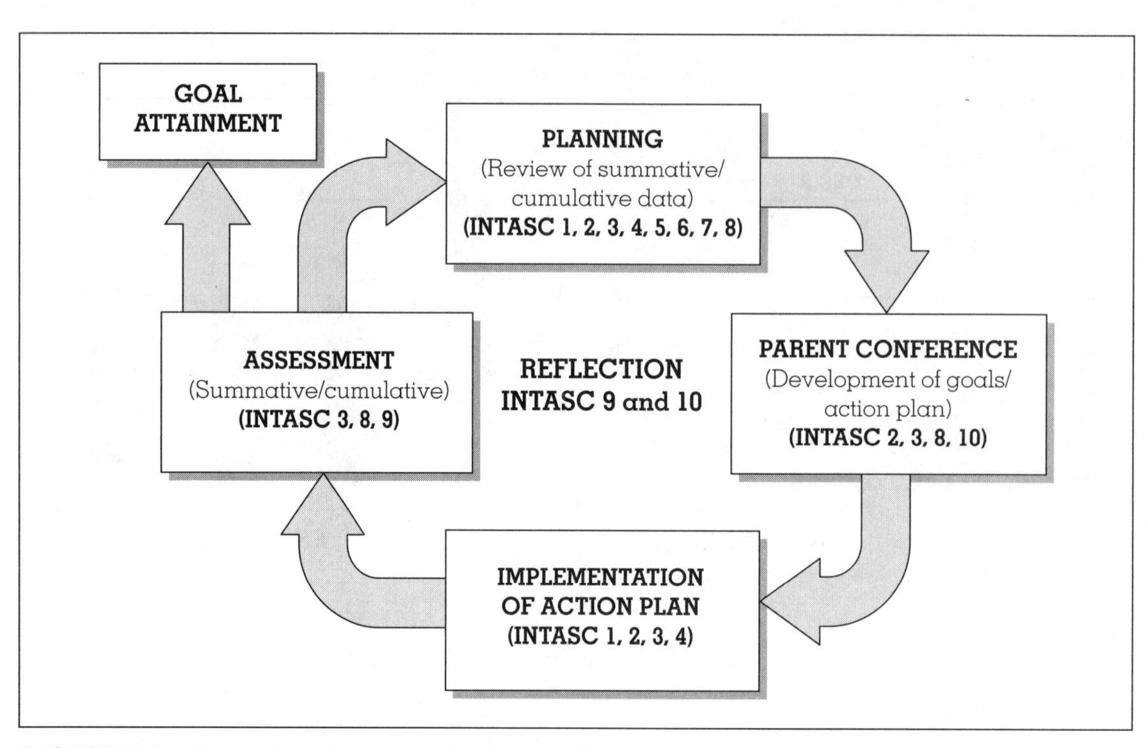

FIGURE 2.8 The cycle of a parent-teacher conference.

Conclusion

It is evident that standards are a driving force in educational reform. Teachers are now being held accountable for higher levels of performance as a result of NCLB and national and state standards. They can no longer merely submit a transcript or proclaim that they have the knowledge, dispositions, and skills required of an effective teacher. Teachers must present authentic evidence of what they know, what they are able to do, and how their teaching increases student achievement. Serious consideration of performance standards, the pillars of stronger accountability for results, and proven educational methods from the NCLB legislation will help teachers create and collect meaningful and focused portfolio entries that demonstrate their teaching effectiveness.

Chapter 2 ACTIVITIES

The intent of this chapter is to emphasize the importance of performance standards and the impact of NCLB. The following activities are designed to get you thinking about the use of standards and data-driven instruction as it relates to portfolio documentation at the pre-service and in-service levels.

Consult with your university professors or school system administrators to determine if you are required to use a prescribed set of standards for your portfolio framework or if you have the option to select a set of standards or themes of your choice.

If you are currently a student, use the Appendix C worksheet to begin thinking about how your coursework relates to the selected performance standards or themes and the identification of artifacts for your portfolio.

If you are a practicing teacher, use the Appendix D worksheet to document your professional development plan.

In this era of high-stakes accountability it is important for teachers to continually demonstrate their competency with data-driven instruction. Create an Excel spreadsheet of mock classroom data with two or more disaggregated variables. Use your data to create a portfolio entry reflecting the Cycle of Data-Driven Instruction. Determine how you are going to represent the data in your portfolio.

CHAPTER 3

Electronic Portfolios

Introduction

The development of National Educational Technology Standards for Teachers (NETS·T) as well as advances in technology and Web-based applications, stimulated initiatives to document performance and learning through the development of an electronic/e-portfolio* (Cambridge, Kahn, Tompkins, & Yancey, 2001). As a result, many teachers and teacher candidates are being strongly encouraged to consider producing or even required to produce an e-portfolio. While national and state standards have driven the development of e-portfolios for both teacher candidates and practicing teachers, teacher education and advance certification programs are far from uniform in their approach to this process (Strudler & Wetzel, 2005).

The goal of producing an e-portfolio is authentic assessment of an individual's performance or achievement in real-life situations tied to technology standards (Kilbane & Milman, 2003). Researchers (Barrett, 1999; Goldsby & Fazal, 2000; Wallace & Porter, 2004) found that teachers who can demonstrate their competence in using technology through an e-portfolio have an advantage in securing a teaching position and are more likely to incorporate technology into their own classroom.

Although most content for portfolios is developed with a computer and requires some technical knowledge and skills, e-portfolios require a more sophisticated understanding of the programs and processes related to this multimedia approach. Because the task of developing an e-portfolio can appear daunting, it is important to understand what is involved before moving in this direction.

The intent of this chapter is to provide an understanding of the elements of e-portfolio development, including:

- an overview of e-portfolios
- the advantages of developing an e-portfolio
- a description of the skills necessary
- information about the variety of hardware and software needed

*The terms *e-portfolio* and *electronic portfolio* are used interchangeably throughout this book.

- information on the options and issues for publishing
- Web resources to help you create an e-portfolio

Whether you are required to develop, or have the option of developing, an e-portfolio, this chapter provides practical information to help you get started as well as additional resources that will offer more in-depth guidelines for the process of e-portfolio development. The portfolio development concept and process presented in the previous and forthcoming chapters of this handbook apply to both paper and e-portfolios. The technical skills, materials, and equipment you use to create hypermedia linking of artifacts in an e-portfolio provide further insights to the reviewer about your technical as well as professional accomplishments.

What Is an Electronic Portfolio?

The e-portfolio, just like the paper portfolio, is a carefully selected collection of exemplary evidence that highlights a teacher's best work and accomplishments. However, unlike the paper portfolio, the e-portfolio is a multimedia approach that allows the teacher to present teaching, learning, and reflective entries in a variety of formats (audio, video, graphics, and text). Because e-portfolios typically use Web-based design, hypermedia links are used to interconnect standards or goals to artifacts for nonlinear access as opposed to section dividers or tabs in a traditional paper portfolio.

The electronic portfolio, sometimes referred to as a digital or multimedia portfolio, is typically published on the World Wide Web (WWW or Web) of the Internet, on DVD, or on CD. Developing an e-portfolio brings together the processes of both multimedia project development and portfolio development. Understanding how these two complementary processes work together, along with using standards as a framework for portfolio development, helps teachers gain the most benefit in demonstrating their growth over time, which is the primary purpose for creating a professional teaching portfolio (Barrett, 2000).

Demonstrating Competency with Technology Standards

Most states have adopted NETS standards, in some cases with state-specific modifications. As a result, many colleges of education now expect teacher candidates to demonstrate competency in the utilization of technology as a graduation requirement. When preparing either an electronic or paper portfolio you may choose to demonstrate your competencies within a section of your portfolio devoted to technology standards, or you may integrate your technology skills within your chosen framework. If you choose to develop an e-portfolio, you will be able to implicitly demonstrate many, but perhaps not all, of your technological skills. Hence, it will be important to consider technology standards throughout the process of portfolio development to ensure you have represented the full complement of NETS or state-level standards required by your program. The six categories in the NETS standards are:

- Technology Operations and Concepts
- Planning and Designing Learning Environments
- Teaching, Learning, and the Curriculum
- Assessment and Evaluation
- Productivity and Professional Practice
- Social, Ethical, Legal, and Human Issues

A complete representation of these standards and their indicators are available at the ISTE website (www.iste.org).

What Are the Advantages of Developing an Electronic Portfolio?

Electronic portfolios have the advantages of accessibility, portability, creativity, proof of teacher technology skills, enhanced self-confidence, and dissemination to a broader community (Kilbane & Milman, 2003). The chart on pages 33–34 provides a broad comparison of electronic and paper portfolios and the relative advantages and disadvantages of each.

As you can see from the comparison chart, e-portfolios allow portfolio reviewers to experience a multimedia presentation. They can watch a lesson, hear student interactions, and listen to a teacher's reflections rather than read about them. The decision to produce a paper or e-portfolio knowing the advantages and disadvantages of each is still individual and highly dependent on the situation, your technical skills, the purpose of your portfolio, and the audience.

Do I Have the Technical Knowledge and Skills?

The minimum level of knowledge and skills necessary for considering the development of an e-portfolio is basic computer literacy. Basic computer literacy requires that you understand the fundamentals of computer hardware and software, and that you know how to use a variety of software applications. More specifically, you need to know how to use your computer to create word-processing documents, incorporate computer graphics and produce audio and video files with hyperlinks connecting related digital artifacts. The general advantage of producing an electronic teaching portfolio is that as you develop your skill and become more versatile in your use of technology, you will advance from literacy to fluency. That fluency will ultimately extend to your learners as you adapt and integrate technology to your planning and delivery of instruction.

If you consider yourself computer literate and need to develop an e-portfolio that requires a higher level of skills than you currently have, you should think about taking a course, a workshop, or seeking out a mentor who has this knowledge and expertise prior to or in conjunction with your e-portfolio production effort. The level of effort required on your part is inversely proportional to the administrative and technical support provided by the organization, school, or workplace that originates the requirement. That is, the more help you can get in the form of equipment, software, and technical and administrative support, the easier the task will be for you (Gibson & Barrett, 2003). For example, many institutions of higher education that require e-portfolios of their new teachers also provide multimedia labs with technical support staff and online systems for straightforward creation of Web-based e-portfolios.

Criteria	*Paper Portfolio*	*Electronic Portfolio*
Accessibility	Can be reviewed anywhere without technological equipment.	Can be reviewed anywhere by a number of individuals with appropriate equipment.
Portability	Often cumbersome to carry.	Easy to carry or distribute on compact disc or via Web.
Audience	Difficult to reconfigure for different reviewer interests and hard to use by multiple simultaneous reviewers.	Easily reconfigured and able to be viewed by multiple simultaneous reviewers.
Creation	No specialized technical skills required. Production process is time consuming and labor intensive.	Steeper learning curve for technical skills. Production process is time consuming and labor intensive but often leads to increased technology application in the classroom.
Reviewer Friendliness	No special equipment needed to view. Sometimes difficult to find specific information.	Appropriate equipment needed for viewing, but easy to find information if hyperlinked.
Storage	Cumbersome to store by owner or institution. No backup copy likely.	Easy to store both master and backup copies. Large storage capacity with multiple modalities.

Criteria	*Paper Portfolio*	*Electronic Portfolio*
Flexibility	Difficult to maintain as dynamic or "living" documentation.	Easily modifiable with updates instantly available if Web enabled or reproducible at low cost on a compact disk.
Technical Competence	Reveals very little about technical proficiency.	Reveals breadth and depth of technical ability across all standards. Generalization of skills to the classroom.
Professional Competency	Captures the essence of your professional growth and learning through documentation and reflective entries.	Captures the essence of your professional growth and learning through documentation and reflective entries using multiple modalities. Video and audio clips enhance performance and personal reflections.
Standards	Establishes a static connection to performance standards and evidence.	Allows easy and immediate cross-mapping to any system of standards through hyperlinks.
Personal Marketability	More challenging for the portfolio developer to make teaching "come alive."	More professional and compelling display of skills with the potential to incorporate audio and video artifacts.

You also have to consider the time that it will take to develop the skills necessary for this type of presentation. If you think that you have an adequate level of technical knowledge and skills, and you have the time to develop an e-portfolio, the overview provided in this chapter will assist you in getting started in this process.

Using Web-Based Commercial Systems for Portfolio Development

With the increasing expectation that teachers and teacher candidates develop e-portfolios to document their growth and learning over time, several Web-based commercial systems (e.g., LiveText, TaskStream, Foliotek) were developed and marketed to individuals as well as to school systems and higher education institutions (Strudler and Wetzel, 2005). Fiedler and Pick (2004) evaluated four portfolio systems—LiveText, TaskStream, The Open Source Portfolio Initiative (OSPI), and Chalk and Wire—using the criteria listed here. These criteria should be considered when you select a commercial portfolio system.

- Planning and goal setting
- Creativity ability
- Facilitated communications between instructor and student
- Collaboration tools
- Connection and linking capabilities
- Organizational flexibility
- Display flexibility and transportability
- Data and information
- Start-up costs and maintenance
- System functionality and usability
- System security

While often costly to individuals, Web-based systems allow for the storage of materials over time, in some cases throughout a teacher education program, and provide the necessary template for portfolio development. Consequently, an infrastructure for including hyperlinks, data, and audio/video clips in a portfolio is easily accessible, which simplifies the technological skills and hardware necessary for e-portfolio development. Nonetheless, as previously mentioned, teacher education programs are far from uniform in their approach to e-portfolios. Moreover, commercial Web-based programs are often cost prohibitive if not provided through an institution, so it is very important to have an awareness of the other methods for developing an e-portfolio because most teacher candidates still utilize the independent approach.

What Computer Hardware Do I Need?

The following hardware is suggested to begin the process of creating an e-portfolio:

- **A computer with**
  - sufficient memory for storage
  - sufficient memory for processing
  - audio-video input capability if using analog sources (e.g., VHS videotape)
- **Internet server access** (if you plan to publish your portfolio on the Internet)
- **Flat-bed color scanner**
- **Digital camera or digital video camera** (if you decide to incorporate video clips in your portfolio)
- **CD burner** (if you plan to publish your portfolio on a CD)
- **DVD burner** (if you plan to publish your portfolio on a DVD)
- **USB flash drive** (for backup or transfer of digital artifacts)

What Computer Software Do I Need?

The required software can be divided into several categories: hypermedia "card" formats, HTML or Web-authoring software, multimedia slideshow or video editing software, Web-based commercial systems, PDF writers, and general utilities. The basis of selection from any of these categories depends on availability of the software, your technical expertise, the purpose of your portfolio, and the type of computer you are using (e.g., Windows or Apple OS). The following chart shows the most commonly cited e-portfolio development software for use by teachers. For further in-depth analysis of numerous applications, their advantages and disadvantages, and their appropriateness for specific electronic purposes, visit Dr. Helen Barrett's numerous websites, Kilbane and Milman (2003), and the sites listed on page 39.

Formats	*Software/Website*
Hypermedia "Card" Programs Software programs that allow the integration of graphics, sound, and movies in a single file. Electronic cards or screens are linked together by developer-created buttons.	**HyperStudio** www.mackiev.com **Toolbook** www.toolbook.com **KidPix** www.learningcompany.com
HTML or Web-Authoring Software Applications that will translate your text and graphics into an HTML format. Web-authoring software will generally allow you to copy and paste word-processing text into a web page. If you are competent with HTML, you can use any text editor to create web pages, but will only be able to edit in a "code view."	**Microsoft Word** www.microsoft.com **Dreamweaver** www.adobe.com/products/dreamweaver **Adobe GoLive** www.adobe.com/products/golive/
Multimedia Slideshow Software Multimedia slideshow software allows the portfolio developer to create electronic slides that incorporate a combination of text, audio, still images, animation, video, and interactivity into a presentation.	**Microsoft PowerPoint** www.office.microsoft.com/enus/powerpoint/default.aspx **Keynote** www.apple.com/iwork/keynote **OpenOffice** www.openoffice.org/ **Google Docs** http://docs.google.com
PDF Writers A universal file format that preserves all of the fonts, formatting, colors, and graphics of any source document, regardless of the application and platform used to create it. Adobe Acrobat is the leading software for creating PDF files. However, there are other software programs that allow for the creation of PDF files. These include OpenOffice, Microsoft Office, and MAC OS.	**Adobe Acrobat** www.adobe.com/products/acrobat/ **PDFCreator** www.pdfforge.org/products/pdfcreator

Formats	*Software/Website*
Video Editing Digital video production software that provides ability to produce video clips combined with still images, titling, audio tracks, and transition and other special effects. It is important to note that some of these programs are system specific.	**Adobe Premiere Pro** www.adobe.com **Adobe Premiere Elements** www.adobe.com/products/premiereel/ **Apple Final Cut Express and Pro** www.apple.com **iMovie** www.apple.com **Pinnacle** www.pinnaclesys.com/PublicSite/us/Home/ **Ulead VideoStudio** www.ulead.com/runme.htm **Windows Movie Maker** www.microsoft.com/windowsxp/downloads/updates/moviemaker2.mspx
General Utilities Software programs that facilitate and enhance the development of an e-portfolio.	**Adobe Illustrator** **Adobe PhotoShop** or **PhotoShop Elements** **Apple iLife (iDVD, iMovie, iPhoto, iTunes)** **Clip Art** **Microsoft Excel** **SoundStudio**

Options and Issues When Publishing an Electronic Portfolio

The most prevalent options of publishing an e-portfolio are via a CD, a DVD, or the Web. Before deciding on any of these methods, you will need to be aware of several important issues. Understanding the pros and cons of CD, DVD, and Web publication will help you to make the appropriate choice.

Publishing on a CD or DVD

A CD allows you to include about 650 MB of content and a DVD allows you to include about 4.7 GB of text, graphics, audio, and video. CDs or DVDs are easy to distribute, store, and duplicate, making it feasible for you to easily distribute multiple copies of your portfolio to individuals or organizations. Most CD or DVD burners produce a CD or DVD for any platform, e.g., Windows or Apple OS. Additionally, the cost of a blank CD or DVD has dropped to less than fifty cents U.S. The cost of a CD or DVD burner has also decreased. Many computers provide CD or DVD burners or combination units (e.g., super drives) as an integral and affordable part of the hardware configuration. These factors make the CD or DVD a ready option for duplicating your e-portfolio.

A slight disadvantage to publishing on a CD or DVD is the difficulty in updating or changing a portfolio once it has been recorded. Making changes requires the rewriting or burning of a new disk. You would need routine access to the appropriate hardware and software to record and republish any changes.

Publishing on the Web

Publishing on the Web is limited by the space available to you on a web server. When teacher candidates graduate, they often lose their space on the university or college's web server that was provided in support of their project. Similarly, teachers who store their web page on a school system server will also lose that space if they change school systems. More recently, vendors of online portfolio builders, like LiveText or TaskStream, that have contracts with colleges or universities offer affordable options for new teachers to continue to share their e-portfolios on the Web after they graduate. Teachers must decide if they want to purchase space on a commercial site or use free space that might include a lot of irrelevant advertising that may distract the viewer from the substance of the portfolio presentation.

The choice of publishing an e-portfolio via the Internet, a DVD, or a CD is clearly an important decision. It can only be made after careful consideration of your individual preferences, your situation, and the hardware and software available to you. Most e-portfolio development software can be used to publish on a CD, DVD, or the Web. Keep in mind that the portfolio reviewer needs to have the necessary hardware and software to access your e-portfolio. Being aware of this consideration will help you to determine whether to develop a paper portfolio or e-portfolio. If you develop both types, then you will surely be prepared for any situation.

Adhering to Intellectual Property Rights and Copyright Laws

A Web-based e-portfolio can be accessed anytime by anyone with online capability. Individuals can password protect their portfolio contents by providing their password only to portfolio reviewers. To further ensure confidentiality, consider deleting personal data, yours or others', that should not be accessible to the public; for instance, names, addresses, phone numbers, and Social Security numbers.

Because the Internet is accessible to so many people, an individual's intellectual property rights can be threatened. Documents on the Web can easily be copied and used by others. In addition, teachers who choose to include materials such as photographs of their students, letters of recommendations, or similar document types must be sure to secure permission for including these items in their portfolio. See Appendix E for a sample permission letter for photographs and videos. Copyright laws must be adhered to if you use clip art, digital photos, or other commercially prepared material.

Resources to Get You Started

There are many articles in professional journals and books that describe how to develop an e-portfolio. At the time of this publication, the best current source of information is available on the Web. Use of popular search engines such as Google, Google Scholar, Excit2, and Info.com provide links to valuable information. These sites will also help you to find items such as portfolio builders, tutorials, and portfolio examples. Public or university libraries make available access to search the ERIC databases and provide another way to access information in the form of articles and research papers about e-portfolios. Check to see if your public library provides online access from your home computer. Using search terms such as *portfolios for teachers, portfolio examples, e-portfolio teacher portfolios, pre-service teaching portfolio, digital teaching portfolio,* and *professional portfolio* will yield many possibilities. You may also want to consult Web-based articles or books on pointers for good Web design.

In addition, numerous sites provide a plethora of information about the development of e-portfolios, including the process, online examples, and rubrics for assessment. Following are some sites that may be helpful in higher-education settings. You will note that most sites include additional links to other e-portfolio resources. However, it is crucial to recognize that many of the links included can expire, are broken, or are no longer available. You may also find that some higher-education sites require a password in order to view examples of teacher candidate portfolios.

Websites Created by Dr. Helen Barrett, University of Alaska

Resource	*Website*
Dr. Helen Barrett's Home Page	http://helenbarrett.com/
ISTE International Society for Technology in Education—National Educational Technology Standards Electronic Portfolio Templates	www.helenbarrett.com/nets.html
Dr. Helen Barrett's favorite Internet sites.	http://electronicportfolios.com/portfolios/bookmarks.html
Portfolio Development "At-a-Glance Guides," Common Software Tools for Creating and Publishing Electronic Portfolios (Updated May 13, 2005)	http://electronicportfolios.com/ALI/index.html
Dr. Helen Barrett on Electronic Portfolio Development (Apple Learning Interchange)	http://newali.apple.com/ali_sites/ali/exhibits/1000156/

Websites with How-to Guides

Resource	*Website*
Florida State University Department of Physical Education This Florida State University site describes their Department of Physical Education's requirement for pre-service teachers to document their competency in relationship to the state's preprofessional practices and national standards for sport and physical education beginning teacher standards. There are links to examples of acceptable and unacceptable documentation as well as a complete portfolio example.	www.fsu.edu/~smrmpe/pencate_portfolios.html
University of Wisconsin-Stout This University of Wisconsin-Stout site provides an e-portfolio guide to developing pre-service and in-service art teaching portfolios. The topics include: What Is an E-Portfolio? Creating Your Portfolio, Example Portfolios, Evaluating Your Portfolio, Reflection, and Helpful Resources.	www.uwstout.edu/art/artedportfolios/index.html
eFolio Minnesota This site is geared toward Minnesota residents as well as students enrolled in Minnesota schools. If you select Gallery from the menu, you will find student portfolio examples.	www.efoliominnesota.com
The Videography for Educators Tips and techniques to assist in the development of quality video are included in this website. It also provides planning documents and video examples to illustrate concepts and skills in video production. The content assumes you are already learning the mechanics of digital video editing applications, are familiar with the operation of video cameras, and are ready to learn the art of video editing.	http://newali.apple.com/cgi-bin/WebObjects/ALIView.woa/wa/DisplayExhibit?AspectName=PLANNING&SiteCode=ali&ExhibitID=1000019

Websites with Electronic Portfolio Examples

Resource	*Website*
Penn State University Teaching with Technology Certificate This site lists portfolios that were approved for a Teaching with Technology certificate. Although these are university instructor portfolios, they provide an example of good portfolio design.	http://tlt.its.psu.edu/support/twt/completed.html

University of Scranton Model Student Portfolio Site This pilot Web-based portfolios site includes model portfolios of students at the University of Scranton. Although not all the individual portfolio links work, there is sufficient information to provide portfolio examples.	http://academic.uofs.edu/organization/msp/students/students.html
University of Florida School of Music Examples of music-education teacher candidate portfolios, templates for both PC and MAC operating systems, as well as a portfolio manual are included on the website.	http://portfolios.music.ufl.edu/studentport.html
Other E-portfolio Examples	http://durak.org/kathy/portfolio/ www.msu.edu/~miazgama/professional.htm

Conclusion

It is obvious that the trend toward wider use of technology in the schools and improved computer literacy among students and teachers has had a profound impact on teacher education. As the power and availability of technology increase and the costs of hardware and software decrease, teachers will be forced to expand their knowledge and skills to keep up with the technological standards for the profession.

Making the decision to develop an e-portfolio is certainly in keeping with this growing trend. While it is exciting to think about the potential benefits of implementing this emerging form of technology, it is also important to understand the amount of technical knowledge and skills needed as well as the issues that affect the development and publication of an e-portfolio. When you begin the process of e-portfolio development with the essential technical literacy, appropriate hardware and software, readily accessible support, and the time needed to prepare a product of this magnitude, you will eliminate many of the frustrations that could impact your success. For a more in-depth discussion and detailed, step-by-step guidelines for all aspects of e-portfolio development, we recommend *The Digital Teaching Portfolio Handbook: A How-to Guide for Educators* (Kilbane & Milman, 2003). Keep in mind that regardless of whether you create a paper portfolio or e-portfolio, the substance and credibility of the documentation (digital artifacts and reflections) are more important than the format in which you choose to present your work.

Chapter 3 ACTIVITIES

Now that you have an overview of the concept of e-portfolios, and have decided that you want to develop one, engage in the following activities to help you get started.

Decide how you will demonstrate your technological skills throughout your portfolio. Will you devote an entire section to technology standards or will you demonstrate your technological competencies within the framework you've already selected for your portfolio, such as INTASC?

Identify and list the software and hardware available to you through your school or college. Use a scanner, digital camera, or spreadsheet to create an initial electronic entry to be used in your portfolio.

Identify the individuals who can provide technological assistance throughout the portfolio development process.

Explore the websites listed throughout this chapter, as well as others available on the Web, to identify and record features you want to consider as you develop your portfolio. For example, ease of navigation and viewing, choice of background and font, amount of information on a page, and other features that impress you in a positive or negative way.

CHAPTER 4

Phase I—Getting Started

Introduction

For some, the portfolio development process can be overwhelming. Many teachers have difficulty making decisions about how to begin this process and where to go next. The Getting Started Phase of Portfolio Development will not only help you get through this roadblock but will also provide the foundation for all the remaining phases. The portfolio development process is highly reflective and requires you to make many decisions throughout each phase. There are three main decisions to be made during Phase I: *Determining the purpose of your portfolio; Considering a set of performances standards;* and *Collecting, selecting, and creating documents.* Understanding and working through these three tasks will help eliminate some of the anxiety associated with beginning this rigorous endeavor.

Determining the Purpose of Your Portfolio

The purpose of your portfolio depends on where you are in your teacher education program or teaching career. Most portfolios fall into the categories described in Chapter I; entrance, working, exit, interview, or showcase portfolio. Review this information so that you thoroughly understand the purpose of each type. Each portfolio's purpose requires a different kind of decision making regarding the selection of materials and the way in which you present them. It is important to note that as a teacher candidate, the purpose of your portfolio evolves as you develop as a teacher and as your audience changes from prospective college, to academic department, to prospective employer. The chart following illustrates a small sampling of some of the different types of decisions you need to make when compiling artifacts that will support the purpose of your portfolio.

Portfolio Type	*Purpose*	*Decisions*	*Potential Evidence*
Entrance	Admission to Teacher Education Program	■ What evidence will I include that will prove that I have an adequate knowledge base to enter this program? ■ What experiences have I had related to teaching? ■ What skills do I have that will demonstrate my potential to become an effective teacher? ■ What values do I have that are indicators of what makes a quality teacher?	■ Transcripts of college coursework ■ Test scores ■ Research paper that demonstrates my thinking and writing skills ■ Camp counselor ■ Day care program assistant ■ Documents that demonstrate superior organizational skills ■ Written scenarios by me or others that validate my ability to motivate students ■ My philosophy of education
Interview	To secure a teaching position	■ What evidence should I include that illustrates my ability to teach? ■ What assets should I include to validate student learning?	■ A video with accompanying lesson plans ■ Supervisor's evaluation ■ Before-and-after test scores ■ Examples of student work

As illustrated in this chart, the questions you ask yourself will differ considerably based on the purpose of your portfolio. Many of the questions you need to consider will evolve, not only from the purpose of your portfolio, but also from coursework and performance standards. Attention to the decision-making process will ensure that you include evidence that is relevant.

Considering a Set of Performance Standards

Much attention has been given to the importance of considering performance standards in the development of a professional portfolio. As stated in Chapter 2, standards and themes provide a credible theoretical foundation for the collection of your documentation. Teacher candidates will most likely use a set of standards identified by their teacher preparation program. In-service teachers will consider national or local standards identified by their individual school or school district. Both teacher candidates and in-service teachers may consider standards identified by their specific subject or specialty area.

Appendix A contains several examples of national standards. Appendix B is a listing of national organizations, which have developed professional standards for their members. You might also consider the use of the six universally understood themes suggested in Chapter 2 since they correlate with key performances articulated in many of the standards. Whichever performance standards or themes you select, your documentation should provide evidence of growth and competency related to those standards or themes.

Collecting, Selecting, and Creating Documents

The next task in this phase involves the collection or creation of evidence to support your portfolio purpose. There are many items that could be included in your portfolio. However, it must be emphasized that each item must be accompanied and supported by an explanation of the artifact, a rationale for inclusion, and a reflection on your growth and learning. Having too many examples may create an unwieldy task for you as well as the reviewer. The key is to be highly selective by sorting out the best from the rest, choosing only those items that are critical and essential to the purpose of your portfolio. Best, however, does not always mean exemplary. Sometimes a lesson gone badly provides important evidence of "lessons learned." You must also include a reflection that indicates how you felt about the lesson, what you would do differently, and your plans for continued growth. In general, current evidence has more value than examples that represent experiences from many years ago. However, you may include major honors or awards you earned earlier in your career that are still significant regardless of when they were received.

The following examples of portfolio documents are organized using the universal themes correlated with the INTASC standards. As you review these ideas for documentation, remember that these examples may apply to more than one standard or theme and should be placed in the portfolio where they are most appropriate. If you are producing an e-portfolio, you can readily cross-map, or hyperlink, your evidence to several standards. All these examples can be converted to digital assets for use in an e-portfolio, and may include audio and video enhancements.

Suggestions for Portfolio Documentation

If you were to document a standard that relates to your *Knowledge of Subject Matter and Educational Theory (INTASC Standard 1),* you might include the following items in your portfolio:

- Highlights of a unit of instruction
- Abstract of a research paper

- Case studies emphasizing the application of learning or human development theory
- Position paper related to subject matter or educational theory
- Transcripts or descriptions of courses, workshops, study groups, and staff development experiences that enhanced your knowledge of subject matter or theory
- Original instructional materials that demonstrate your knowledge of subject matter
- Test results that show your competency in content areas such as the National Teacher's Exam (NTE) or PRAXIS
- Notes, letters, and written feedback from other professionals regarding your subject-matter competency

If you were to document a standard that relates to your ***Knowledge of Development and Learning (INTASC Standard 2),*** you might want to include the following items in your portfolio:

- Samples of observational data (e.g., checklists, running records, anecdotal notes)
- A lesson plan that provides evidence of differentiated planning and instruction based on ability levels (e.g., reading groups, small-group math lessons), as well as work samples and photographs. The plan must convey the different teaching strategies used for the different ability levels
- A lesson plan that indicates evidence of differentiated planning and instruction based on assessment data (particularly for subgroups)
- A lesson plan and photos that demonstrate your appreciation for a child's development in areas other than math, reading, science and social studies (e.g., art, physical education, drama, and music)
- Copies of various assessment tools used to determine a child's background knowledge and abilities
- Lesson plan or work sample that demonstrates the use of prior knowledge to introduce a new curricular goal/objective
- Photos of children working together as evidence of peer group teaching/mentoring and/or collaborative work
- Work samples/photos/reflections demonstrating your ability to take advantage of teachable moments, rather than just planned instructional experiences for your students
- A copy of a referral to a specialist or an administrator that conveys concerns about a child's development and requests follow-up/guidance
- A flyer or agenda from a Family Learning Night that indicates a willingness to involve families in a child's development and learning
- A newsletter or parent handbook that includes information on child development, learning, or parental involvement in education

All standards include aspects of ***Planning, Delivery, and Assessment of Instruction (INTASC Standards 3, 4, 7, and 8).*** Here are some ideas that might be appropriate for documenting your competencies in these areas:

- An overview of a long-range unit of instruction
- An explanation of how you use knowledge of the learner to plan instruction
- Sample lesson plans
- An explanation of how you modify instruction to meet the needs of all students
- Pictures of students engaged in a learning activity
- A video tape demonstrating your teaching
- A web illustrating your repertoire of strategies used for instruction
- A list of strategies used to create a multicultural perspective
- Samples of student work
- Samples of assessment tools used to diagnose learning needs
- Samples of rubrics used to assess student performance
- A written "think-aloud" about your decisions regarding the use of assessment results to diagnose and plan further instruction
- A chart illustrating before and after assessment of student learning
- Documentation of how you use technology for planning, delivery, and assessment
- Pictures of bulletin boards, plays, special events, special projects, field trips, and guest speakers
- A professional development plan for increasing effectiveness in planning, delivery, and assessment of instruction
- Results of solicited feedback from students regarding your effectiveness as a teacher
- Notes or written feedback from an administrator, supervisor, or mentor teacher regarding the effectiveness of your instruction

***Classroom Management and Organization* (*INTASC Standard 5*)** are familiar terms to all educators. However, this terminology is not always used in state and national standards. Classroom management and organization competencies are imbedded throughout many standards. It is obvious that effective classroom management impacts all teaching performance. Therefore, some evidence of your skills and dispositions regarding classroom management should be placed in the portfolio regardless of whether the standards specifically use this term or not. The examples listed here are some ideas to help you document your competency in this area.

- A statement of your philosophy of classroom management and discipline
- A description of your policy and procedures for managing your classroom
- A diagram of the classroom
- A description of a situation in which you were successful in changing inappropriate student behavior to on-task behavior
- A student contract
- Pictures of bulletin boards and centers that relate to management and organization of the classroom

- A description of strategies used for instructional management or behavior management
- A sample of how you keep accurate records (grades, attendance, checklists, progress notes)
- Notes, letters, and written feedback regarding the effectiveness of your classroom management

How you interact with students, colleagues, parents, and community has a significant impact on your success as a teacher. The state and national standards that are labeled Social Context, Social Development, Family Outreach, Family Partnerships, and Collaboration with Colleagues each include performances that require effective ***Human Relationships (INTASC Standard 6).*** Here are a few examples of documents that could support these categories.

- A letter of introduction or newsletter written by you to the parents of your students or school community
- An explanation of special strengths you have in creating positive working relationships with students, other teachers, parents, administrators, and supervisors
- A description of experiences working with diversity in the classroom and what you do to make all students feel included
- A summary of what you do to involve the broader educational community in the instructional program for students
- A document or graphic organizer that explains or shows what you have done to enhance collaboration with colleagues
- Notes and letters from students, parents, school, or university professionals regarding your interpersonal skills
- A description of how your interpersonal style fosters positive and productive working relationships

Professionalism (INTASC Standard 9) can be documented by including any item that demonstrates your commitment to the profession. The examples here are some ways to document professionalism:

- A current professional development plan
- A current résumé
- A list of memberships in professional organizations
- A list of professional books you have read
- A description of leadership positions held
- Evidence of degrees, honors, awards, and recognition received
- Evidence of your volunteer work, special projects, programs, and participation on committees related to education
- Research, articles, and papers written or coauthored
- Letters from administrators commenting on your professional qualities: responsibility, reliability, punctuality, attitude, etc.

- Evaluations
- A written statement of your goals for future professional growth

It is critical to remember that if you choose to include photographs or a video of your students, parents, or colleagues in your portfolio, then you will need to secure permission from the individual or the student's parent or legal guardian. See Appendix E for a sample letter of permission for both photographs and videos. Appendix G is a sample format for introducing and explaining a video that you wish to include in your portfolio.

These examples of portfolio content are provided to stimulate your thinking and are by no means exhaustive. Consider these ideas as you collect, select, and create your portfolio artifacts. Please see Appendix F for a worksheet to help you think about what you already have and what you need in order to begin the collection of documents for your portfolio.

Determining the Appropriateness of Your Artifacts

Here are some questions to consider as you make important decisions about what artifacts to select for your portfolio. Answering these questions helps you determine whether the document is worthy of inclusion.

- Do the artifacts align with the purpose of your portfolio?
- Do the artifacts support a performance standard or theme?
- Are the artifacts credible and do they support progress toward your professional growth, learning, and goals?
- Are the artifacts items that provide substance and meaning to your portfolio?
- If this artifact were eliminated, would it detract from the credibility of your portfolio?

Martin-Kniep (1999) suggests that teacher candidates assemble professional portfolios with no more than five items that represent the following outcomes:

- The ability to communicate with a variety of audiences effectively
- The ability to reflect on one's practice and to set goals to further one's professional development
- The ability to identify and use effective curriculums or programs to meet the needs of different kinds of learners
- The ability to work collaboratively
- One's best work in the area of assessment or evaluation (p. 6)

She also reported that "most teacher candidates like having clear expectations of what to include in their portfolio while having the freedom to select appropriate and personally meaningful evidence" (p. 6). The final selection of artifacts will be based on the purpose of the portfolio, the audience, and your personal preferences for documentation.

Phase I for Electronic Portfolios

As noted earlier, the process for developing a professional portfolio is applicable to paper and electronic versions when dealing with the content. Both require that you determine the purpose; consider a set of performance standards; and collect, select, and create artifacts. However, they differ in the way that they are produced.

When developing an e-portfolio, there are additional components that need to be integrated into the process and that relate to the more technical aspects of preparation for electronic publication. Figure 4.1 presents an overview of the process for Phase I—Getting Started. The items in

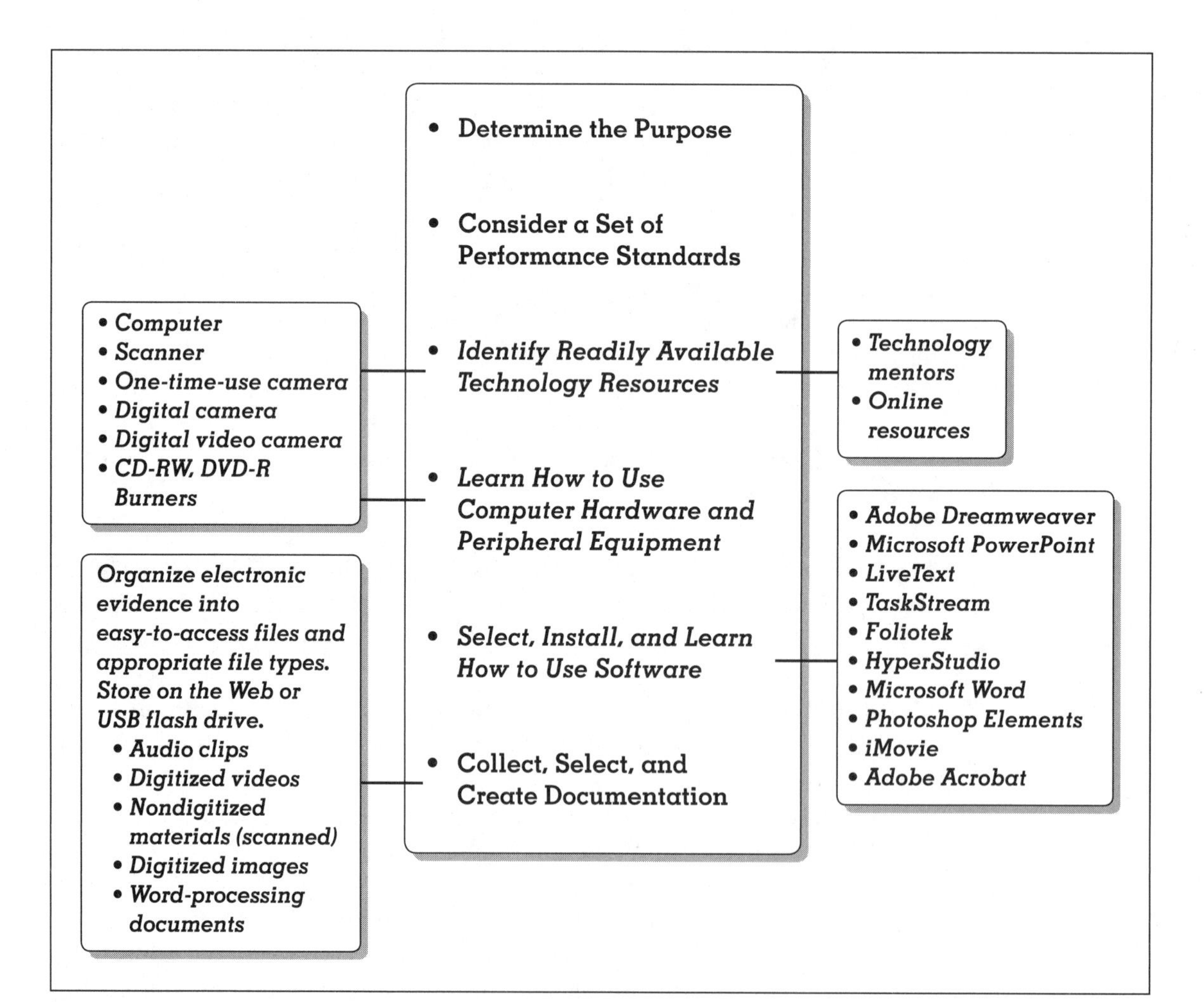

FIGURE 4.1 Phase I—Getting Started.

italics identify the differences in the process when adapting this phase to e-portfolio development.

You will notice that the process for developing an e-portfolio in Phase I—Getting Started includes three additional components: (1) identifying readily available technology resources; (2) learning how to use computer hardware and peripheral equipment; and (3) selecting, installing, and learning how to use software. Consider the following suggestions as you work through Phase I:

- Explore the availability of technical experts at your school or in your community who can provide support while you are engaged in this effort. You will probably find computer hardware and peripheral equipment like scanners, video cameras, and audio equipment available for your use at these sites.
- Use the one-page guidelines for creating and publishing e-portfolios developed by Dr. Helen Barrett (http://electronicportfolios.com/ALI/index.html). These "At-a-Glance Guides" include a vast amount of information about digitizing and storing your artifacts using a variety of hardware and software applications.
- Consider keeping a "one-time use" camera with your school materials so that you can take photos that can be utilized in your portfolio to support the standards, goals, or universal themes you are using as a framework for your portfolio.
- As you consider the use of the variety of software available, select an application that you have experienced. For example, if you are already familiar with Microsoft Word, use the web-page development features of that application to design, build, and publish your first web pages of assets for your e-portfolio. Be aware that each kind of software is designed for different purposes. A leading-practices approach suggests that you invest your time in learning an application dedicated to website management (e.g., Dreamweaver) for designing, building, and managing your e-portfolio. Dr. Helen Barrett's "At-a-Glance Guides" also include one-page guides with instructions on using various software to construct an e-portfolio (e.g. Microsoft Word, Excel, PowerPoint, iPhoto, Keynote). Other online resources on this page include how to publish a portfolio on the Internet and on a CD.
- Organize your materials into easily accessible files and store them on the Web or flash drive. The collection, grouping, cataloging, and retrieval are referred to as digital asset management (DAM). The use of Web technology standards is important for DAM. For example, you can create a file folder structure delineated by type of asset (audio, video, document, etc.), folders for raw or compressed data (Web-ready), and production (portfolio ready). It may be helpful to think of DAM as comparable to the library card-catalog system or as a modern-day electronic file cabinet to collect, group information, catalog information, and retrieve items as you need them.

- Use file-naming conventions that are succinct and intuitively reflect the content of the file. One caution is to never use special characters, such as "!," "@," "#," etc.

Conclusion

It is obvious that the collection, selection, and creation of assets are important elements in the portfolio development process. However, artifacts cannot stand alone. Each one must be accompanied by an introductory explanation and rationale for inclusion in your portfolio as well as a reflective entry that communicates your growth and development as a teacher and professional. Chapter 5 provides guidance on how to enhance your portfolio documentation with meaningful introductions, explanations, and reflections.

Chapter 4 ACTIVITIES

The information in this chapter was intended to help you begin the process of portfolio development. Use these activities to focus your thinking about what you need to do to get started.

Write a clear statement about the purpose of your portfolio. This can be used as an introductory entry in your portfolio.

Write a rationale for your selection of the standards or themes you will use as a framework for your portfolio. This may also be used as an introductory entry in your portfolio.

Write your philosophy of education.

Use the worksheet in Appendix F to help you make decisions about what artifacts that you already have or documents that you need to develop in support of the standards.

CHAPTER 5

Phase II—Enhancing Your Evidence

Introduction

The Enhancing Your Evidence phase of portfolio development is one of the most vital steps in the process. The work that you do during this time can make the difference between developing a pretty paper or electronic "page turner" or a respectable testimonial of your professional accomplishments. This phase has three components: *Connecting standards to portfolio documentation; Supporting your documentation;* and *Displaying your documentation.*

Most teachers begin to get serious about the enhancement phase when they are preparing their portfolio materials for use in an interview or presentation. Regardless of the intent, careful attention to the attributes in this phase facilitates the creation of a professional portfolio that represents you well under all circumstances.

Connecting Standards to Portfolio Documentation

In Phase I you identified a set of standards or themes that informed your decision making in the selection of portfolio evidence. In essence, each document that you create or select should support your competency in meeting the performance identified in the standard or theme. You need to communicate to the portfolio reviewer the relationship between your documentation and performance standards. One of the most effective methods for achieving this is to create a chart that cross-references your materials with the performance standards or themes. The portfolio reviewer can see at a glance the relationship between the standards or themes and your evidence. The following charts are included to help you understand the concept of cross-referencing standards with portfolio content. Consider including one of these organizational formats in your portfolio. The chart in Figure 5.1 provides further credibility to your documentation. Furthermore, it is possible that the reviewer may be specifically looking for your ability to integrate standards with your portfolio content.

Evidence and Standards Cross-Reference Chart

Portfolio Evidence	***INTASC Performance Standards***									
	1	*2*	*3*	*4*	*5*	*6*	*7*	*8*	*9*	*10*
Philosophy of Education	*	*			*					
Lesson Plan (Mathematics)			*	*			*	*		
Unit Plan Social Studies			*	*			*	*		
Sample Tests								*		
Student Work			*							
Behavior Management Plan					*					
Professional Development Plan										

See Chapter 7 for actual portfolio entries from teacher candidates who used these formats.

Standards and Evidence Cross-Reference Chart

Performance Theme	***Evidence***
Knowledge of Subject Matter	*Research paper* *Unit of Instruction* *Travel Related to Study of Africa* *Case Study*
Planning, Delivery, and Assessment of Instruction	*Lesson/Unit Plans* *Sample Tests/Student Work* *Video* *Observational Feedback and Evaluations*
Human Relationships	*Letters to Parents* *Letters from Parents* *School Newsletter* *Special Projects*
Classroom Management	*Classroom rules* *Case study* *Seating arrangement* *Reflection*
Professionalism	*Lists of Membership in Professional Organizations* *Professional Development Workshops and Certificates of Completion*

FIGURE 5.1 Cross-reference charts.

Supporting Your Documentation

Most instructional materials cannot stand alone. Narratives need to be provided for the portfolio reviewer to fully understand the significance of each item included in your portfolio and its relevance to your teaching competencies. Writing meaningful introductions, clear explanations, and insightful reflections provides context for the evidence you are presenting. Therefore, it is important that you give careful attention to how you communicate your thoughts in each of these informative entries.

Introductions

Introductions are narratives that are usually found at the *beginning* of the portfolio or at the onset of each *new section.* The intent of an introduction is to provide an overview of the forthcoming material. An introduction, which occurs in the beginning of the portfolio, often includes the purpose of the portfolio and a philosophy of education. The introduction can also include an overview of the standards or themes that are being used, a rationale for the inclusion of the documents, and an organizational chart cross-referencing documentation with standards. Section introductions may include some of the same type of information. However, these introductions are more specific to the standard, theme, or goal that you are using as the framework for your portfolio.

Explanations

Explanations are narratives that provide information about the document presented. They provide a better understanding of the evidence that cannot be captured by the document alone. An explanation can include a rationale for the selection of the evidence, a description of the event, and the teacher/student learning outcomes resulting from the experience. Explanations should be written for each document. They can range from a *full page* to a *short caption* connected to an image or other entry. Some items, such as transcripts, résumés, and letters of recommendation, are self-explanatory. Nevertheless, it is beneficial to have an introduction to the portfolio section that includes these types of documents. Including an explanation enhances nearly all entries. If you intend to produce an electronic teaching portfolio and include digital video or voice-overs, the video or audio narrative can reduce the amount of explanation required. It is good practice to have someone read your explanations to determine whether they clearly describe the relevance of the documentation to the standard or theme. A major indicator that your explanation needs further clarification is if the reviewer has difficulty understanding your rationale for the selection of an artifact.

Reflections

Reflection is a highly complex thinking process cultivated over time. It is a process that requires careful and analytical thinking about issues related to the teaching profession. Typically, reflection involves systematically and insightfully thinking about what you are doing, why you are doing it, how you are doing it, and the effects of your instruction on student learning. The intent of reflection is to develop the ongoing awareness of a teacher's own thoughts, feelings, teaching decisions, and learner reactions. It should lead to insightful change of behavior toward the improvement of instruction and the increased probability of learning.

Portfolio reflective entries are written thoughts, feelings, insights, and questions that represent your personal analysis of professional issues. Written reflections may communicate to the portfolio reviewer information about how you make teaching decisions, how you apply theory to classroom practice, how your teaching has made a difference in the lives of learners and the goals of the school, and how you intend to increase your teaching effectiveness and student learning. Figure 5.2 illustrates a process for writing effective reflections.

When actual teaching materials are combined with reflections, the reviewer begins to understand the thought processes that result in decisions that shape the teacher's actions and promote growth. Reflections allow the reviewer to gain insight into teacher decision making and learning that resulted from the event or instructional situation. They bring meaning to the documentation of your performance and demonstrate your ability to analyze your performance and growth from an experience. When explanations and reflections are part of the evidence of your performance, they provide the reviewer with information about what occurred as well as your insights related to the teaching and learning experience.

Writing reflective entries that include your thoughts, feelings, and insights may be a difficult task for some individuals. After you use the process for writing effective reflections, try the sentence starters in Figure 5.3 to facilitate your thinking and help you move forward in writing reflective entries. These are only a few ways to begin a reflective entry. Each individual's reflections are unique to that person's specific experiences, writing style, and own way of processing those experiences. Appendix H is a worksheet that will structure the reflective writing process. Use this worksheet as a template for writing reflective entries for your portfolio.

Combining Introductions, Explanations, and Reflections

All portfolio entries are a result of your experiences as a teacher. In order to communicate an experience in your portfolio you must select appropriate materials that embody the critical aspects of the experience. Once again,

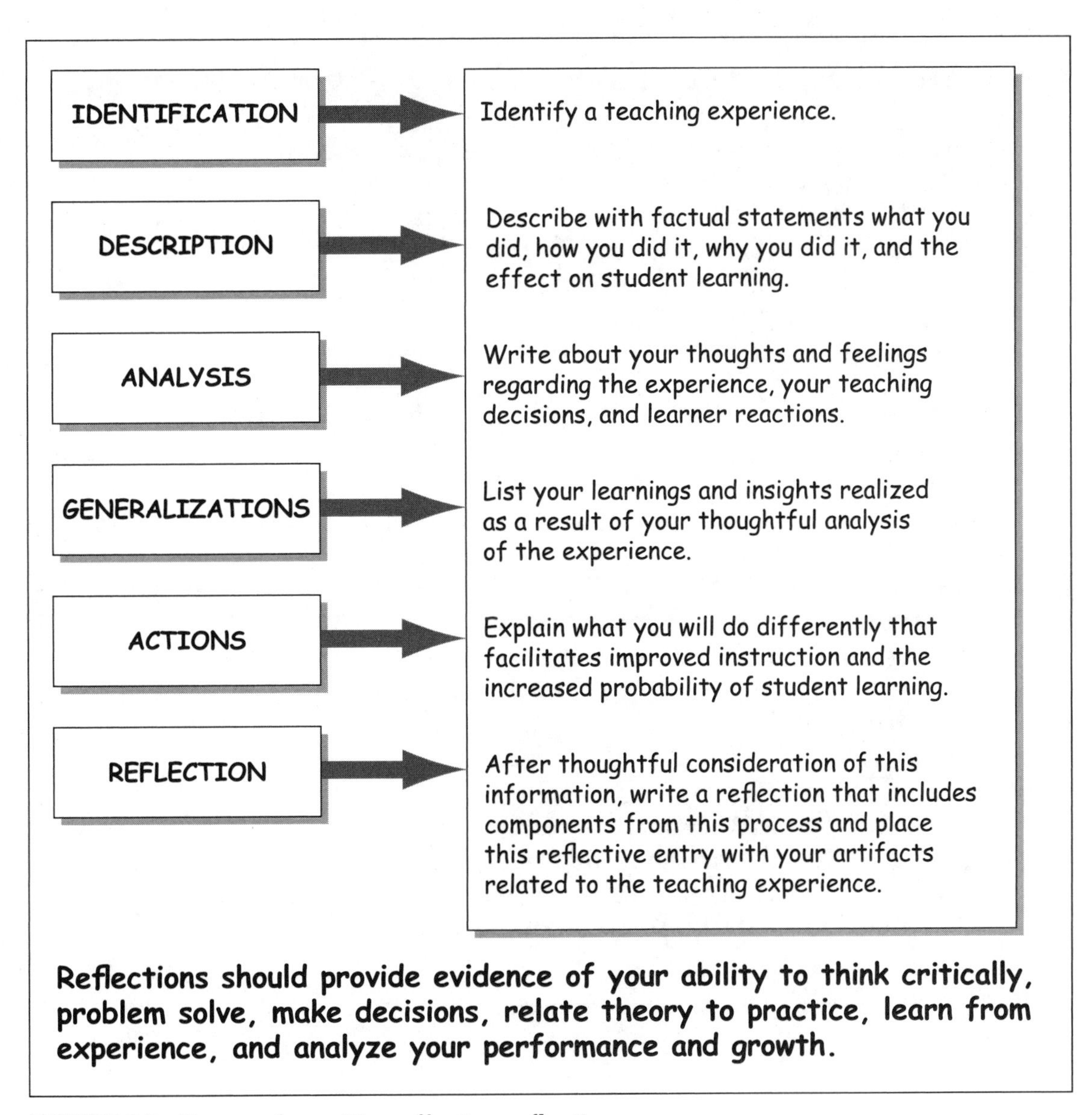

FIGURE 5.2 Process for writing effective reflections.

these items by themselves cannot tell the entire story. They must be supported by introductions, explanations, and reflections.

Figure 5.4 illustrates how the experience of conducting a parent-teacher-student conference can become a portfolio entry. The introduction provides information about why this teacher chose to create this entry for her portfolio. It also explains the relationship of these documents to the INTASC Standards. Each element is presented with an explanation that helps the reviewer understand the thinking behind the inclusion of these items. Finally, the entry includes a reflection about the teacher's thoughts and feelings in

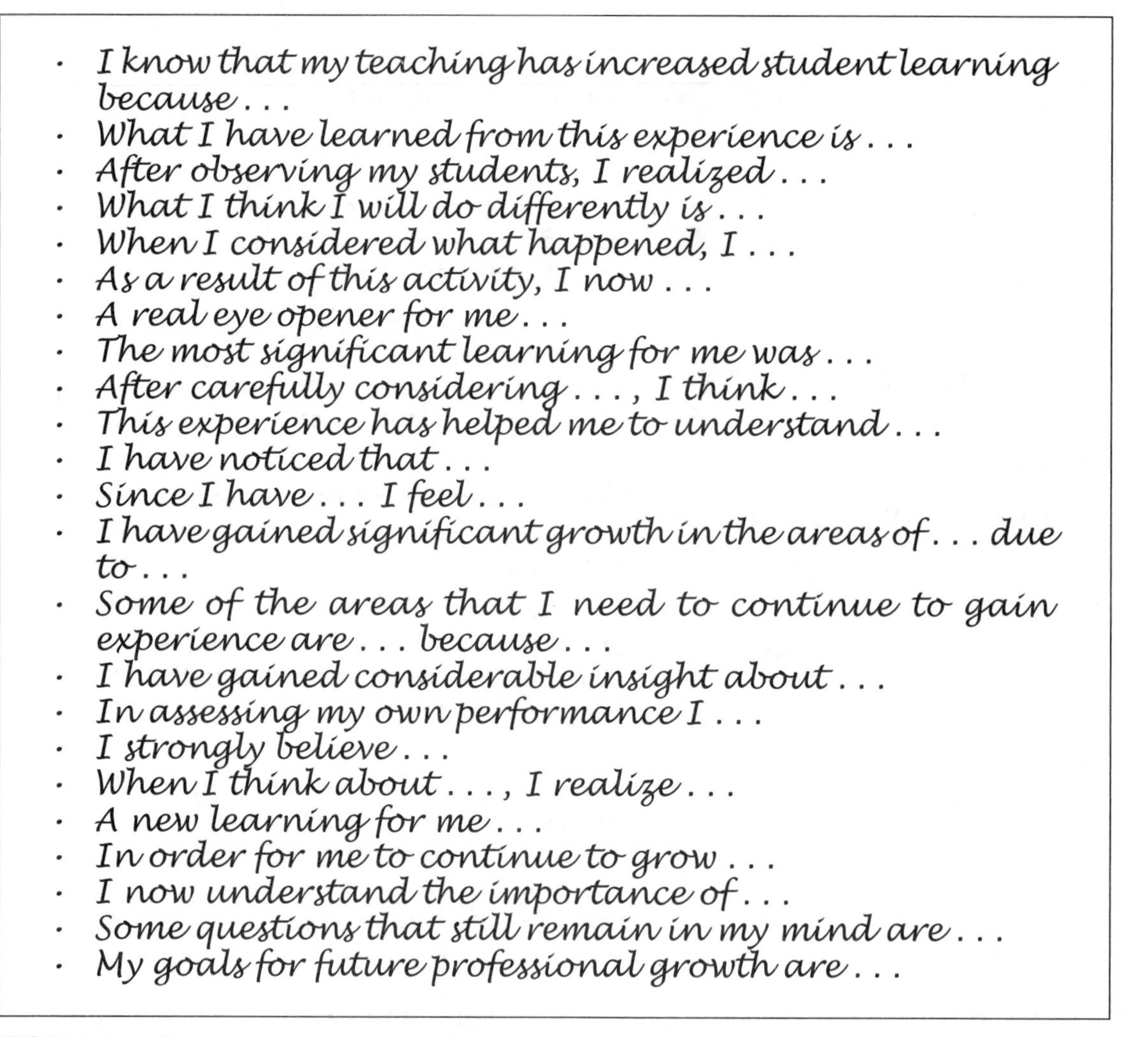

- I know that my teaching has increased student learning because . . .
- What I have learned from this experience is . . .
- After observing my students, I realized . . .
- What I think I will do differently is . . .
- When I considered what happened, I . . .
- As a result of this activity, I now . . .
- A real eye opener for me . . .
- The most significant learning for me was . . .
- After carefully considering . . . , I think . . .
- This experience has helped me to understand . . .
- I have noticed that . . .
- Since I have . . . I feel . . .
- I have gained significant growth in the areas of . . . due to . . .
- Some of the areas that I need to continue to gain experience are . . . because . . .
- I have gained considerable insight about . . .
- In assessing my own performance I . . .
- I strongly believe . . .
- When I think about . . . , I realize . . .
- A new learning for me . . .
- In order for me to continue to grow . . .
- I now understand the importance of . . .
- Some questions that still remain in my mind are . . .
- My goals for future professional growth are . . .

FIGURE 5.3 Sentence starters for reflective entries.

relation to the process and outcomes of conducting a parent-teacher-student conference. The accompanying graphic in Figure 5.5 provides a format for displaying the parent-teacher-student conference information and documents in a three-page portfolio entry.

Displaying Your Documentation

Blending the elements of an appealing visual display with meaningful documentation is a key component in enhancing your portfolio. Up to this point you have concentrated on collecting and developing high quality evidence that reflects the complexities of teaching and your competence as a

Parent-Teacher-Student Conference

Introduction

I have chosen to include my experience in conducting a parent-teacher-student conference because I believe that this illustrates my ability to assess student learning, communicate student performance, and build a positive working relationship with both students and parents. Furthermore, this experience supports the INTASC Principle 8, related to assessment, and INTASC Principle 10, related to fostering relationships with parents.

Assets with Explanations

Letter to parent(s) arranging conference

I sent this letter two weeks in advance to have the flexibility of scheduling for both myself and the parents. I received a response regarding the conference two days after I sent it and was able to confirm the date, time, and place immediately.

Organization plan for conference

There were several critical points, both positive and negative, that I wanted to communicate to the student and parents. The issues were regarding his academic performance. By pre-planning the way in which I wanted to deliver this information I came to the conference feeling confident and well prepared.

Samples of student work

I selected specific samples of the student's work that supported his academic performance including classwork, homework, and tests. I was then able to substantiate my assessment with authentic documentation.

Action plan to improve performance

I created a blank contract that enabled the parents, student, and me to cooperatively develop an action plan for improvement in the identified areas.

A copy of report card and written comments

I included this because this is the formal document that is used to report the assessment of student performance. After some introductory relationship building conversation, I introduced the report card as an opening to the discussion of the student's academic progress.

Note from parents

I included this because it illustrated the level of satisfaction that both the parent and student felt regarding the process that was used to negotiate a plan for facilitating the student's improvement.

Reflection

As a beginning teacher, I drew from all the basic theoretical principles about building human relationships and providing negative feedback that I could remember from my mentor teacher and college coursework. I wanted to create a climate that allowed everyone to feel comfortable during a discussion that imparted negative information. By using student work, and a set of performance criteria to keep the conversation on a professional level, I was able to work out a mutually agreeable contract with ease. I feel that through preplanning, accurate record keeping, and a genuine concern for feelings within a professional climate, I was able to demonstrate my ability to assess student performance and build a productive working relationship with the parents and student.

FIGURE 5.4 A portfolio entry combining introductions, explanations, and reflections.

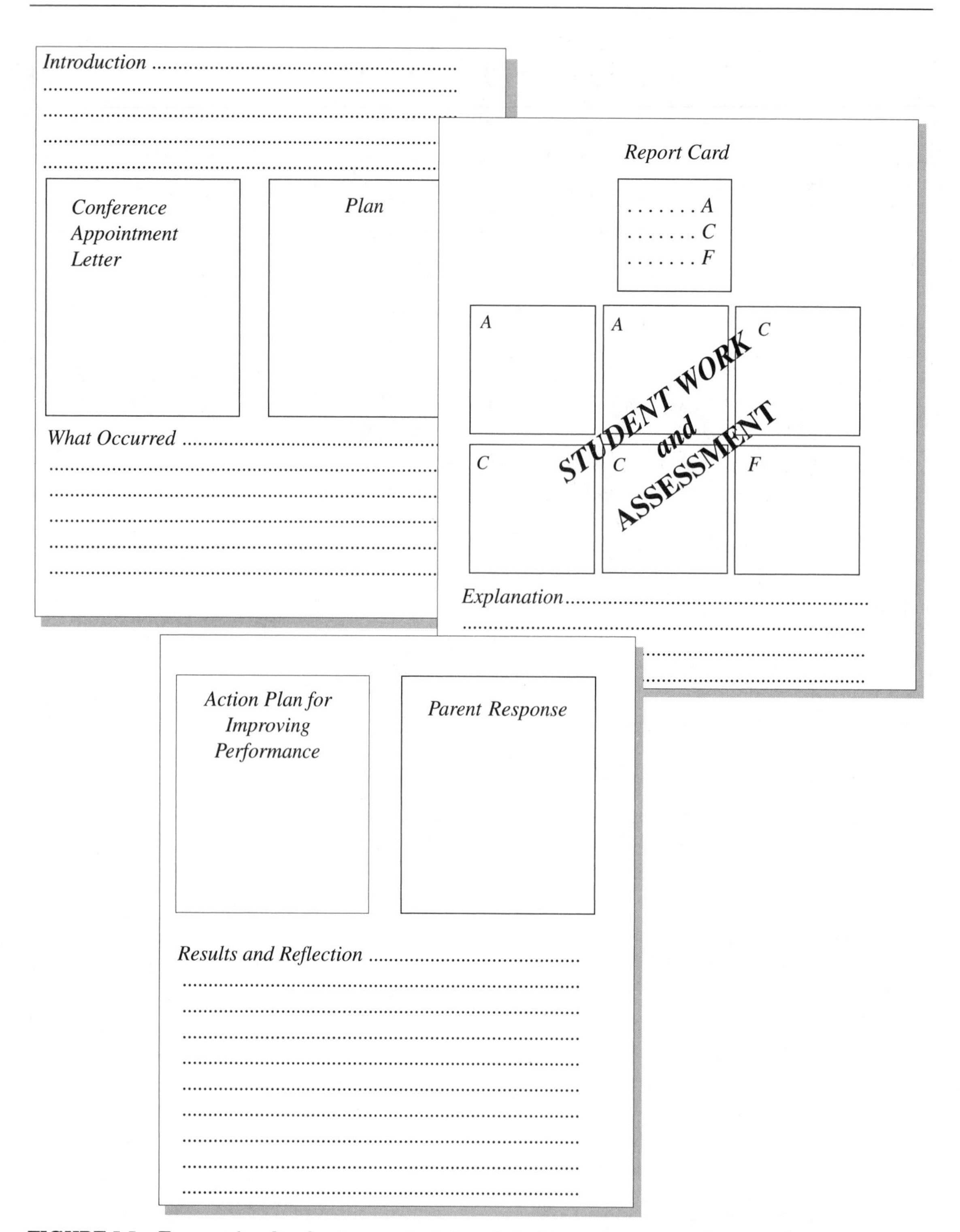

FIGURE 5.5 Format for displaying materials related to a parent-teacher-student conference.

teacher. This component requires you to make decisions on how you will represent these entries on each page of your portfolio. The decisions you make in how to display your portfolio documentation will highly influence the way in which the reviewer perceives your work. The main idea is to have items with significance and substance that are displayed in a professional manner. There are three areas for decision making during this component: *packaging the contents*, *organizing the documentation*, and *designing the layout*.

Packaging the Contents

Packaging the contents is the simplest of these decisions. Choosing something small and easy to carry, such as a loose-leaf notebook, seems to work well for most people. A loose-leaf notebook provides the flexibility to add, remove, or reorganize the documentation as needed. For example, items from one type of portfolio can be fine-tuned or adapted for inclusion in a portfolio used for another purpose. However, some people have used file crates, bookbags, and other creative ways to present their work. Select the packaging appropriate to your purpose and individual preference. Many teachers have found that inserting each entry into a clear plastic sheet protector prevents the documents from getting soiled or torn and makes it easier to handle.

Organizing the Documents

You will need to make a decision about how to organize and categorize the documents in your portfolio. This decision will be unique to you, the purpose of your portfolio, and the types of materials you have collected. Some individuals have organized their portfolio around standards, themes, content areas, goals, or other categories unique to their purpose. A table of contents is essential to the portfolio regardless of how you choose to organize the material. Using a table of contents in combination with color-coded section tabs is a logical and highly effective approach to organizing and categorizing your evidence. This organizational approach represents your thinking, highlights the main sections of the portfolio, and allows easy access to your documentation.

Designing the Layout

Portfolio design refers to the way you format your documentation. Formatting relates to the layout of the content and accompanying narratives on a single page or set of related pages. Visual design is an important consideration when preparing your portfolio for presentation and refers to the textures, colors, shapes, pictures, drawings, content placement, and the like.

Dull, drab, stylistically monotonous pages of content can present a *boring* script and leave the reader with a similar impression of the writer. When making decisions about formatting your documents, consider the following aspects of visual design:

Quantity	• How many documents can you effectively display on one page?
Quality	• Are your documents clear, legible, and meaningful?
Variety	• Have you selected different ways to represent your experiences and competencies such as charts, graphic organizers, photographs, student work, and your own original materials?
Arrangement	• Are your documents arranged in a logical order on the same page with careful consideration to spacing and size?
Aesthetics	• Have you considered the use of color, borders, and different styles and sizes of lettering?

Phase II for Electronic Portfolios

The components in Phase II as noted in this chapter are applicable when developing an e-portfolio. The only difference is in the implementation. Figure 5.6 presents an overview of the process for Phase II—Enhancing Your Evidence. The items in italics identify the differences in the process when adapting this phase to e-portfolio development.

When you begin Phase II—Enhancing Your Evidence, the differences in implementation are obvious. For example:

- When organizing the content of your e-portfolio, you will use hyperlinks to connect standards to portfolio evidence or move from one section to the next.
- Create electronic folders to store your artifacts related to your standards, goals, or universal themes.
- In the area of packaging, instead of a loose-leaf notebook, you can house your materials on the Web or on a CD or DVD.
- The organization of your evidence is accomplished through planning a layout or storyboard and constructing internal navigation links as opposed to organizing with color-coded tabs. Paying particular attention to techniques in storyboarding will facilitate the flow of the design of your work.
- When creating an e-portfolio for the first time, many individuals adapt one of the templates readily available online or create one of their own. Using a template provides consistency for the layout of the entire port-

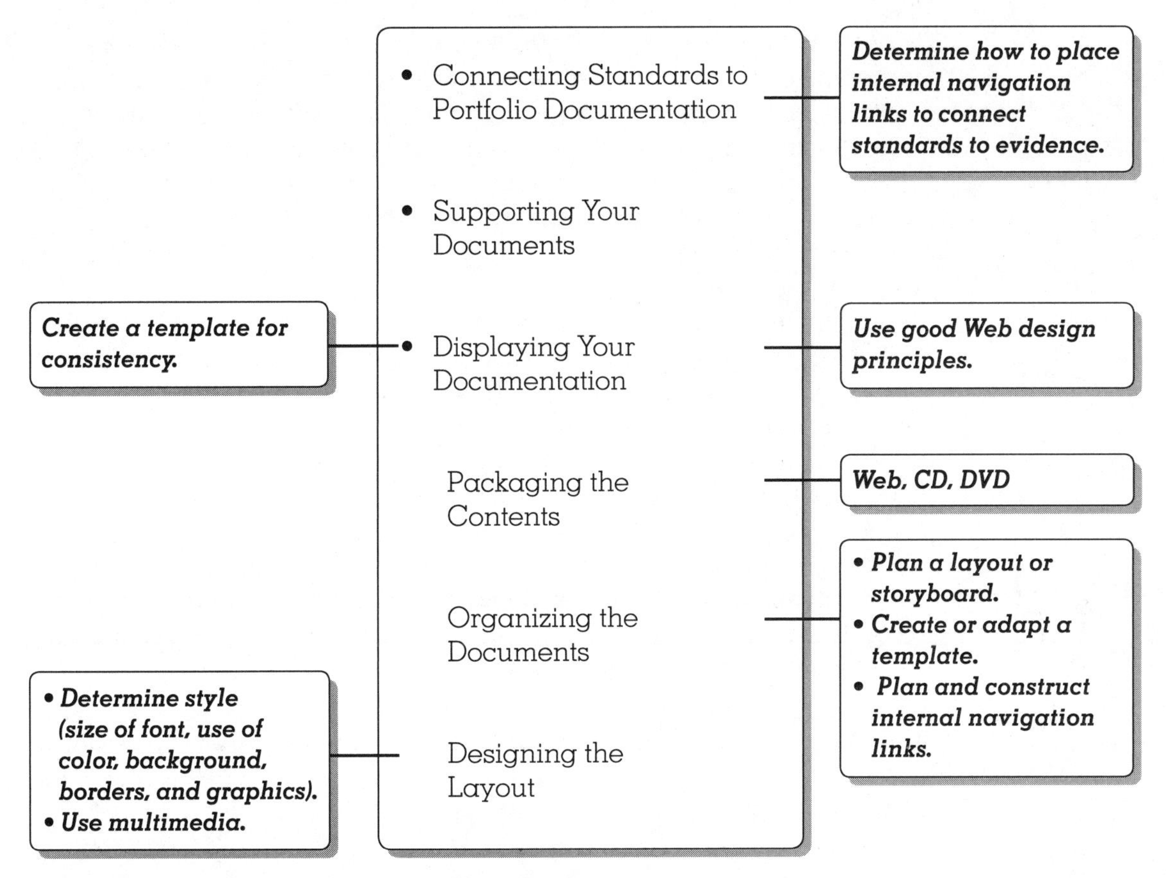

FIGURE 5.6 Phase II—Enhancing Your Evidence.

folio and eliminates the task of duplicating your work each time you include a new document. Consider the graphic elements you want to include on each page. Select your background color or design, table of contents, font color and style, and the navigational links you want on each page, as well as the creation date. Kilbane and Milman (2003) discuss in greater detail the components of creating a template file.

Designing an e-portfolio is the same as designing a paper portfolio; that is, you are making decisions about the quality of the presentation of your evidence.

- Consider good Web design principles, including the use of color and contrast, font size and style, choice of background, and placement of graphics and text.
- Consider developing a template for your portfolio that provides the organizational format for each link with graphic elements listed here. ISTE provides an example of e-portfolio templates in HTML and PowerPoint format to assist you in using the technology standards as a framework for your e-portfolio (http://electronicportfolios.com/nets.html).

- Try to make each page user friendly. If your organizational system is too complex and your reviewers are novices on the computer, they may become frustrated and not take the time to access your information.
- Try to keep each page short and simple. Interest dissipates when a page contains only text and is too long. Use short paragraphs with space between them. When you chunk the content instead of creating one long page, use links that allow the viewer to "drill down" to more related information if they want it.
- Be sure to provide navigation links so the reviewer can return to the original starting point. In other words, do not bury information so deeply that the viewer has to click more than three times to navigate to it and then gets lost once at your site.
- If you publish on the Web and choose to include sophisticated designs like Flash animation, remember, there is a huge disparity among Internet connections and transfer rates. Downloading a page full of pictures, animations, or graphics may take a long time depending on the Web connection available to the viewer. Viewers who have to wait more than ten seconds for a page to download and open quickly lose interest and will even leave your site rather than wait.

You need to make decisions about using multimedia evidence, including whether you will use video and audio, where you will place this electronic information, and what format or software you will use.

Conclusion

There is no question that without introductions, explanations, and reflections, your portfolio will lack credibility. Furthermore, if these elements are carefully thought through and clearly written, your portfolio will be a far better product. While you may have quality documentation and exceptional narratives, if they are not displayed in a professional manner, the overall presentation of your portfolio will be diminished.

Chapter 5 ACTIVITIES

These activities will guide your thinking and facilitate your progress as you attempt to enhance the quality and the presentation of the evidence in your portfolio.

Design a table of contents or homepage for your portfolio.

Design a template for your e-portfolio.

Provide an explanation—either narrative or cross-reference chart—of how you have organized your portfolio to show the relationship between the documents presented and the standard(s) they support. If you are creating an electronic portfolio, determine where to place internal navigation links to connect the standards to your artifacts.

Select an artifact that you would like to include in your portfolio. Write an introduction, explanation, and reflection to accompany this artifact.

Arrange your artifacts with accompanying narratives in a logical, well-organized visual display.

If you are creating a portfolio based on your professional goals:

- Develop an introductory narrative to explain your goals and action plan for achieving them.
- Design a portfolio entry that represents your professional development plan and outcomes.

CHAPTER 6

Phase III—Using Your Portfolio

Introduction

There are many different situations where you will be expected to present a professional portfolio. Chapter 1 briefly identified some of these situations when describing the different types of portfolios. To summarize, the *entrance* portfolio is used to screen applicants for admission to a teacher education program. The *working* portfolio is used to document and evaluate ongoing teaching performance and growth over time. The *exit, interview,* or *showcase* portfolios are used in a presentation or interview for the purpose of program completion, employment or job advancement. This chapter focuses on how to use your portfolio during an exit, interview or showcase portfolio presentation.

There are two distinct components to Phase III: *Self-evaluating your portfolio* and *Presenting your portfolio.* The self-evaluation component is a process designed for use by a teacher to reflect on the overall effectiveness of the portfolio before using it for an interview or presentation. The self-evaluation component for electronic portfolios requires not only assessing your portfolio for its content, but also assessing the technical aspects. The presentation component identifies several recommendations for using your portfolio during an interview as well as options for publication of an e-portfolio.

Self-Evaluating Your Portfolio

Developing a portfolio is a time-consuming and rigorous process. As you move toward the final product, you will be eager to present your work to others. However, it is in your best interest to first invest some time in evaluating your own work. The self-evaluation process focuses on four major areas:

- Introduction and organization of the portfolio
- Performance standards or themes
- Documentation
- Introductions, explanations, and reflections

These areas directly align with the portfolio development process as described in the preceding chapters. To help guide you through this process, we have developed several questions that address attributes that promote a quality portfolio. By addressing these questions, you are able to make decisions that enhance the substance and presentation of your documentation before sharing your portfolio in a more formal setting. Even the best portfolio can benefit from the self-evaluation process.

Evaluating the Introduction

The general introduction sets the stage for the entire content of your portfolio. It is the opening statement that includes information regarding your educational philosophy and the purpose of your portfolio. It may also include a professional development plan related to your career goals.

- Is my introduction meaningful, informative, and relevant to the purpose of my portfolio?
- Are my philosophical beliefs expressed clearly?
- Is my professional development plan correlated with the purpose of the portfolio?
- Does my introduction demonstrate consistent, correct use of grammar, punctuation, word choice, spelling, and sentence formation?

Evaluating the Organization

Portfolio organization refers to the way the portfolio is assembled. It includes the packaging of your artifacts and the manner in which they are displayed.

- Are the contents packaged appropriately?
- Is the evidence organized effectively?
- Are the documents easily accessible?
- Does the overall appearance reflect a professional image?

Evaluating the Use of Performance Standards, Themes, or Goals

Performance standards identify the knowledge, dispositions and skills that a teacher should know and be able to demonstrate. They provide the conceptual framework for portfolio development and documentation. *Goals* identify areas for professional development and correlate with performance standards or themes. *Themes* are generic categories that are inherent throughout the performance standards.

- Are performance-based standards, themes, or goals used as the foundation for my portfolio documentation?
- How have I communicated the use of standards, goals or themes, and supporting evidence to the reviewer?

Evaluating the Documentation

Documentation refers to the evidence selected to support your professional competencies. They may be a combination of teacher-made materials, student work, evaluation documents completed by others that validate your professional performance, and additional materials as appropriate to the purpose of the portfolio.

- Is all my evidence relevant to the purpose?
- Are my documents directly related to a standard(s), theme(s), or goal(s)?
- Does the documentation provide substantial evidence in support of my competency and growth toward that standard(s), theme(s), or goal(s)?
- Do I have a variety of examples organized thoughtfully and displayed effectively?
- Are my examples accompanied by introductions, explanations, and reflections?
- Are my evaluative documents current and completed by professionals who have first hand knowledge of my performance?
- Does my documentation show significant evidence to support student learning or the results of my instruction?

Evaluating Introductions, Explanations, and Reflections

Introductions, explanations, and reflections are narrative entries that provide information about specific portfolio artifacts in each section of your portfolio. They provide insight about the portfolio developer's thoughts related to teaching and learning.

- Are my introductions at the beginning of each section clearly articulated and do they provide a rationale for inclusion of the forthcoming documents, linkage to my philosophical beliefs, and comments about how the documents support the standard, theme, or goal?
- Do my explanations provide significant information to help the reviewer understand the relevance of this evidence and how it supports my ability to teach, impact student learning, or demonstrate leadership?
- Do my reflections provide evidence of my ability to think critically, problem solve, make decisions, relate theory to practice, learn from experience, and analyze my performance and growth?
- Do my introductions, explanations, and reflections demonstrate consistent, correct use of grammar, punctuation, word choice, spelling, and sentence formation?

To complement the information just presented, we have designed a worksheet to structure the self-evaluation process (see Appendix I). This worksheet is intended for use by the portfolio developer. However, it could be given to other individuals for their input prior to using your portfolio in an actual interview or presentation.

Now that you have an understanding of how to self-evaluate your portfolio, you need to be aware of the fact that portfolio reviewers will identify specific criteria to evaluate your documentation. Being aware of these criteria will help you further assess the effectiveness of your own portfolio and be better prepared to use your portfolio during an interview.

Appendix J contains an example of an overall portfolio assessment instrument developed by the authors. This instrument includes criteria that may be used by individuals who are evaluating your performance and are reviewing your portfolio documentation. It is a Likert scale that rates ten essential aspects of the portfolio on a continuum from 1 to 5. This comprehensive, generic assessment tool is intended to help you to evaluate the overall quality of your portfolio. You may give this to a peer, colleague, professor, or administrator to use in a practice portfolio presentation or mock interview.

Appendix K provides examples of actual guidelines and rubrics used by teacher education programs at Villa Julie College and George Mason University. The guidelines identify the required portfolio contents and the rubrics identify the criteria used to evaluate the documentation. This information may be useful for individuals who are interested in seeing how teacher education programs implement the portfolio development process and evaluate portfolio documentation.

Presenting Your Portfolio

The presentation of your portfolio is the culminating component in the portfolio development process. It is the point at which teachers share their portfolio for the purpose of gaining employment or supporting career enhancement. The portfolio, in this phase, is a carefully selected collection of exemplary evidence that highlights a teacher's best work and accomplishments.

Following are some helpful hints drawn from many conversations with teacher candidates, in-service teachers, administrators, and personnel directors about their firsthand experiences with the use of portfolios during interviews. While these helpful hints are geared to the job interviews, they can apply to other portfolio presentation situations. Keeping these suggestions in mind can dramatically improve the quality of your professional interview with personnel staff or school administrators.

- **Bring your portfolio to all interviews.** Be ready to present your portfolio at every interview. Let the interviewer know that you have brought your portfolio with you and would appreciate the opportunity to share portions of it. Be aware that you may not have the option of sharing your portfolio during large-scale interview situations where many teachers are tightly scheduled. However, you should still have your portfolio with you. Some interviewers are very impressed by the effort you devoted to preparing this product and they will at least glance through it and make a notation that you have developed a professional teaching portfolio.

- **Be prepared to present your portfolio to the principal.** Most teachers have found that they are more likely to have the opportunity to share their portfolio during a one-on-one interview with the school principal. In fact, many administrators expect to see a portfolio at this time. This interview is typically longer and more personalized with sufficient time to review your portfolio. Both teacher candidates and in-service teachers claimed that their portfolios were a critical aspect of this more personal interview. Be prepared to present your portfolio during this type of interview.

  When presenting an e-portfolio, make certain you have access to technology that can access your website or operate your CD or DVD. Many teachers today have their own laptop and come prepared to share their e-portfolio, thus not being dependent on the reviewer's technology resources.
- **Know the location of your documentation.** Be familiar with the organization of your portfolio so that when the opportunity presents itself you can locate an example of your work without searching frantically through the materials. The use of a detailed table of contents with color-coded tabs for each portfolio section will assist you in locating examples quickly. If you produce an e-portfolio, make use of the hyperlinking capability in redundant ways so you can access the example you want from any page of your e-portfolio. A site map, the equivalent of a table of contents, is very useful for quickly finding what you want.

  Know the contents of your portfolio so well, that you can unobtrusively work your portfolio into the interview. There will be times during the interview when a question is asked that directly relates to one or more of your portfolio documents. Take advantage of this situation to bring your portfolio to the attention of the interviewer. You might say, *Let me show you a document that . . .* Sharing this evidence may bring more credibility to your response.
- **Position your portfolio strategically.** When sharing your paper portfolio, place it in a position so that it is facing the interviewer. This may mean that you will have to explain your documents from an inverted view. Practice this maneuver prior to your interview. When sharing an e-portfolio it is more effective for both the interviewer and interviewee to be facing the screen.
- **Keep your portfolio a reasonable size.** Do not present a massive portfolio. The documentation presented in your portfolio should include a limited number of examples that can easily be reviewed during the interview time. Be highly selective, including only the most essential information relevant to the purpose of the interview. The content in an e-portfolio is compact because it's a digital representation of your qualifications.

- **Be sensitive to the interview process.** Do not dominate the interview by sharing your portfolio page by page unless requested by the interviewer. Allow the interviewer to determine the structure of the interview.
- **Conduct a "mock" interview.** Practice responding to interview questions using your portfolio. If possible, select a classmate or colleague to role-play the interview with you. Rehearsing prior to the real interview may build your self-confidence and facilitate a smooth transition from the interviewer's question, to your response, to sharing a portfolio entry. Identify the portfolio items that directly relate to, or support your response to the typical interview questions posed here.
  - What is your philosophy of education?
  - What are your *best practices* in the area of classroom management and discipline?
  - What strategies have you found to be most effective in teaching (*insert subject here*)?
  - How do you differentiate instruction to accommodate the various ability levels?
  - What accommodations have you made in your classroom for working with limited-English-speaking students?
  - How have you incorporated the use of technology in your planning, delivery, and assessment of instruction?
  - How do you promote productive working relationships with parents, colleagues, and community?
  - How do you deal with difficult parents?
  - What are your most effective motivational strategies?
  - What methods of assessment do you use to determine student learning?
  - What do you consider to be your strengths?
  - What are your greatest challenges as a teacher?
  - What are your goals for continued professional growth?
  - Tell me about your involvement in professional projects, activities, or organizations related to teaching.
  - What is your most significant learning as a result of creating a professional portfolio?
- **Leave a small sampling of your documents.** Create a small version of your portfolio that you can give to the interviewer. Some principals may ask you to leave your portfolio with them so that they can take more time to review its contents. If this is not something that you feel comfortable doing, prepare a small sampling of materials that can be left with the interviewer. Consider including your *philosophy*, a *lesson plan* with a *reflection about your teaching effectiveness and student learning*, a *current resume*, a *recent evaluation*, and one or two *letters of recommendation*. Of course, when you produce an e-portfolio in a Web-based design, you can leave a CD, DVD, or PDF version of your portfolio with the interviewer.

Phase III for Electronic Portfolios

Many of the components in Phase III are applicable when developing both an electronic or paper portfolio. Figure 6.1 presents an overview of the process for Phase III—Using Your Portfolio. The items in italics identify the differences in the process when adapting this phase to e-portfolio development. The self-evaluation component for e-portfolios requires you to assess the technical aspects of your portfolio. The Presenting your Portfolio component requires you to consider several methods for publication of your artifacts in a digital format.

Evaluating the Technical Aspects of Your Electronic Portfolio

As mentioned previously, investing time in the self-evaluation of your portfolio prior to presentation is well worth the effort. Evaluating the meaningfulness of your introductions and logic of your organization; the use of performance standards or themes; the relevance and quality of your documentation; the quality of your introductions and explanations; and the insightfulness of your reflections are critical and essential elements of the self-evaluation process.

In addition to these areas, an e-portfolio must also be evaluated on the technical aspects. The following questions focus on the aspects that are

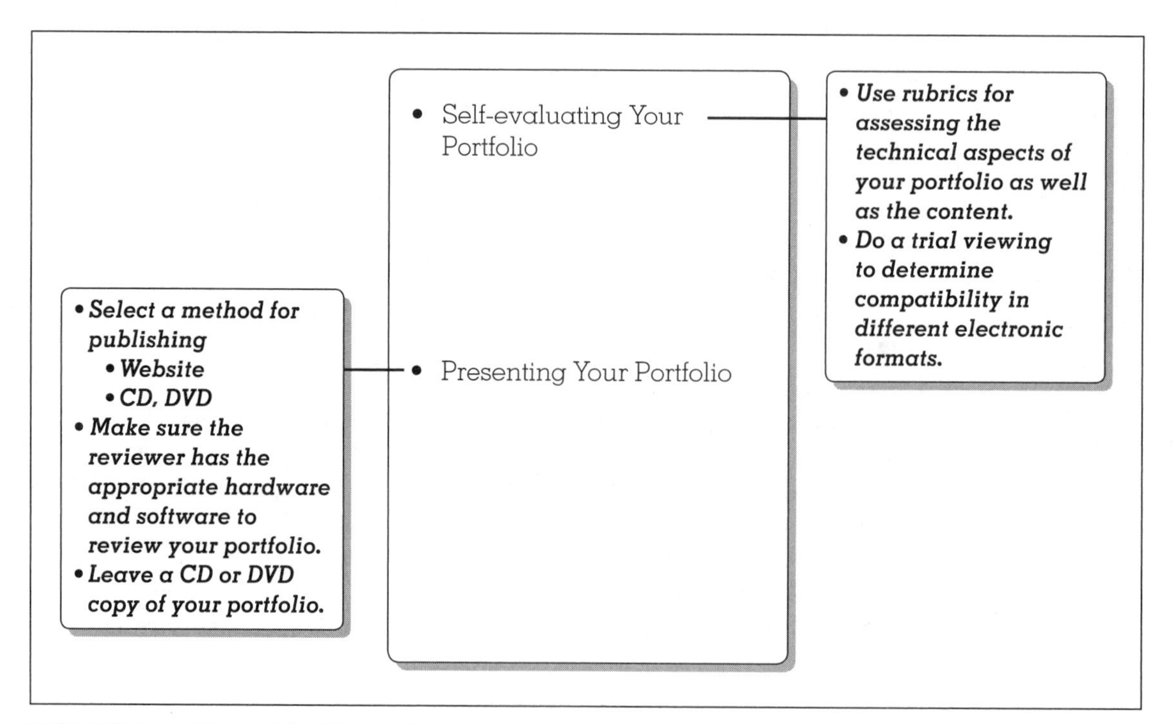

FIGURE 6.1 Phase III—Using Your Portfolio.

related to the mechanics and design features. When used in conjunction with the content assessment, you will have a more comprehensive self-evaluation of your e-portfolio. Consider these questions before publication of your e-portfolio:

- Do my narratives demonstrate consistent, correct use of grammar, punctuation, word choice, spelling, and sentence formation?
- Is the content of my portfolio logically organized and the information meaningfully connected?
- Do I have multilinked pages, with all links clearly labeled and working with an easy-to-use navigation system?
- Are my graphics and photographs clear, high quality, and relevant?
- Are my video clips short, meaningful, and audible?
- Does my visual display demonstrate effective use of quality design principles for the choice of background; size and style of lettering; color selection; and placement of text, graphics, and digitized images?
- Does my e-portfolio work for viewers with various hardware and software configurations?

Some of these technical aspects can be improved by having a colleague review and provide feedback. Seeking feedback from others will provide the opportunity to make constructive changes before publishing on the Web or on a CD or DVD. Planning trial viewings of your e-portfolio using different Web browsers and locations will help you pick up problems in loading time, size of font, and quality of colors. Be aware that color variations may be the result of the calibration of your reviewer's monitor, and cannot be overcome by design changes. Appendix L is a worksheet for you or a colleague to use when assessing the technical aspects of your e-portfolio.

Presenting Your Electronic Portfolio

There are many differences between electronic and paper portfolio development in the presentation component of Phase III. E-portfolio development offers several publication methods—on the Web, a CD, or a DVD. You need to select the method most appropriate to your skill level and the availability of software and hardware. Chapter 3 discusses e-portfolio publication options and issues. Knowing about these options and issues will help you make a decision regarding the best presentation mode for you. Consider the following suggestions when presenting your portfolio:

- If you choose the CD or DVD option, provide individual copies to reviewers.
- Check with the reviewer to determine if they have the appropriate hardware and software to review your portfolio.

If you decide to publish your portfolio on the Web, put your Web address on your resume. Be sure to let potential employers know that you have a web page. Before or after your interview, consider sending an e-mail to a potential employer with an embedded link to your Web-based e-portfolio.

Conclusion

Evaluating the effectiveness of your electronic or paper portfolio and practicing how to use your portfolio are two of the most constructive activities you can engage in to prepare yourself for your portfolio presentation or interview. The *self-evaluation* process helps you to fine-tune your portfolio product, while the *presenting your portfolio* process, provides helpful hints in using your portfolio in a professional setting. Anticipating interview questions and being prepared to share well-organized, quality, supporting documents helps you appear more competent and knowledgeable when presenting your portfolio.

You have now learned about the entire process of portfolio development. This process is applicable to the development of either a paper portfolio or an e-portfolio. The final chapter includes samples of documents from the professional portfolios of novice and experienced teachers. They are included to help you see the many ways you can represent your teaching experiences and organize your documentation. All examples can be represented in either paper or electronic form.

Chapter 6 ACTIVITIES

Use these activities to help you evaluate and present your portfolio.

Use the Self-Evaluation Worksheet, Appendix I, to determine the effectiveness of your portfolio before using it in an interview.

Use the results of your self-evaluation to determine the items that need revision and make the appropriate changes.

Ask a peer or colleague to use this worksheet to provide you with feedback on your portfolio.

If you are presenting your portfolio in an electronic format, use the assessment tool located in Appendix L to evaluate the technical aspects of your portfolio.

Use the interview questions from this chapter to conduct a mock interview using your portfolio. Ask your interviewer (peer/colleague) to provide you with feedback to enhance your presentation in a real interview.

Make a short version of your portfolio to leave with your interviewer.

CHAPTER 7

Examples of Portfolio Entries

Introduction

This chapter is filled with examples of portfolio documents that are representative of the many ways you can present your professional experiences and accomplishments. The entries have been selected from elementary and secondary teachers' electronic and paper portfolios and are intended to provide you with ideas for the many types of evidence that could be included in your portfolio. All examples can be represented in either paper or electronic portfolio format. Many of the examples include pictures of students. Due to issues of confidentiality, we were not able to publish some of the original photographs. In those instances, a camera icon is used in place of a photograph.

Portfolio entries such as letters from parents, students, supervisors, and administrators; samples of certificates and awards; transcripts; test scores; and written evaluations have intentionally been omitted. These are documents that speak for themselves and do not require a lot of creativity on your part. However, they are an important part of your portfolio and should be included in your documentation.

The examples include items that address the organization of the portfolio and instructional evidence that represents the many aspects of teaching. All the artifacts presented are intended to stimulate your thinking about different and creative ways to represent your teaching experiences in your professional portfolio. Keep in mind that there is no right or wrong way to present your work. Every portfolio is a product that reflects the uniqueness of the individual creating it.

Examples

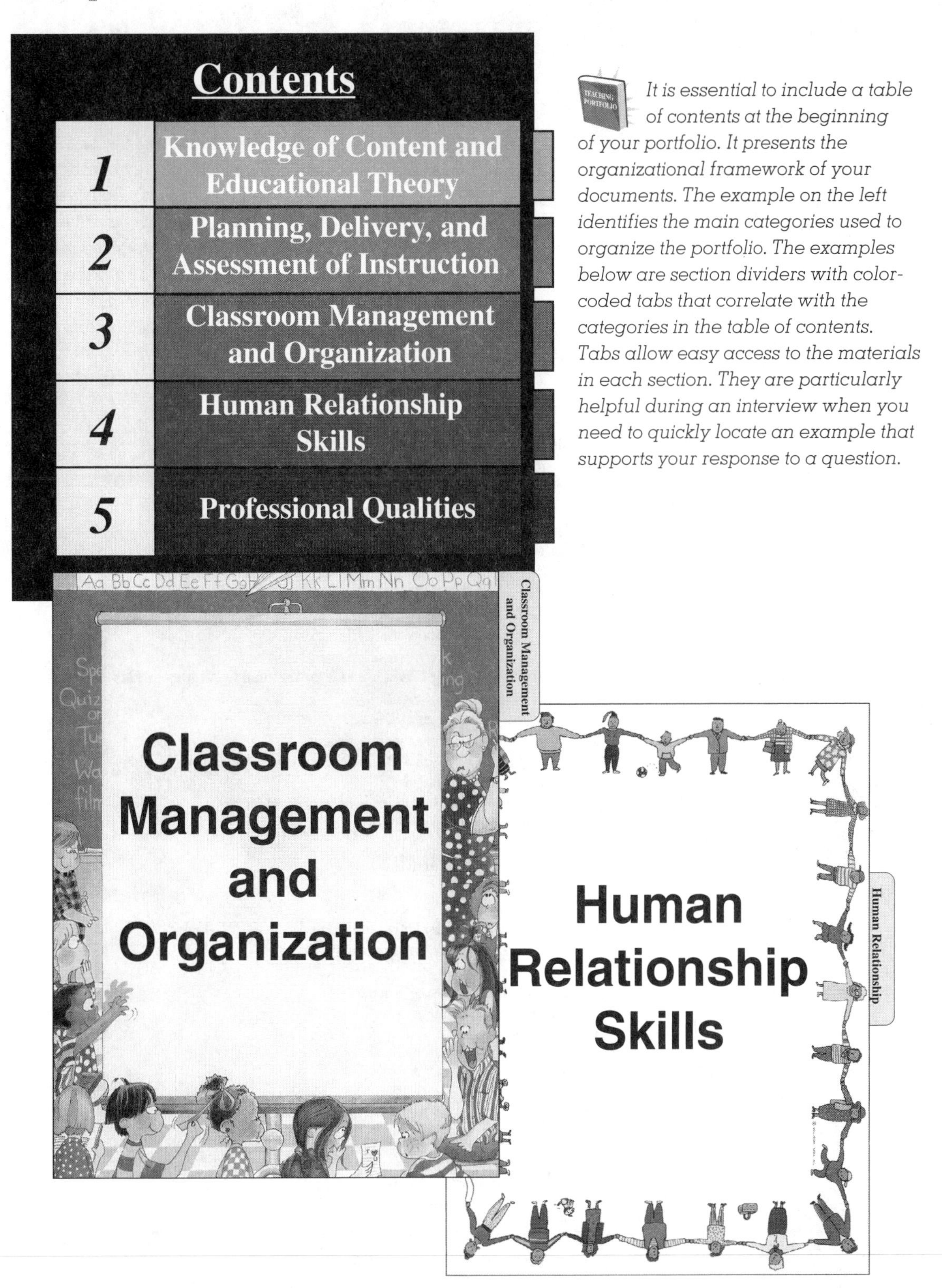

Contents
1
Knowledge of Content and Educational Theory
2
Planning, Delivery, and Assessment of Instruction
3
Classroom Management and Organization
4
Human Relationship Skills
5
Professional Qualities
Classroom Management and Organization
Classroom Management and Organization
Human Relationship Skills
Human Relationship

It is essential to include a table of contents at the beginning of your portfolio. It presents the organizational framework of your documents. The example on the left identifies the main categories used to organize the portfolio. The examples below are section dividers with color-coded tabs that correlate with the categories in the table of contents. Tabs allow easy access to the materials in each section. They are particularly helpful during an interview when you need to quickly locate an example that supports your response to a question.

These examples of tables of contents include a listing of all items in each section of the portfolio. The portfolio reviewer can see at a glance the types of artifacts that have been included to support each category. Adding page numbers would allow quick access to a specific entry.

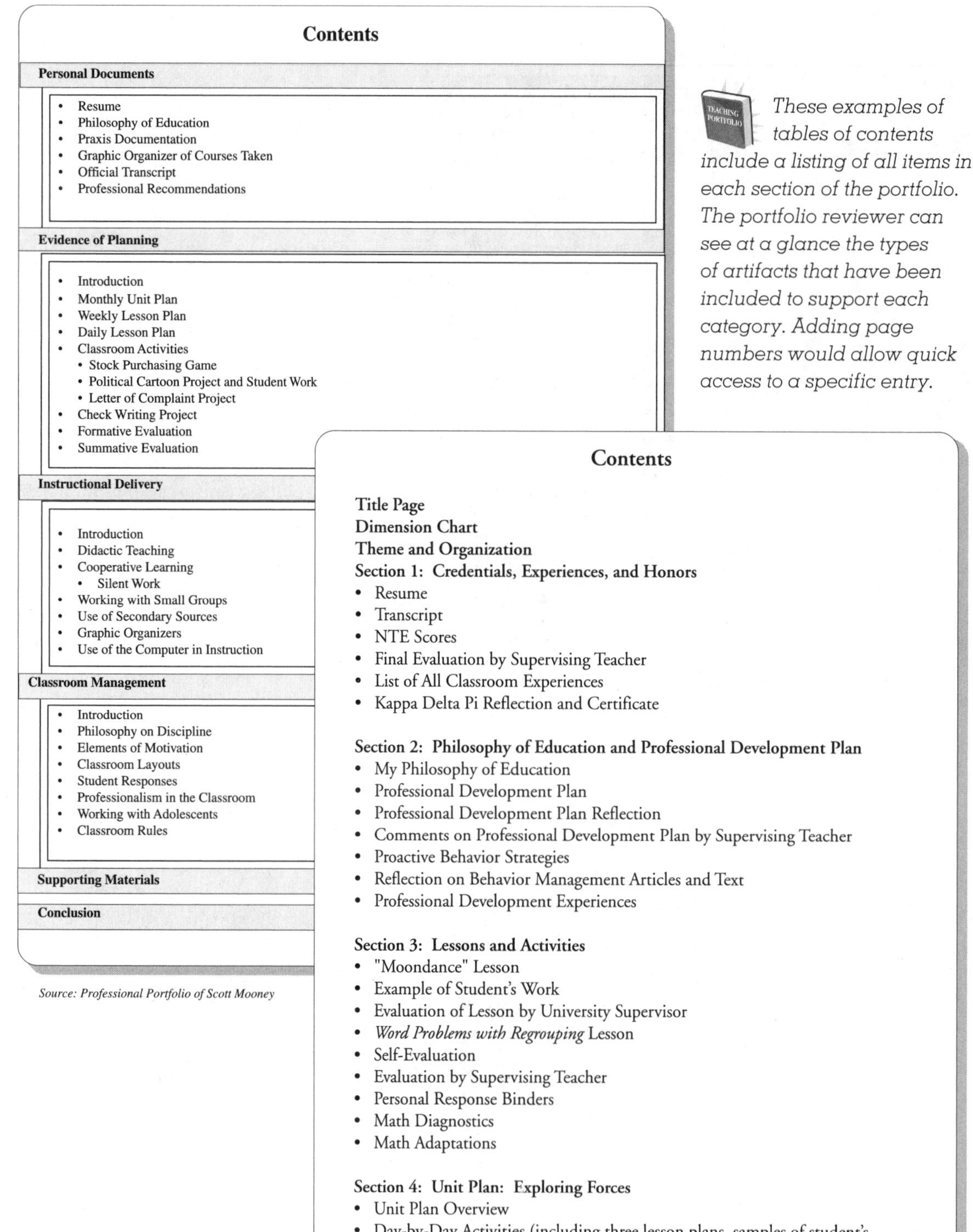

Contents

Personal Documents

- Resume
- Philosophy of Education
- Praxis Documentation
- Graphic Organizer of Courses Taken
- Official Transcript
- Professional Recommendations

Evidence of Planning

- Introduction
- Monthly Unit Plan
- Weekly Lesson Plan
- Daily Lesson Plan
- Classroom Activities
  - Stock Purchasing Game
  - Political Cartoon Project and Student Work
  - Letter of Complaint Project
- Check Writing Project
- Formative Evaluation
- Summative Evaluation

Instructional Delivery

- Introduction
- Didactic Teaching
- Cooperative Learning
  - Silent Work
- Working with Small Groups
- Use of Secondary Sources
- Graphic Organizers
- Use of the Computer in Instruction

Classroom Management

- Introduction
- Philosophy on Discipline
- Elements of Motivation
- Classroom Layouts
- Student Responses
- Professionalism in the Classroom
- Working with Adolescents
- Classroom Rules

Supporting Materials

Conclusion

Source: Professional Portfolio of Scott Mooney

Contents

Title Page
Dimension Chart
Theme and Organization
Section 1: Credentials, Experiences, and Honors

- Resume
- Transcript
- NTE Scores
- Final Evaluation by Supervising Teacher
- List of All Classroom Experiences
- Kappa Delta Pi Reflection and Certificate

Section 2: Philosophy of Education and Professional Development Plan

- My Philosophy of Education
- Professional Development Plan
- Professional Development Plan Reflection
- Comments on Professional Development Plan by Supervising Teacher
- Proactive Behavior Strategies
- Reflection on Behavior Management Articles and Text
- Professional Development Experiences

Section 3: Lessons and Activities

- "Moondance" Lesson
- Example of Student's Work
- Evaluation of Lesson by University Supervisor
- *Word Problems with Regrouping* Lesson
- Self-Evaluation
- Evaluation by Supervising Teacher
- Personal Response Binders
- Math Diagnostics
- Math Adaptations

Section 4: Unit Plan: Exploring Forces

- Unit Plan Overview
- Day-by-Day Activities (including three lesson plans, samples of student's work, self-evaluations, peer evaluation, evaluation by supervising teacher, and evaluation by college supervisor)
- Supplementary Activities

Source: Professional Portfolio of Emily Anne Cosden

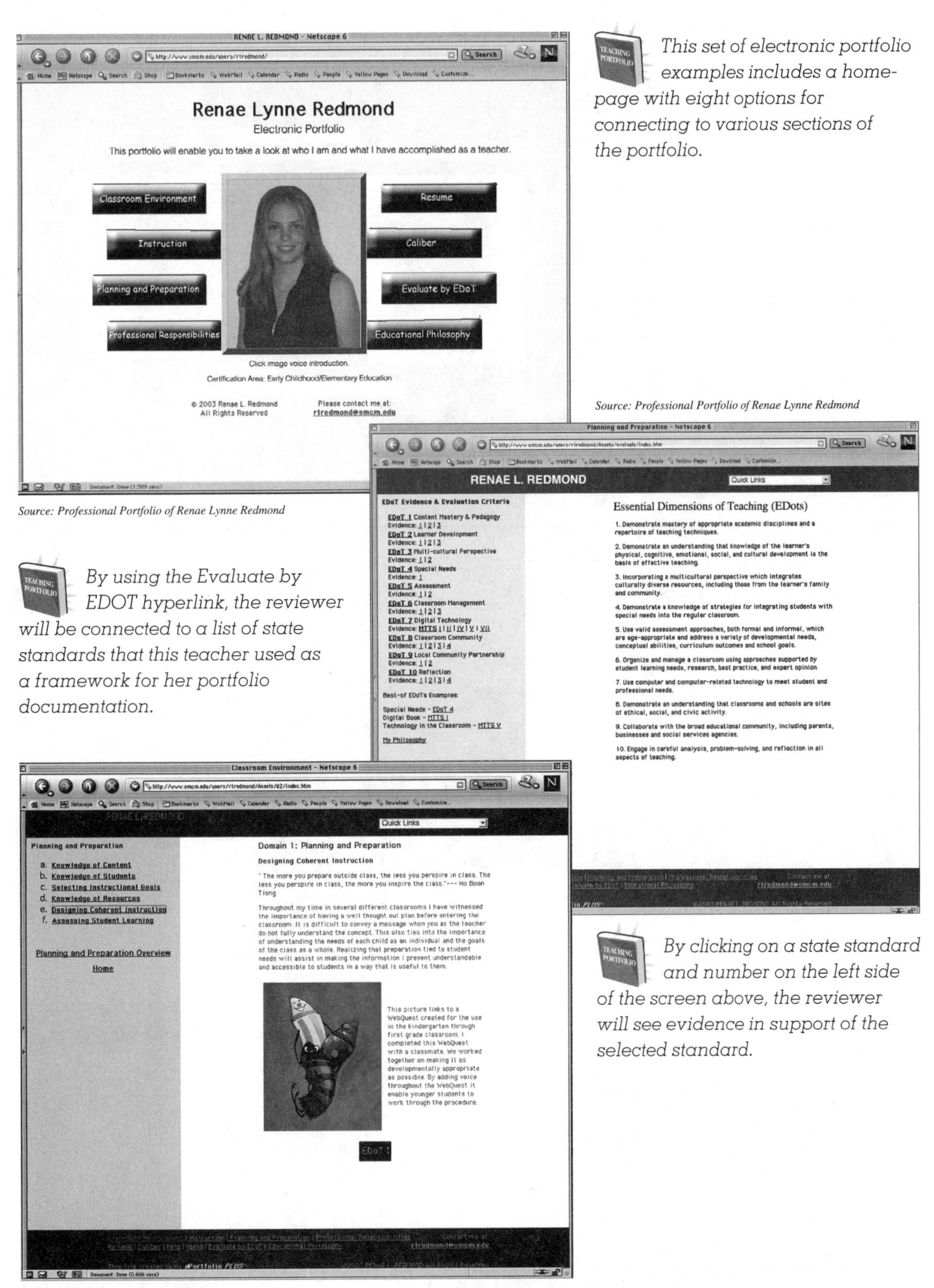

This set of electronic portfolio examples includes a homepage with eight options for connecting to various sections of the portfolio.

Source: Professional Portfolio of Renae Lynne Redmond

Source: Professional Portfolio of Renae Lynne Redmond

By using the Evaluate by EDOT hyperlink, the reviewer will be connected to a list of state standards that this teacher used as a framework for her portfolio documentation.

By clicking on a state standard and number on the left side of the screen above, the reviewer will see evidence in support of the selected standard.

Source: Professional Portfolio of Renae Lynne Redmond

This teacher's electronic homepage includes photographs of her students, four major hyperlinks using Danielson's Domains, and a personalized audio message. The screens below highlight evidence supporting the Professional Responsibilities domain.

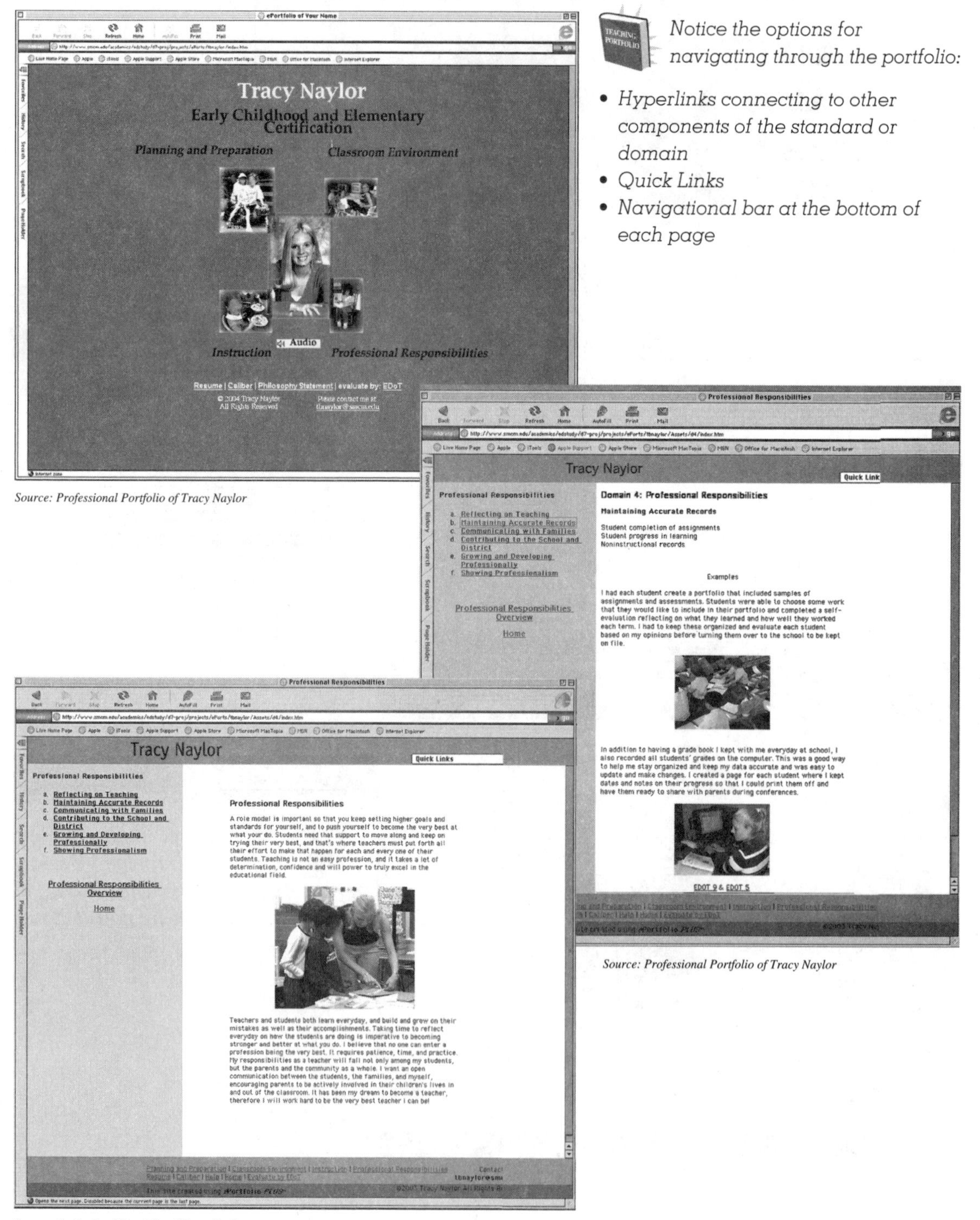

Notice the options for navigating through the portfolio:

- *Hyperlinks connecting to other components of the standard or domain*
- *Quick Links*
- *Navigational bar at the bottom of each page*

Source: Professional Portfolio of Tracy Naylor

Source: Professional Portfolio of Tracy Naylor

Source: Professional Portfolio of Tracy Naylor

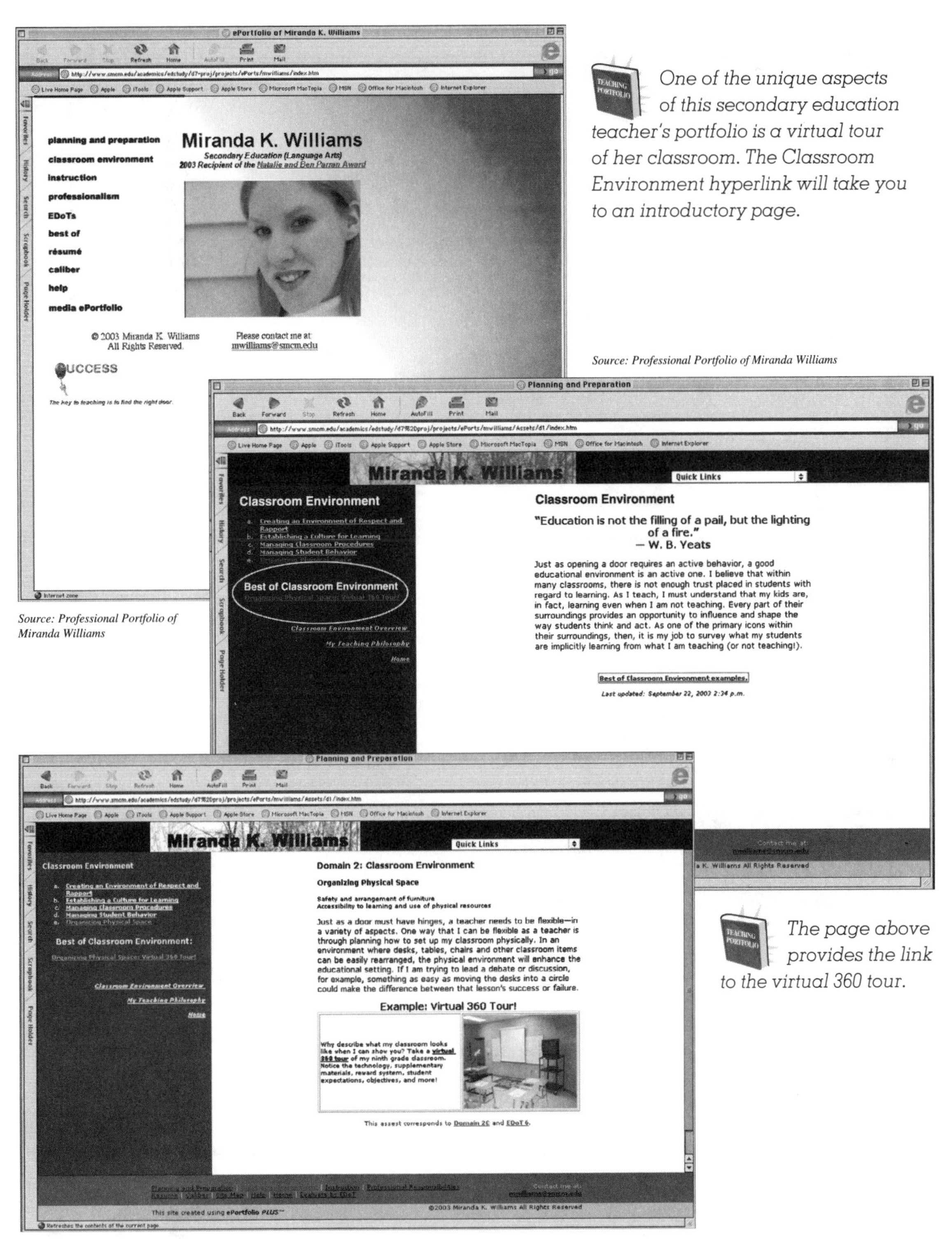

One of the unique aspects of this secondary education teacher's portfolio is a virtual tour of her classroom. The Classroom Environment hyperlink will take you to an introductory page.

Source: Professional Portfolio of Miranda Williams

Source: Professional Portfolio of Miranda Williams

The page above provides the link to the virtual 360 tour.

Source: Professional Portfolio of Miranda Williams

Here the reviewer can see a video of the classroom and the physical setup that supports effective classroom management. Notice the variety of links that provide quick access to other parts of the electronic portfolio.

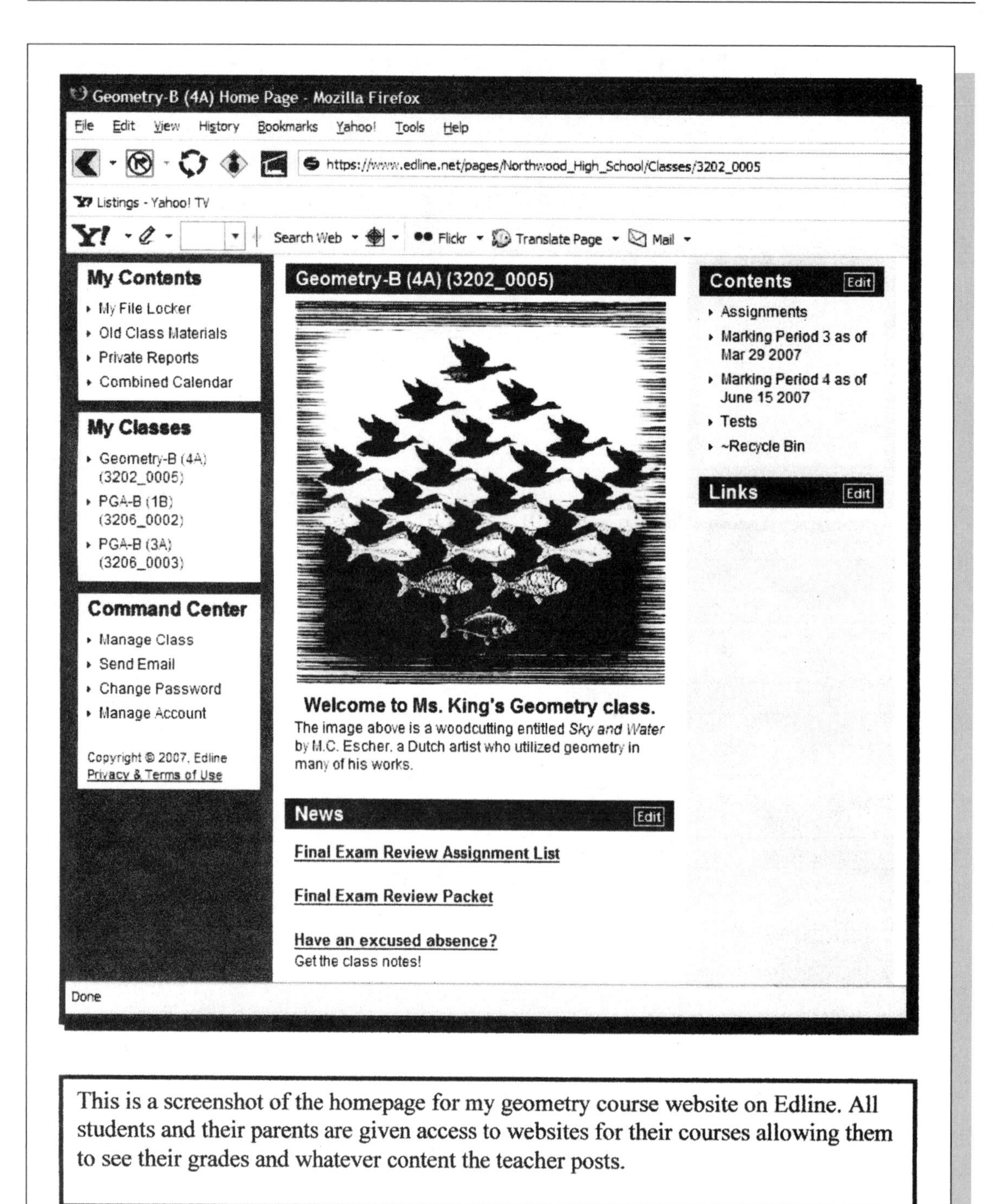

This is a screenshot of the homepage for my geometry course website on Edline. All students and their parents are given access to websites for their courses allowing them to see their grades and whatever content the teacher posts.

Source: Professional Portfolio of Kimberly King

This example not only illustrates organization of a homepage but it is also set up to provide information about the course(s) and communication between teacher, parents, and students.

Source: Professional Portfolio of Rosanna Calabrese

Patchwork Portfolio of Rosanna Calabrese

TANYA LOVED LISTENING TO HER GRANDMOTHER TALK ABOUT THE PATCHWORK QUILT AS SHE CUT AND STITCHED TOGETHER THE SCRAPS OF COLORFUL FABRIC. A SCRAP OF BLUE FROM BROTHER JIM'S FAVORITE OLD PANTS, A PIECE OF GOLD LEFTOVER FROM TANYA'S CHRISTMAS DRESS, A BRIGHT SQUARE FROM TANYA'S HALLOWEEN COSTUME—ALLFIT TOGETHER TO MAKE A QUILT OF MEMORIES.

from The Patchwork Quilt
Valerie Floundry

As individual scraps of fabric in a patchwork quilt tell a unique story and come together to create a unified work of art, it is my hope that the individual patches of this portfolio tell the story of my professional development and achievement as a teacher candidate. This document is truly my quilt of memories.

This set of artifacts introduces a portfolio developed around the theme of Patchwork quilts. It includes an introductory narrative and graphic linking performance standards with the theme. These introductory artifacts provide a rationale for the organization and thematic framework of the portfolio.

Source: Professional Portfolio of Rosanna Calabrese

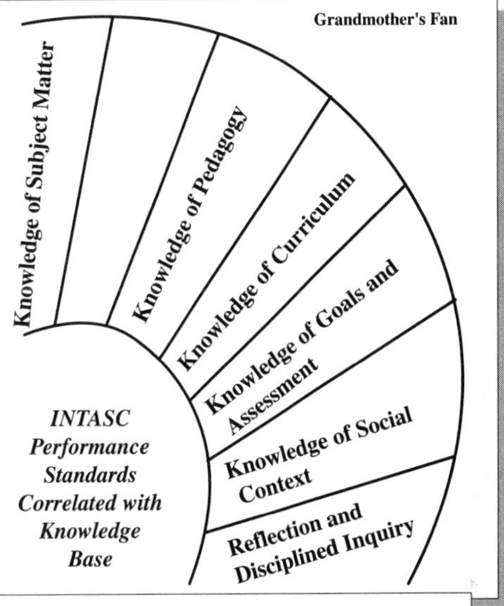

Quilts

It is a pleasure to share this professional portfolio with you. It is my hope that the pages genuinely document my achievement of the standards established for teacher candidates.

The theme of this professional portfolio is "quilts." Quilts are works of art that are created to tell stories or document life experiences. Each patch is special and has been designed for a special purpose or inspiration. Together the patches create a unified work of art that tell an even greater story. I believe that education mirrors these qualities of a quilt. Education is a multifaceted discipline that is made of up very special methods of inquiry, ways of knowing, and pedological strategies. Each classroom is a unique community comprised of individual learners with their own fears, interests, talents, and abilities. Education and the classroom are unique quilts that tell the story of our society's present and fosters its future.

I have chosen the College of Education standards for teacher candidates as the organizational framework for this portfolio. These standards are a compilation of expectations of graduates of the College of Education as well as the Interstate New Teacher Assessment and Support Consortium (INTASC) Principles. INTASC standards articulate various beliefs, dispositions, and performances teacher candidates should possess. I believe that through my education, as well as experience in the classroom, I have achieved those standards.

In order to present a theme that is genuine and valid, I spent a great deal of time researching the history and various attributes of quilts. Each section, which is a series of documents demonstrating my achievement of the INTASC standards, begins with a web of attributes of the respective standard. The designs of the graphic organizers are actual traditional quilt patches. The names of the design are under the patches.

This portfolio is a work in progress, as I continue to develop with each experience and reflection. It may never be finished, as I feel I will never be completely developed. It would be a shame to declare myself educated at the completion of my undergraduate degree. Bishop Crieghton once said, "The true objective of education is to leave a man continually asking questions." I have not asked all my questions yet, and I hope I never cease exploring and learning.

Source: Professional Portfolio of Rosanna Calabrese

Introduction

This professional portfolio is designed to give the viewer a small glimpse into the type of professional educator I am both in and out of the classroom. In this portfolio I have included many examples of my personal and professional work. The reader will find that adolescent development is the focus of my teaching. Inside I have attempted to highlight aspects of my professional development while keeping in mind my first priority—the academic and social development of young adults.

Becoming a professional teacher will enable me to not only impart my knowledge of the social studies to my students but also to help mold and construct successful
society. I will strive t
active members of the
country. Students n
instructors in all that li
become one of a num
for all my students.

Source: Professional Portfolio of Scott Mooney

Portfolio introductions may also be narratives, without graphics, explaining the focus of the portfolio and the teacher's philosophy of education. If narratives are used, they should be no longer than one page. Narrative entries that are lengthy may not be read by the reviewer.

Philosophy of Education

Society pulls students in many different directions. Children have been taught to spend more time watching television than working on schoolwork. Subsequently, teachers have been forced to design activities that constantly re-engage their students. I feel that it is the teacher's job to provide an enriching environment in which the student can grow mentally and academically. This environment must attempt to counteract the media-generated negativity that is constantly battering our young students.

Students learn in numerous unique ways. The teacher should provide varying classroom activities to allow for each of these students to showcase his or her own distinctive method of learning. Students in my classroom will be empowered to achieve, as well as receive motivation to take risks and responsibility for their own education.

Choices should be made available for the student to actively participate in the learning process. Teachers should feel support in trying new ideas and finding new ways to stimulate and propagate academic growth. We as teachers should assume that students can and will achieve to their highest level. We should take the stance that we do not know all, and that we are merely resources to the student along their larger educational journey.

Source: Professional Portfolio of Scott Mooney

Philosophy of Education

My philosophy of education is perpetually evolving. Whether I am a novice or a master at my craft, I will always be a learner and a teacher. Each day I learn from my students, my school, and my community. I then transform these lessons into knowledge that I can use to better understand and help my students, to better serve my school, and to better contribute to my community. Although I cannot definitively state my philosophy of education in a short, concise paragraph, there are four major components that guide my thinking as an educator.

Individual Learner's Needs -- All students can learn; however, it cannot be assumed that they learn in the same ways. In order to meet the needs and concerns of each student, a variety of approaches is necessary to address all learning styles, levels of ability, and levels of motivation.

Student Empowerment -- Students will be motivated to learn if they are given democratic control of their learning. When students are given choices regarding the framework of content material, structure of the class, and classroom policies and procedures, they will take ownership in the process that is rightfully theirs.

Classroom and School as a Community -- School is more than a place to receive an academic education. It is important that students feel as if they belong so that they can form real, lasting social connections. To achieve this goal, students, staff, and parents must get involved in activities and work together, as a team, inside and outside of the classroom to build community.

Teacher as a Lifelong Learner -- Le
a lifelong process. This process req
commitment to learn more in the content are
educational research and strategies, and ong

Realizing that there are differences
whether it be in culture, learning ability,
education, in my classroom, will unite differ
attained by a cooperative effort from everyo
be understood and before my students ca
question, and reflect for themselves, I must
as they must understand each other. With t
in mind, I enthusiastically welcome the cha
a positive impression on the lives of studen

Source: Professional Portfolio of Rosanna Calabrese

This set of items illustrates two ways of representing a philosophy of education. The example on the left begins with a general introduction to the philosophy, then highlights four major components of the philosophy. The final paragraph provides a short conclusion.

This graphic organizer links various elements of a teacher's philosophy of education. It can be shown during an interview when the question "What is your philosophy of education?" is asked. It allows you to have a visual reminder of the important attributes of your philosophy.

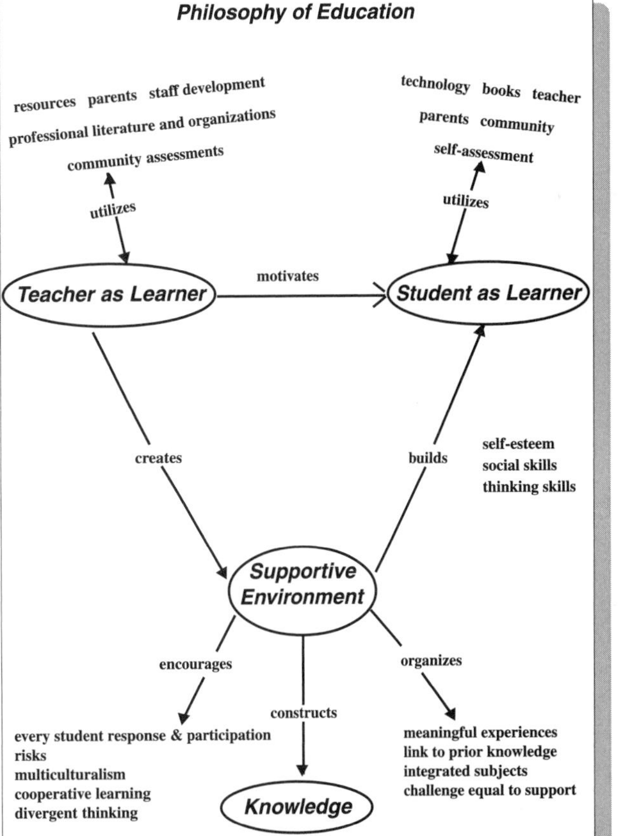

Source: Professional Portfolio of Lauren T. Costas

Essential Dimensions of Teaching

Throughout my portfolio I mention the Essential Dimensions of Teaching in numerous instances. These dimensions are ten performance-based standards for guiding career-long development that the State of Maryland requires all future-teaching candidates to demonstrate in order to be considered a highly effective educator. The dimensions are as follows:

Teachers Candidates and Teachers Will:

1) Demonstrate mastery of appropriate academic disciplines and a repertoire of teaching techniques.
2) Demonstrate an understanding that knowledge of the learner's physical, cognitive, emotional, social and cultural development is the basis of effective teaching.
3) Incorporate a multicultural perspective which integrates culturally diverse resources, including those from the learner's family and community.
4) Demonstrate a knowledge of strategies for integrating students with special needs into the regular classroom.
5) Use valid assessment approaches, both formal and informal, which are age-appropriate and address a variety of developmental needs, conceptual abilities, curriculum outcomes and school goals.
6) Organize and manage a classroom using approaches supported by student learning needs, research, best practice, and expert opinion.
7) Use computer and computer-related technology to meet student and professional needs.
8) Demonstrate an understanding that classrooms and schools are sites of ethical, social, and civic activity.
9) Collaborate with the broad educational community, including parents, businesses, and social service agencies.
10) Engage in careful analysis, problem-solving, and reflection in all aspects of teaching.

The small footprint labels in the bottom corners of each page are to help in identifying pieces of my work that demonstrate each of the above dimensions.

Reflections and captions found on both blue and yellow paper (with the mountain symbol) throughout my portfolio are also explanations that identify aspects of my teaching that meet these ten dimensions.

Source: Professional Portfolio of Kate Maczis

These two introductory portfolio entries explain how performance standards and portfolio documentation are related. The entry on the left lists the standards used, and the chart below cross-references each standard with the supporting documents. The teacher also included icons on each portfolio document that supported a standard. The icons alerted the reviewer to the connection between the artifact and the standard.

Essential Dimensions of Teaching
Portfolio Guide

Artifacts	Dimensions 1	2	3	4	5	6	7	8	9	10
Computer Software							*			
Software Evaluation: Bailey's Bookhouse							*			
Software Integration Project	*			*	*		*			*
Computers and Special Needs: Research Paper				*			*			
Preschool Inventory							*		*	
Daily Assessment Packet				*			*			
Reflections and Interpretations of the Woodcock-Johnson Psycho-education Battery					*		*			
Performance Assessment Task	*				*		*			
Case Study of Caitlin/Parent Conference Materials		*							*	
Case Study of Kevin		*								
Lesson: Reading for a Literary Experience: Who's in the Shed?	*				*		*			*
Lesson: Exploring Three-Letter Words Using Sound Boxes and Letter Tiles						*	*			*
Lesson: The Gingerbread Man: Using Illustrations to Create A Story	*			*	*	*				*
Lesson: Examining Point of View and Story Elements in Fairy Tales: The Three Little Pigs	*				*					*
Lesson: Aquarium Visit Follow-up Activities	*				*		*		*	
Lesson: Insect Memory Game	*			*	*	*	*			*
Literature Assignment	*				*					
Lesson: Jelly Beans for Sale: Understanding the Value of a Quarter	*			*		*	*			
Lesson: Converting Written Time into Digital Time	*			*	*		*			
Lesson: Maps for Parents				*	*	*	*		*	
Theme Development	*	*								
Curriculum Assignment	*	*							*	

Source: Professional Portfolio of Kate Maczis

Theme and Organization

When I began the process of constructing my portfolio, I decided to choose a theme that would reflect my feelings about being an educator. The theme "Committed to a World of Learning" came to me one day as I was driving home from Milbrook. I was sitting in traffic thinking about what I could say that would represent my dedication to the learning process. Throughout my entire life I have enjoyed learning. In my career as a teacher, I hope to pass my love of knowledge on to my students.

The organization of my portfolio is also somewhat deliberate. For example, I chose not to have a multiculturalism section because I believe that multiculturalism should be so ingrained in teaching that it cannot be separated out. Every aspect of teaching (lessons, parent involvement, and related experiences) is permeated by multiculturalism. I also chose not to have a separate section for assessment. Every day in the classroom I assess students' progress. The assessments may be formal or informal, but all are an integral part of teaching. Similarly, I do not have a section about technology. The key focus of technology in education is to integrate the technology so it becomes a part of teaching, just as motivation of manipulatives. The sections that I did choose to create incorporate multiculturalism, assessment, and technology. I created the parent involvement section to highlight and draw attention t
relationships with parents. The lesson pl
lessons and small group activities that w
needs. Finally, the related experiences s
have participated in outside of the classr

Source: Professional Portfolio of Emily Anne Cosden

The introductory entries presented here are two more examples of how to let the portfolio reviewer know your thinking behind the organization of the portfolio documentation. The chart below is a different version of how you can cross-reference performance standards with all the documents that relate to the standard.

Dimension 1	Reflection on Behavior Management Articles and Text
	Professional Development Experiences
	Lesson: "Moondance"
	Lesson: "Word Problems with Regrouping"
	Math Adaptations
	Unit Plan: Forces
	Lesson: "In, On, Under, and Through"
Dimension 2	Theme and Organization
	Philosophy of Education
	Word of the Month
	Math Diagnostics
	Friday Folders and Anecdotal Records
	Individual Behavior Charts
	Behavior Certificates
Dimension 3	Theme and Organization
	Professional Development Exercises
	Philosophy of Education
	Personal Response Binders
	Classroom Reflection
	Seating Arrangement
	Word of the Month
	Lesson: "In, On, Under, and Through"
	Newsletters
Dimension 4	Theme and Organization
	Letter from Ms. Prucino, IST teacher
	Math Adaptations
	Lesson: "Moondance"
	Reflection on Special Education Experience
	Lesson: "In, On, Under, and Through"
Dimension 5	Theme and Organization
	Philosophy of Education
	Professional Development Experiences
	Lesson: "Moondance"
	Friday Folders and Anecdotal Records
	Math Diagnostics
	Informal Literacy Interview
	Formative and Summative Assessments from Unit Plan: Forces
Dimension 6	Philosophy of Education
	Proactive Behavior Strategies
	Reflection on Behavior Management Articles and Text
	Classroom Meetings
	Seating Arrangement
	Individualized Goal Charts
	Behavior Certificates

Source: Professional Portfolio of Emily Anne Cosden

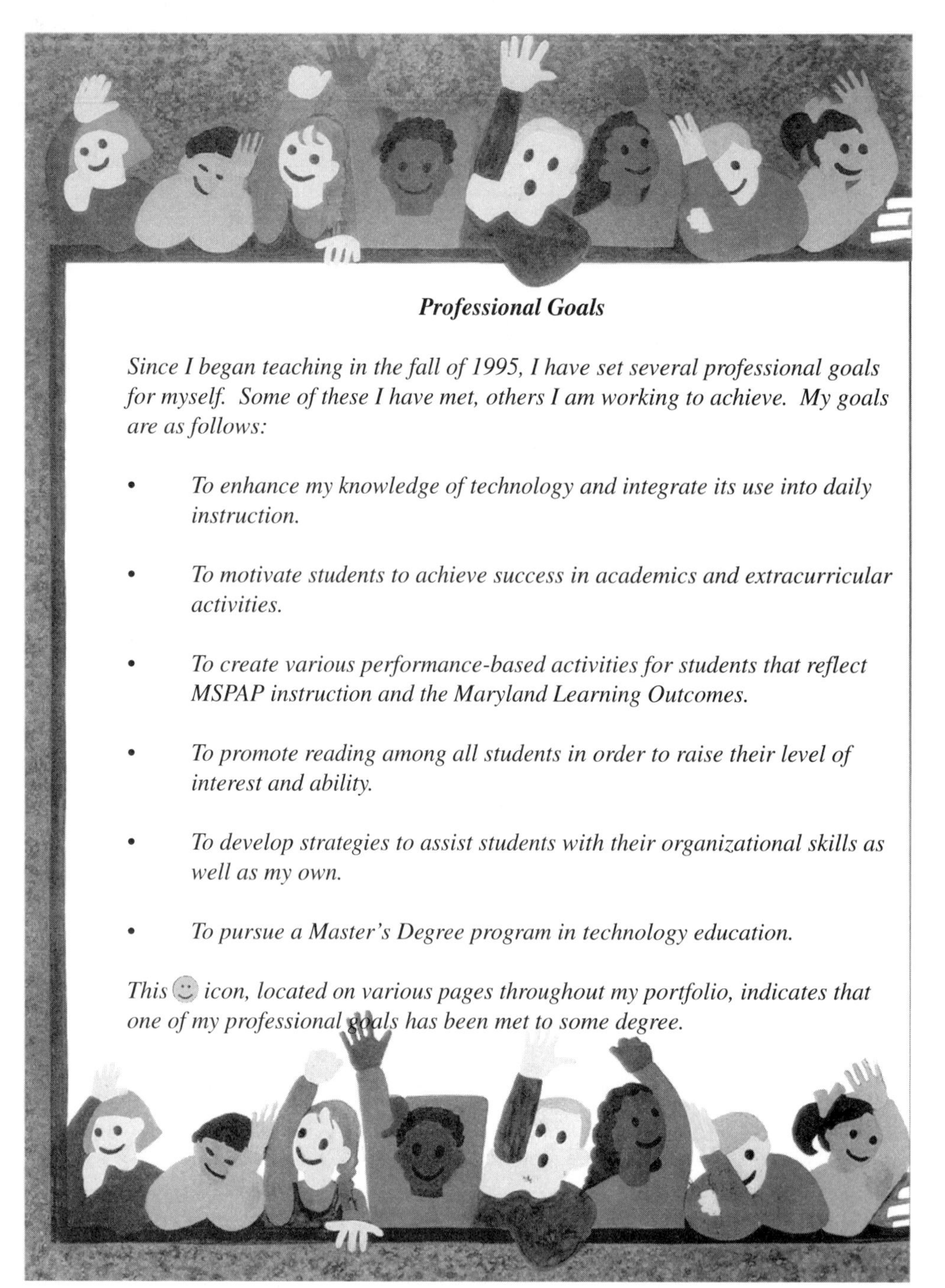

Professional Goals

Since I began teaching in the fall of 1995, I have set several professional goals for myself. Some of these I have met, others I am working to achieve. My goals are as follows:

- *To enhance my knowledge of technology and integrate its use into daily instruction.*
- *To motivate students to achieve success in academics and extracurricular activities.*
- *To create various performance-based activities for students that reflect MSPAP instruction and the Maryland Learning Outcomes.*
- *To promote reading among all students in order to raise their level of interest and ability.*
- *To develop strategies to assist students with their organizational skills as well as my own.*
- *To pursue a Master's Degree program in technology education.*

This ☺ icon, located on various pages throughout my portfolio, indicates that one of my professional goals has been met to some degree.

Source: Professional Portfolio of Ryan Imbriale

Including a list of your professional goals provides information to the portfolio reviewer about your future interests and commitment to growth.

Source: Professional Portfolio of Maria Giovanna Marsili

Short- and Long-Term Goals

I have learned a great deal over the past three years of teaching. I have always loved children and have wanted to make a difference in their lives. Thanks to my experience in the classroom, I now know how to make a positive change in children's lives. As an educator, I have set and achieved many goals. My main goals, which are stated on my Professional Development Plan (PDP), were to explore ways to adapt my lessons to meet the individual needs of my students, to implement multicultural activities, and to maintain effective classroom management. I am very fortunate that I set these goals because they helped me stay focused on becoming a more effective educator.

I feel as if I set realistic short- and long-term goals for myself. My short-term goals included establishing a good rapport with my students, establishing classroom management, and learning techniques and strategies from the experienced teachers I worked with. My long-term goals were to become a more effective educator, to make my students feel comfortable and excited about learning, and to truly know how it feels to be a classroom teacher. I feel as if my internship has given me the opportunity to achieve my goals.

As a part of my one-year intensive internship, I was expected to observe other teachers. I decided to observe a first-year fourth-grade teacher, the music teacher, a third-grade teacher, and a fifth-grade teacher. I greatly enjoyed these experiences. I learned how other teachers interact with their students, various management techniques, and what students are held accountable for in other grades. I was especially grateful for the time I spent with the music teacher. It is not very often that classroom teachers have the time to visit special area classrooms. This was a very enlightening and interesting experience.

I definitely plan on establishing short- and long-term goals for my first year of teaching. Some of my goals for my first year of teaching will remain the same. As I am faced with a new group of students, I will need to establish a good rapport and classroom management techniques that will work for those students. One short-term goal I want to work on is incorporating the reading standards into my lessons. I feel this is very important and I did not have much practice doing so in my internship. I al ways intend on pursuing my goal of becoming a more effective educator. I think when teachers lose sight of this goal, their students suffer. I want my students to have the

Professional goals may also be effectively communicated in a narrative form or chart. Many teachers often use both a narrative introduction and an accompanying chart. The chart below shows how a teacher's professional development plan relates to the INTASC standards.

Professional Development Plan

INTASC Performance Standards	Action Plan	Implementation
The Learner The teacher candidate stimulates student reflection on prior knowledge and links new ideas to already familiar ideas, making connections to students' experiences, providing opportunities for active engagement, manipulation, and testing of ideas and materials, and encouraging Students to assume responsibility. The teacher candidate assesses individual Differences, and designs and delivers Instruction appropriate to students' stages of development, cultural backgrounds, Learning styles, strengths, and needs.	1. What do the students already know (and have done) about the topics I will teach? 2. How can I get the children interested in activities and stimulate them to learn? 3. How do I adapt my lessons to work for the different learning levels represented in my classroom?	1. I will review what the students have already done with my mentor teacher before teaching a lesson and I will activate the students' prior knowledge by asking review questions at the beginning of a lesson. 2. I will implement child-centered activities in a manner that excite children. Examples of this are the patterning activities I have done and the measurement activities I will implement in the future. 3. I will make appropriate adjustments, including using different manipulatives for different groups.
Goals & Assessment The teacher candidate uses a variety of formal and informal assessment techniques to enhance his or her knowledge of learners, evaluate student's progress and performances, and modify teaching and learning strategies.	1. What kinds of formal and informal assessments are done in kindergarten?	1. I will take part in observing and administering some formal assessments that are used, including Title I assessments and ISM assessments. I will also discuss with my mentor teacher how the many informal assessments, such as observations, collection of homework, and questions are used in kindergarten.
Subject Matter The teacher candidate evaluates teaching resources and curriculum materials for their comprehensiveness, accuracy, and usefulness for representing particular ideas and concepts.	1. What curriculum objectives are children in kindergarten expected to pass? 2. How can I makeup lessons to cover multiple objectives accurately?	1. I have looked at some curriculum guides already and plan to study more over the next few weeks. 2. I have made up some lessons that cover one main objective, but within these lessons, the student think critically, explore and use multiple skills to draw conclusion to their thinking.

Source: Professional Portfolio of Denise Logsdon

Professional Development Plan

My student teaching experience helped me to obtain various goals for my teaching career and has also encouraged me to achieve others. Over the next three years, my goals are to . . .

π Attend an NCTM Annual Conference . . .
In order to learn from and share with other teachers and build networks with colleagues; obtain resources for the classroom; learn about the latest technology in mathematics teaching.

π Work toward obtaining a Master's Degree in Education . . .
In order to further my understanding of teaching and work with experienced teachers.

π Work toward obtaining an advanced degree in Mathematics . . .
In order to develop my understanding of higher level mathematics and use this understanding to create meaningful lessons.

π Create and implement discovery lessons in the classroom . . .
In order to aid students in developing a higher and deeper level of mathematical understanding.

π Develop and implement strategies for organization . . .
In order to help my students develop organizational skills for the present and for the future.

π Develop and implement creative activities in the classroom . . .
In order to motivate student learning and create an open and exciting learning environment.

π Collaborate with colleagues and utilize journals and other resources . . .
In order to stay up to date on technology and teaching strategies and develop successful relationships with other teachers.

π Improve upon student-teacher interaction and daily assessment . . .
In order to develop meaningful relationships with students and give important feedback to further student success.

Source: Professional Portfolio of Julianne Cochran

TEACHING PORTFOLIO *This professional development plan was created by an undergraduate student. It demonstrates the teacher's commitment to continued professional growth in the beginning stages of her career.*

This is an example of how a teacher presented her professional development plan in an electronic format.

Source: Professional Portfolio of Renae Lynne Redmond

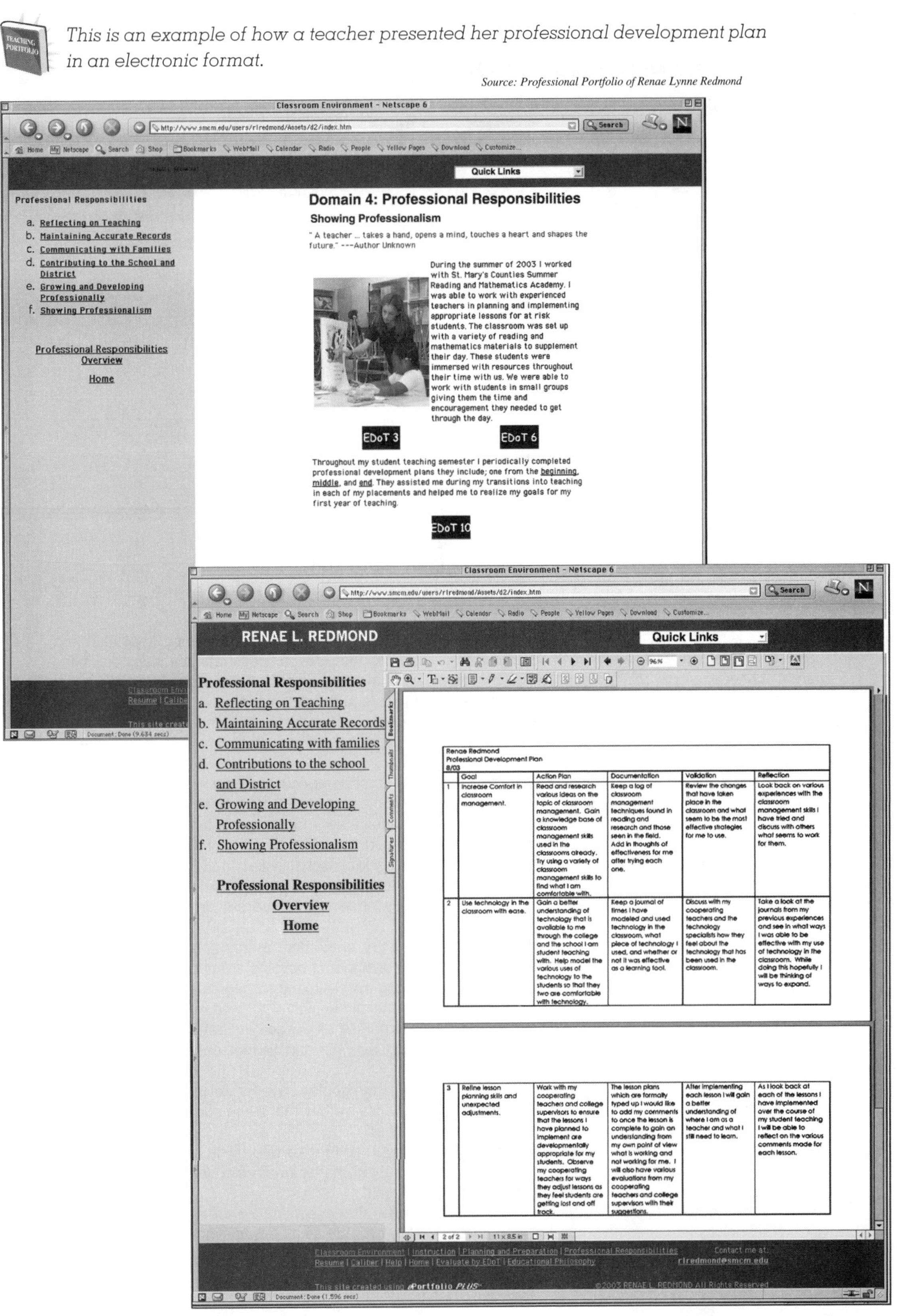

Renae Redmond
Professional Development Plan
8/03

	Goal	Action Plan	Documentation	Validation	Reflection
1	Increase Comfort in classroom management.	Read and research various ideas on the topic of classroom management. Gain a knowledge base of classroom management skills used in the classrooms already. Try using a variety of classroom management skills to find what I am comfortable with.	Keep a log of classroom management techniques found in reading and research and those seen in the field. Add in thoughts of effectiveness for me after trying each one.	Review the changes that have taken place in the classroom and what seem to be the most effective strategies for me to use.	Look back on various experiences with the classroom management skills I have tried and discuss with others what seems to work for them.
2	Use technology in the classroom with ease.	Gain a better understanding of technology that is available to me through the college and the school I am student teaching with. Help model the various uses of technology to the students so that they two are comfortable with technology.	Keep a journal of times I have modeled and used technology in the classroom, what piece of technology I used, and whether or not it was effective as a learning tool.	Discuss with my cooperating teachers and the technology specialists how they feel about the technology that has been used in the classroom.	Take a look at the journals from my previous experiences and see in what ways I was able to be effective with my use of technology in the classroom. While doing this hopefully I will be thinking of ways to expand.
3	Refine lesson planning skills and unexpected adjustments.	Work with my cooperating teachers and college supervisors to ensure that the lessons I have planned to implement are developmentally appropriate for my students. Observe my cooperating teachers for ways they adjust lessons as they feel students are getting lost and off track.	The lesson plans which are formally typed up I would like to add my comments to once the lesson is complete to gain an understanding from my own point of view what is working and not working for me. I will also have various evaluations from my cooperating teachers and college supervisors with their suggestions.	After implementing each lesson I will gain a better understanding of where I am as a teacher and what I still need to learn.	As I look back at each of the lessons I have implemented over the course of my student teaching I will be able to reflect on the various comments made for each lesson.

Source: Professional Portfolio of Renae Lynne Redmond

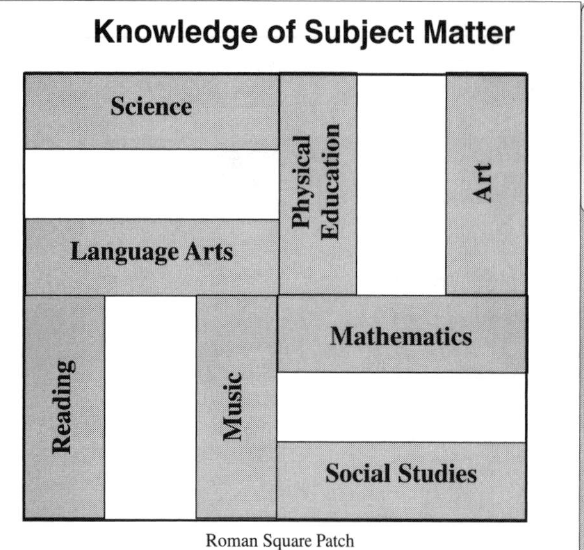

Roman Square Patch

Knowledge of Subject Matter

Standard: The teacher candidate understands the central concepts, assump
are cen
knowle
c) Scie

These examples are introductions to a portfolio section that documents a teacher's knowledge of subject matter. They are part of the portfolio that is based on the theme of Patchwork Quilts. Included is the specific standard being documented, a philosophy statement, an explanation of how the teacher's goal was achieved, and a listing of portfolio entries that support the teacher's knowledge and practice toward the achievement of this standard.

As each scrap of fabric in a patchwork quilt
tells a unique story and
comes together to create a unified work of art . . .

. . . it is my belief that individual disciplines possess unique characteristics. Because education is a profession that employs its own methods of inquiry, research, and pedagogical strategies, each discipline area—Language Arts, Math, Science, Social Studies, and Fine Arts—has its own methods. I believe that in order to present students with learning experiences that are authentic, meaningful, and demonstrating the interconnectedness of knowledge and skills, it is imperative to be articulate in the distinct dimensions of each area. This involves knowing and practicing the various methods of inquiry and developmental theories within each discipline.

I have attended to this goal by actively researching current perspectives and ways of knowing within each disciplinary area. As a result of my knowledge of subject matter, I have been able to define the objectives within each discipline, as well as set developmentally appropriate goals for my students. I use this knowledge to design and develop integrated thematic units that elicit a variety of student engagement and use of thinking skills. When students are participating in learning activities that combine these skills and ways of knowing, they are able to see the unified work of art, the integration of knowledge and skills. I have chosen the following artifacts to document my knowledge and active practice of subject matter knowledge in the classroom:

- **Dienes' Levels of Mathematical Learning**—This entry demonstrates my knowledge of different stages of mathematical learning. I used this model to design and develop a unit on fractions.
- **Poyla's Four Steps to Problem Solve**—By articulating the skills and strategies available to problem solve, I am able to expose my students to a fundamental dimension of applied mathematics.
- **Language Arts**—I created this web to graphically organize an author illustrator study on Maurice Sendak. I have illustrated the several dimensions of Language Arts and the methods in which I employed them in a thematic unit.
- **Reading**—This graphic organizer illustrates the three main goals I have for readers in my classroom community and the actions I take to attend to these goals. I believe that these goals allow me to focus my planning and include all dimensions of subject matter.
- **Hands On Science**—This page reflects a general approach I take to provide contexts for science inquiry in my classroom. When purposes and goals of subject matter inquiry are clearly stated, students are empowered to make their own focused investigations.
- **Technology**—Technology plays an active role across all subject matter areas in my classroom. Technology has become a new form of functional literacy and has its own distinct qualities.

Source: Professional Portfolio of Rosanna Calabrese

Evidence of Planning

Planning is the first step toward creating a quality atmosphere in the classroom. I have been witness to many teachers who have suffered from a lack of planning, and their classroom environment became the unfortunate casualty of that lack of foresight. The reader will see that I have the skills necessary to create a structured environment in which the primary responsibility of the student is to become a successful learner. Unit, weekly, and daily lesson plans are the first step in the creation of a quality environment. These plans allow the teacher to become more familiar with the material as well as initiate a thought process that will lead to more detailed investigation into the subject matter.

I have also included numerous examples of activities I designed and implemented in the classroom. I do not rely solely on the planning of curriculum guides in my teaching and feel more than comfortable designing thought-provoking activities for classroom use. These activities are goal oriented with state and national objectives kept in minds at all times. The use of political cartoons, letters of complaint with their appropriate scoring rubric, and a check-writing project are illustrated. Also included are examples of both formative an

Source: Professional Portfolio of Scott Mooney

The two narratives shown here are section introductions to the planning and instructional delivery categories of the portfolio. They provide the portfolio reviewer with a short philosophy and rationale for including the selected artifacts.

Instructional Delivery

The successful teacher will be able to vary instruction in a number of different ways to accommodate as many students as possible. In a setting full of different nationalities, socioeconomic backgrounds and races, a teacher who can find methods to reach all groups is priceless. This environment forces educators to provide instruction that varies not only day to day but intra-class period also. Teaching block classes allows the instructor to vary instruction far more than does a shorter class period. I have found that it is easier to reach more students in the block-scheduled school due to the longer period of time in class that you have to observe cognition and comprehension.

The reader will find included in this section a number of examples of varying instructional delivery methods. From didactic teaching to cooperative learning methods, structured individual work time to working with small groups, I have attempted to place as many styles as possible into my repertoire. Students deserve to have the most advantageous environment in which to comprehend information. I attempt to provide as much scaffolding as possible, without actually providing answers, during difficult topics. My use of graphic organizers is illustrated as one method that I employ to help students grasp abstract or complex material. Another method I use to aid students' understanding is through the use of computers in class. I believe that making a student more comfortable with technology, and then using that technology to assist in the teaching process, will alleviate some of the pressure placed on the student. Creating a comfortable environment and providing the proper tools to succeed are essential to each other and to the learning process.

Source: Professional Portfolio of Scott Mooney

Source: Professional Portfolio of Lauren T. Costas

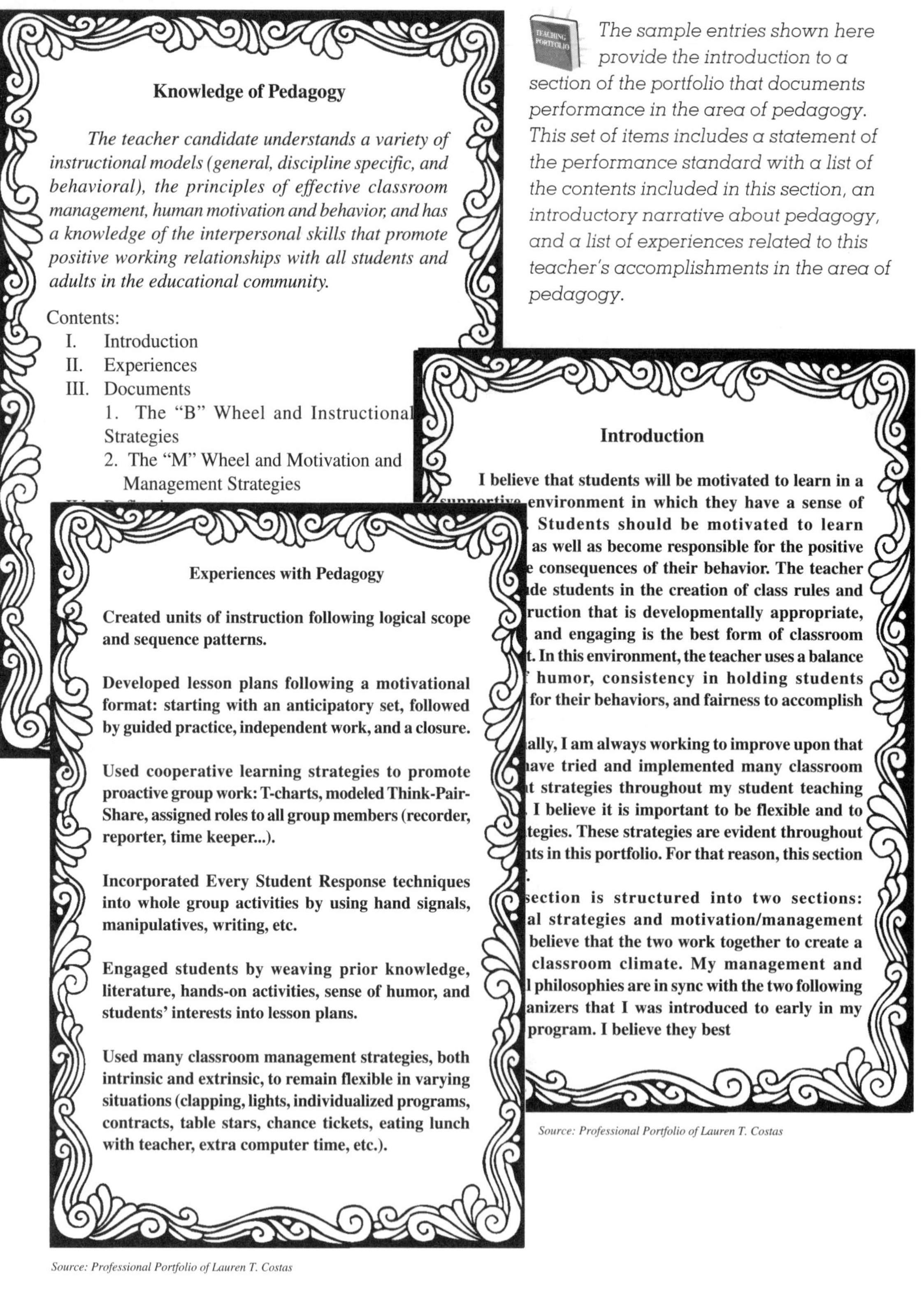

Knowledge of Pedagogy

The teacher candidate understands a variety of instructional models (general, discipline specific, and behavioral), the principles of effective classroom management, human motivation and behavior, and has a knowledge of the interpersonal skills that promote positive working relationships with all students and adults in the educational community.

Contents:

I. Introduction
II. Experiences
III. Documents
1. The "B" Wheel and Instructional Strategies
2. The "M" Wheel and Motivation and Management Strategies

Introduction

I believe that students will be motivated to learn in a supportive environment in which they have a sense of . Students should be motivated to learn as well as become responsible for the positive e consequences of their behavior. The teacher de students in the creation of class rules and ruction that is developmentally appropriate, and engaging is the best form of classroom t. In this environment, the teacher uses a balance humor, consistency in holding students for their behaviors, and fairness to accomplish

ally, I am always working to improve upon that ave tried and implemented many classroom t strategies throughout my student teaching I believe it is important to be flexible and to tegies. These strategies are evident throughout ts in this portfolio. For that reason, this section .

ection is structured into two sections: al strategies and motivation/management believe that the two work together to create a classroom climate. My management and l philosophies are in sync with the two following anizers that I was introduced to early in my program. I believe they best

Source: Professional Portfolio of Lauren T. Costas

Experiences with Pedagogy

Created units of instruction following logical scope and sequence patterns.

Developed lesson plans following a motivational format: starting with an anticipatory set, followed by guided practice, independent work, and a closure.

Used cooperative learning strategies to promote proactive group work: T-charts, modeled Think-Pair-Share, assigned roles to all group members (recorder, reporter, time keeper...).

Incorporated Every Student Response techniques into whole group activities by using hand signals, manipulatives, writing, etc.

Engaged students by weaving prior knowledge, literature, hands-on activities, sense of humor, and students' interests into lesson plans.

Used many classroom management strategies, both intrinsic and extrinsic, to remain flexible in varying situations (clapping, lights, individualized programs, contracts, table stars, chance tickets, eating lunch with teacher, extra computer time, etc.).

Source: Professional Portfolio of Lauren T. Costas

The sample entries shown here provide the introduction to a section of the portfolio that documents performance in the area of pedagogy. This set of items includes a statement of the performance standard with a list of the contents included in this section, an introductory narrative about pedagogy, and a list of experiences related to this teacher's accomplishments in the area of pedagogy.

As you select materials that illustrate your teaching effectiveness, it is important to include a variety of artifacts. However, it will be more meaningful for the portfolio reviewer to see a set of items that are related to the context and sequence of instruction. The first seven examples focus on portfolio documents that represent the context and sequence of an instructional unit.

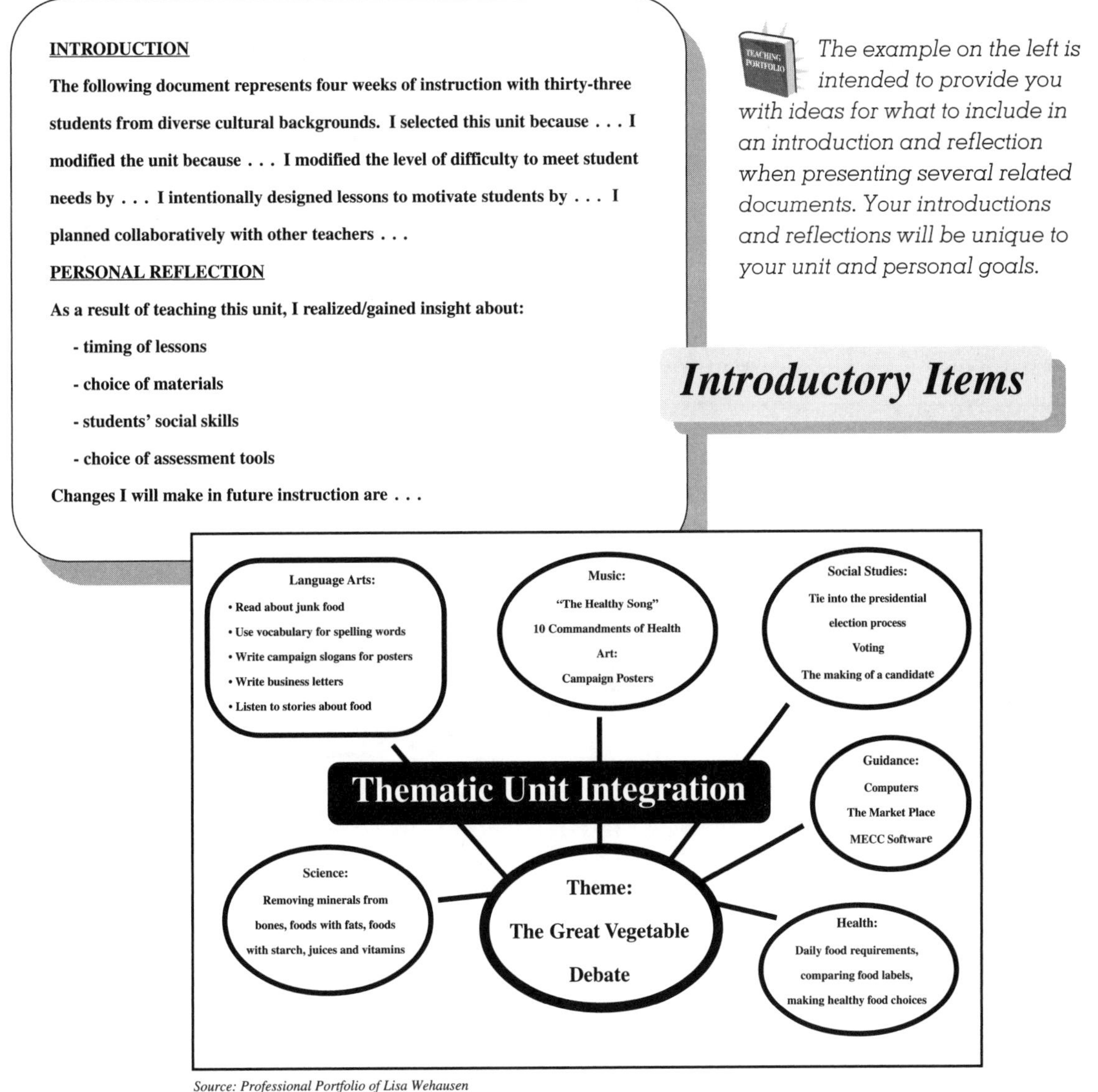

INTRODUCTION

The following document represents four weeks of instruction with thirty-three students from diverse cultural backgrounds. I selected this unit because . . . I modified the unit because . . . I modified the level of difficulty to meet student needs by . . . I intentionally designed lessons to motivate students by . . . I planned collaboratively with other teachers . . .

PERSONAL REFLECTION

As a result of teaching this unit, I realized/gained insight about:

- **timing of lessons**
- **choice of materials**
- **students' social skills**
- **choice of assessment tools**

Changes I will make in future instruction are . . .

The example on the left is intended to provide you with ideas for what to include in an introduction and reflection when presenting several related documents. Your introductions and reflections will be unique to your unit and personal goals.

Source: Professional Portfolio of Lisa Wehausen

This graphic organizer allows the portfolio reviewer to see your interdisciplinary approach to instruction at a glance.

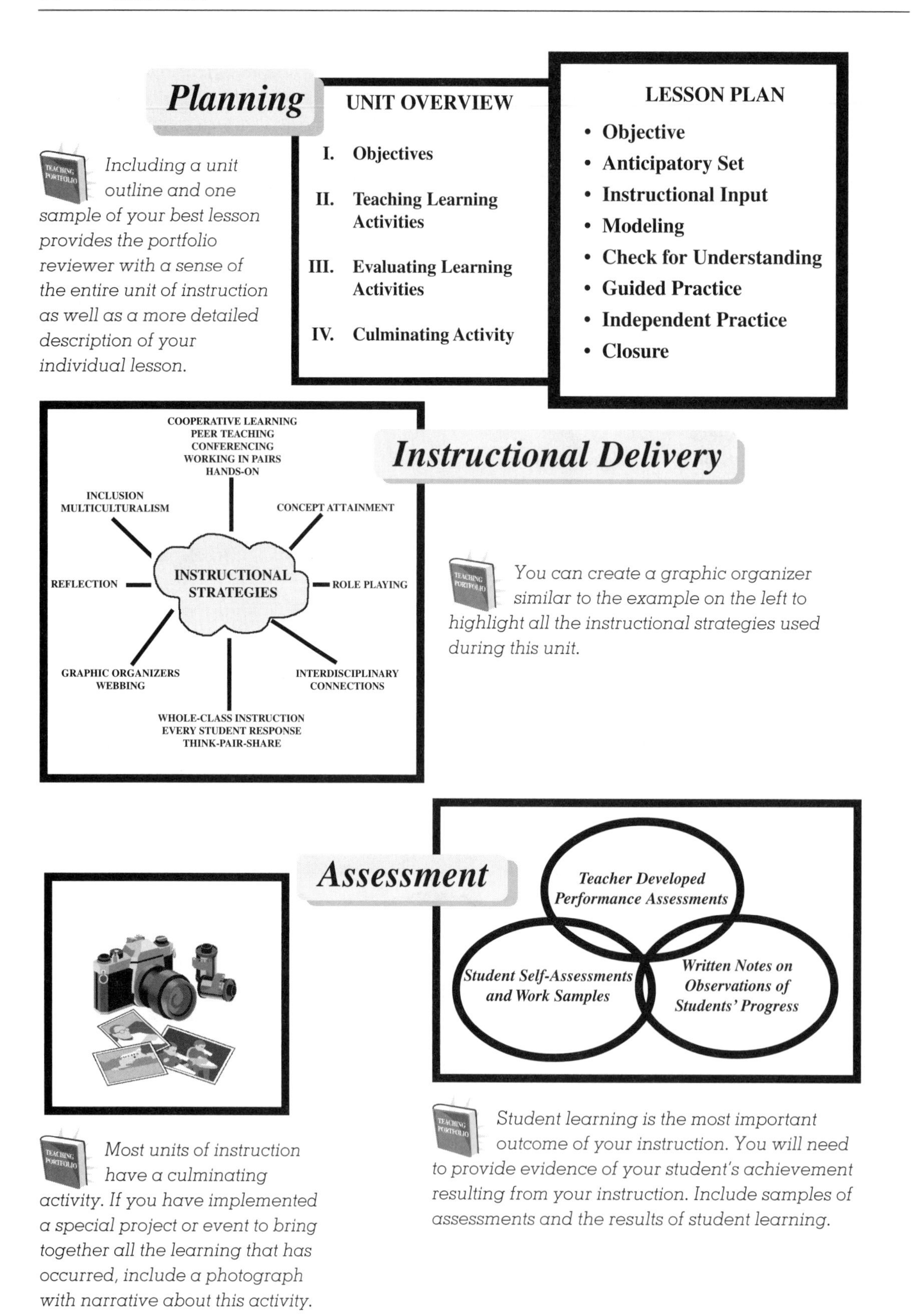

Planning
UNIT OVERVIEW
I. Objectives
II. Teaching Learning Activities
III. Evaluating Learning Activities
IV. Culminating Activity
LESSON PLAN
• Objective
• Anticipatory Set
• Instructional Input
• Modeling
• Check for Understanding
• Guided Practice
• Independent Practice
• Closure
Instructional Delivery
INSTRUCTIONAL STRATEGIES
COOPERATIVE LEARNING
PEER TEACHING
CONFERENCING
WORKING IN PAIRS
HANDS-ON
CONCEPT ATTAINMENT
ROLE PLAYING
INTERDISCIPLINARY CONNECTIONS
WHOLE-CLASS INSTRUCTION
EVERY STUDENT RESPONSE
THINK-PAIR-SHARE
GRAPHIC ORGANIZERS
WEBBING
REFLECTION
INCLUSION
MULTICULTURALISM
Assessment
Teacher Developed Performance Assessments
Student Self-Assessments and Work Samples
Written Notes on Observations of Students' Progress

Including a unit outline and one sample of your best lesson provides the portfolio reviewer with a sense of the entire unit of instruction as well as a more detailed description of your individual lesson.

You can create a graphic organizer similar to the example on the left to highlight all the instructional strategies used during this unit.

Most units of instruction have a culminating activity. If you have implemented a special project or event to bring together all the learning that has occurred, include a photograph with narrative about this activity.

Student learning is the most important outcome of your instruction. You will need to provide evidence of your student's achievement resulting from your instruction. Include samples of assessments and the results of student learning.

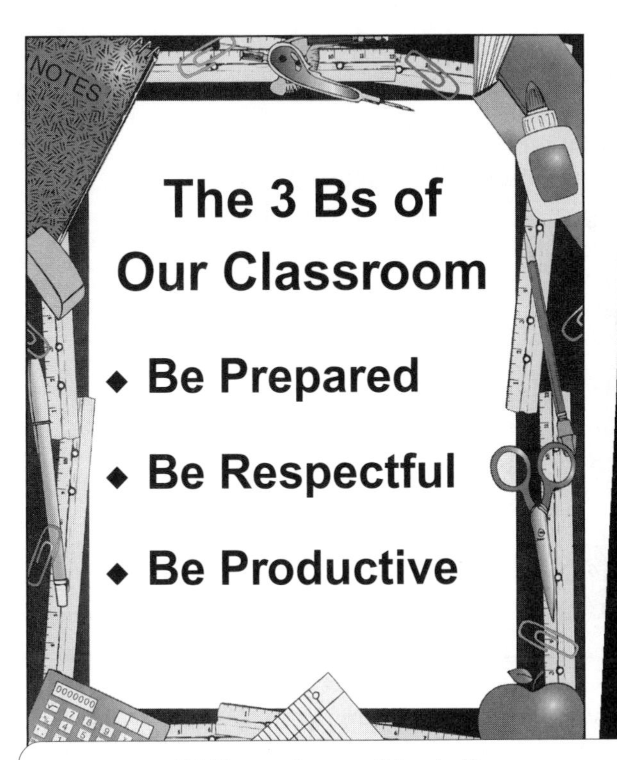

NOTES
The 3 Bs of
Our Classroom
◆ Be Prepared
◆ Be Respectful
◆ Be Productive

CREATING A POSITIVE CLIMATE IN MY ART ROOM

The establishment of a positive and productive classroom environment is, aside from the quality of teaching, the most important function of a teacher. Without a healthy and enjoyable learning environment, it is impossible for students and teachers to reach their full educational potentials.

I believe that the best way to create an effective classroom climate is for the teacher to recognize and accommodate the physical and emotional needs of the students, interests and motivation, individual learning styles, ability levels, and the development of interpersonal communication skills through group involvement. It is my goal for this environment to be as aesthetically pleasing as it is functional. To accomplish this, I will employ the use of visual aids of various art and life objects, student works, sculpture and models, good lighting, and even occasional soft music to promote better concentration.

interesting and nurturing classroom character nbined with effective teaching strategies and style l provide students, and teachers alike, with an oyable and rewarding educational experience that l provide a foundation for learning based on piness and success.

Source: Professional Portfolio of Mat DeMunbrun

Philosophy on Discipline

I expect all students to show both their classmates and me proper respect at all times. By using a variety of methods to ensure that the students work as a team, I attempt to foster a feeling of togetherness and responsibility for one another in the students. Working in groups during class, using proper names when referring to classmates, participating in group projects, and participating in community activities as a class are just a few of the methods I will employ to ensure that the class works together. I believe that if the students feel that their success depends on their classmates, and their classmates' success depends on them, they will work wholeheartedly toward a mutual goal. Along with the components of motivation that I have listed on the following page, I will take the following steps in resolving conflict:

- Wait Time
- Proximity Control
- Informal Conference with Student
- Formal Conference with Student
- Personal Performance Contract
- Extra Involvement in Academic Setting
- After School Detention if Applicable
- Parental Contact
- Guidance Contact
- Parent/Teacher Conference
- Administrative Contact
- Formal Referral

I work very hard to develop and maintain a working relationship with every student. I will never rest if a student requests assistance or guidance. I will also attempt to carry a student only so far. Students, as young adults, need to realize that they are increasingly responsible for their own actions, consequently, they will need to meet me halfway. My relationship with students is based on their attitude alone. I never use other's opinions to develop my own. A relationship is a two-way street and I expect truth and commitment to that relationship.

Source: Professional Portfolio of Scott Mooney

The portfolio documents shown here and on the following page provide examples of different entries related to managing and organizing the classroom. Examples explaining your classroom rules, room arrangement, strategies for discipline, and your approach to creating a positive classroom climate reveals valuable information that provides insight to the portfolio reviewer about your potential to effectively manage the classroom.

Seating Arrangements

I have found it necessary, in some cases to assign students seating as a method of classroom management. The seating arrangements serve two purposes: discipline and lesson implementation. In some cases, students need to have their seats moved if they are sitting near a friend whom they may continuously talk to, or if they are particularly disruptive. In other cases, seating assignments can be used to place a student who needs extra help next to someone who can help. Additionally, the way I set up my room can aid in lesson implementation. Students are generally sitting with a partner, which helps when pairs are required for the day's lesson. The class is set up so that groups can easily be initiated by simply turning a few chairs around. Furthermore, the arrangement of the desks and the seating of the students aids me in my most effective form of discipline—proximity control. There is extra space between the desks so that I can wander between them as I check student progress. The desks are generally facing center, so that the students can see each other, and m

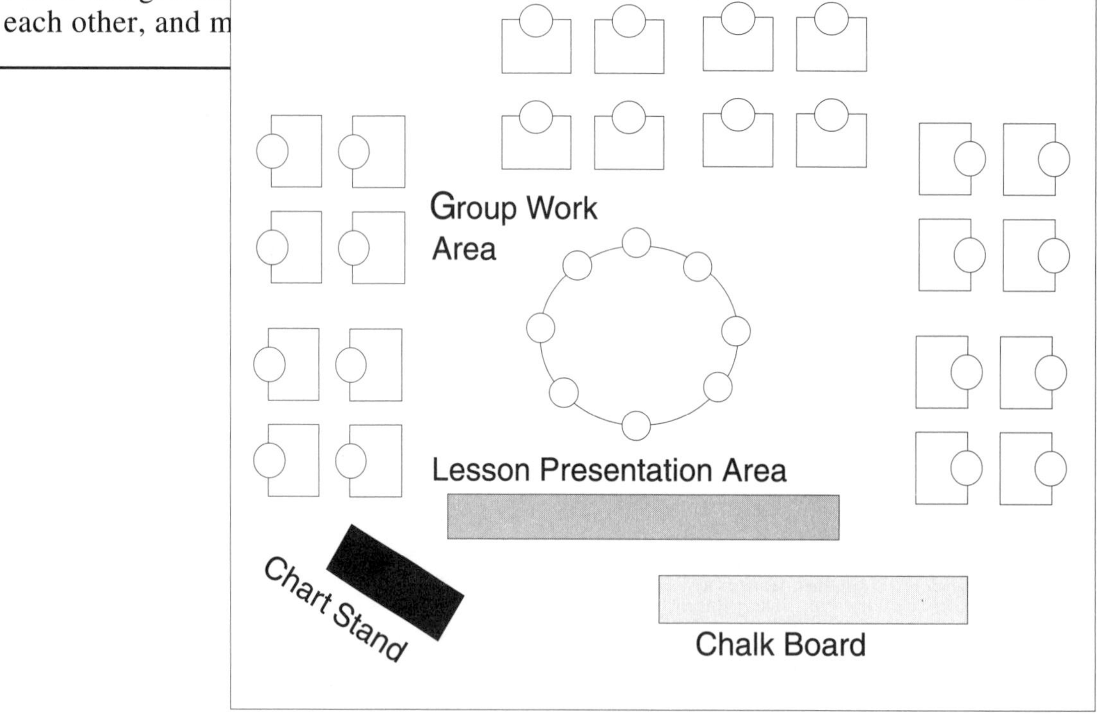

A narrative description discussing your rationale for organizing the classroom allows the portfolio reviewer to understand your thinking and decision making about the arrangement of the classroom. A seating chart provides a visual that correlates with the written explanation.

This series of electronic entries was selected to illustrate the use of a reoccurring design format. Each page of this electronic portfolio is organized with this template.

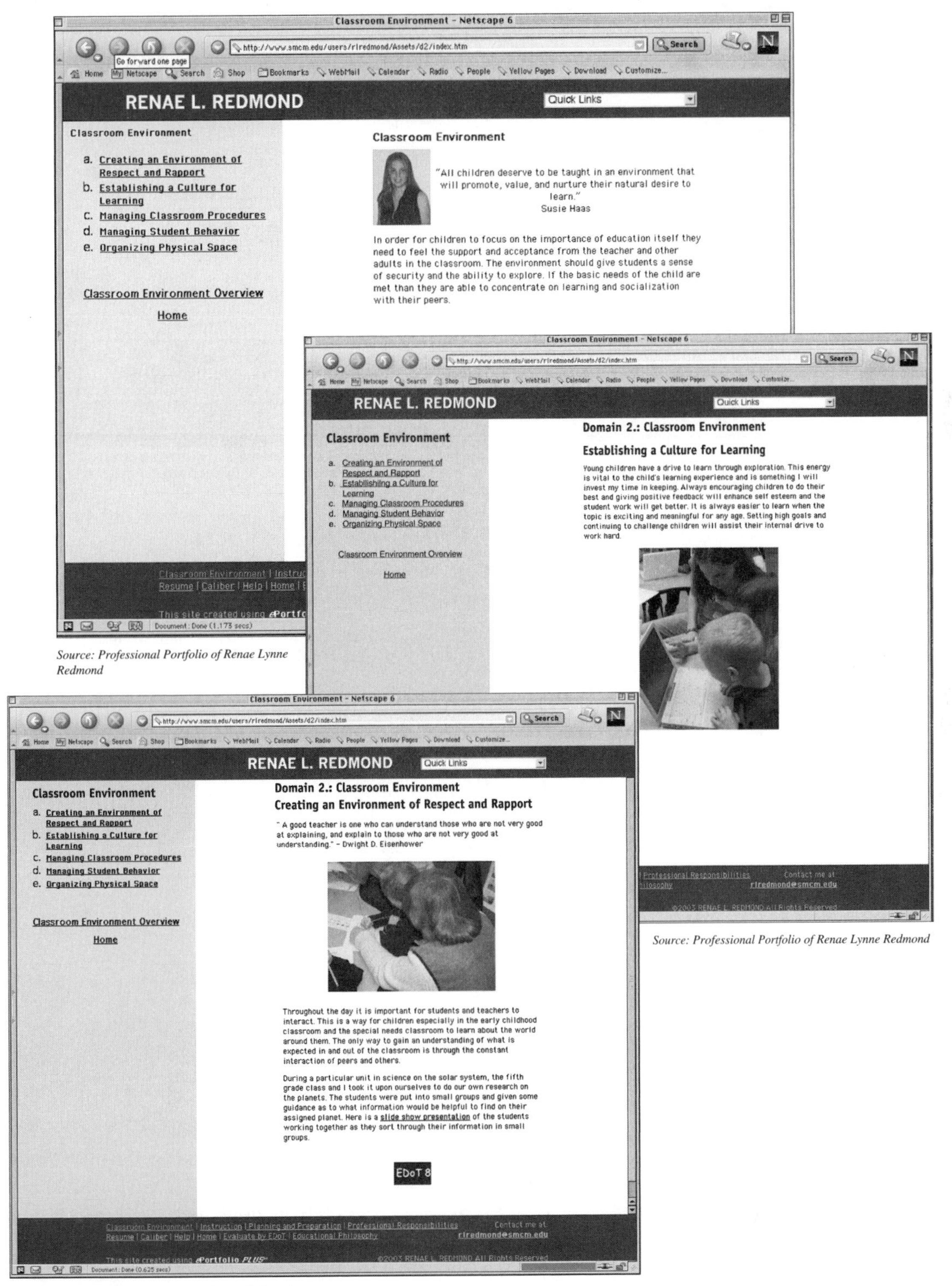

Source: Professional Portfolio of Renae Lynne Redmond

Source: Professional Portfolio of Renae Lynne Redmond

Source: Professional Portfolio of Renae Lynne Redmond

Reflection on Behavior Management Articles and Text

Several weeks into the semester, my cooperating teacher gave me the article, "Some First Steps for Improving Classroom Discipline," and the text, *Teaching Children to Care: Management in the Responsive Classroom.* She recommended that I read the article and selected chapters from the text that were beneficial to her during her first year of teaching. Both texts highlight behavior strategies that can be used in the classroom to maintain a positive environment. After reading the selections, she and I sat down and discussed what I had read. We brainstormed times when we used the techniques in the classroom and reflected on their success or failure. The following chart outlines the behavior strategies that I have used in the classroom and how effective they were for me.

Source: Professional Portfolio of Emily Anne Cosden

Strategy	Source	Description	Reflection on Effectiveness
No Means No	"Some First Steps For Improving Classroom Discipline" by David Hopkins	Say what you mean and mean what you say.	Highly effective with all students in the class. Students react positively when expectations are established and constant.
Limit Setting	"Some First Steps for Improving Classroom Discipline" by David Hopkins	Relax Move slowly Turn, look, wait Prompt (hand, verbal, or eye)	Highly effective with some students, moderately effective with others. Some students respond with exaggerated back talk.
Dealing with Back talk	"Some First Steps for Improving Classroom Discipline" by David Hopkins	Types of Behaviors: •Helplessness •Denial •Blaming •Accusing teacher of professional incompetence Action: Provide opportunities for positive attention getting.	Highly effective with all students. Verbally responding to any form of back talk reinforces it with the student. Many students who need attention get it negatively through back talk.
Self-Controls	*Teaching Children to Care: Management in the Responsive Classroom* by Ruth Sidney Charney	Give students the power to make decisions after modeling effective self-control.	Highly effective with most students, but must be done from first day of school. Beginning self-control training during the year is very difficult.
Appropriate Comments	*Teaching Children to Care: Management In the Responsive Classroom* by Ruth Charney	Specific (name a behavior or accomplishment Positive ("Show me what you will do" not "Don't do that") Comments must be encouraging (they support children's efforts).	Highly effective with all students. Many students have had experiences of frequently being told "no" or "stop." This strategy redirects a specific behavior in a way that does not embarrass or hurt the child.

Source: Professional Portfolio of Emily Anne Cosden

Evidence that supports your commitment to learn more and improve your classroom management provides the portfolio reviewer with additional information about you as a professional teacher. This entry is an example of implementing various behavior management strategies and reflecting on the effectiveness of each strategy.

WEEKLY LESSON PLANS

History - Colonies	Mods 1,2,3,5,6		Mrs. Imbriale
10/14 SWBAT: differentiate between indentured servitude and slavery.	Warm-Up: List the types of farming practiced in the following colonial regions: ① New England ② Middle ③ Southern	I. Review Outline Map II. Definition A. indentured servant B. slave III. Primary Source Document - I.S.	Homework: None!
10/15 SWBAT: compare the lives of an indentured servant and a slave using primary source documents	What is the primary difference between an indentured servant and slave?	I. Review I.S. Primary Source II. Read slave document III. Complete Venn diagram	Homework: Current Events Abstract
10/16 SWBAT: investigate the conditions of the Middle Passage by analyzing a graphic.	List 10 words that you feel would best describe the conditions on a slave ship.	I. Review differences from yesterday II. Analyze the graphic of the slave ship - answer quest. III. Brief discussion	Homework: Vocabulary ① slavery ② indentured servant ③ middle passage ④ witchcraft * ⑤ brochure *
10/17 SWBAT: express their feelings regarding slavery by composing an essay	Identify the name given to the journey from Africa	I. Pre-Writing II. Rough Dr III. Peer Edit	Homework: "Think It
10/18 SWBAT: illustrate an African-American slave tale.	Why do people tell stories?	(Explain im of oral sto II. Illustra III. Write b caption	

Weekly Planning

Source: Professional Portfolio of Merritt Imbriale

Subject US History Unit Colonies - Slavery Topic African-American Storytelling

Mod all Date 10/18/96 Text/Materials Needed The People Could Fly by Virginia Hamilton, paper, colored pencils

MSPAP Outcome/Skills people of nation and world, skills and processes, valuing self and others; Soc. St./Language Usage/Reading/Writing

Focusing Students Attention/Warm-Up Why do people tell stories?

Statement of Objective Students will be able to: illustrate an African-American slave tale.

Introductory/Developmental Activities Display riddle on the board (p. 159) Telling riddles was second to ... Briefly discuss importanc...

Guided Practice Activities Have ... aloud. ("Carrying the Running-Aways") Students should follow along with their own copy of the story.

Independent Activities/Meaningful-Use Tasks Draw an illustration of the story we read. Be sure to label your picture. Then, write a 2 sentence caption for your picture. Be creative; use color.

Assessment Activities Students will be assessed on the picture drawn (labels, creativity, etc.) and the caption.

Closure Activity Ask 2-3 students to share their pictures. Then, read aloud another riddle to enforce storytelling and the message.

Homework Complete illustration, if necessary. Have a great weekend! Reminder: Technology papers/projects due 10/24!

Daily Planning

Source: Professional Portfolio of Merritt Imbriale

TEACHING PORTFOLIO

Many working portfolios include authentic evidence of planning. By providing an example of your weekly plan with the example of a more detailed daily lesson plan, you are demonstrating your skills in long- and short-term instructional planning.

Writing explanations and reflections within the text of the lesson design allows the reviewer to understand the teacher's thoughts and feelings for each element of the lesson.

Lesson Plan: Frequency Tables and Line Plots

Friday, April 2nd, 2004

MATH LAB: (A.K.A. Pre-Algebra)

Objectives:

- The student will review the concepts of frequency tables and line plots in order to apply their knowledge to real life data.
- The student will roll dice to generate data which they will use to create a frequency table, a line plot, and calculate mean, median, and mode.

1) Warm-Up: **(5 minutes)** *I used the Warm-Up time to my advantage today. For instance, I was able to check everyone's homework for completeness (which I record onto my seating chart and later into my grade book), take attendance, and fill out excused absence forms and progress reports. I was also able to pass out calculators which would be needed for the lesson.*

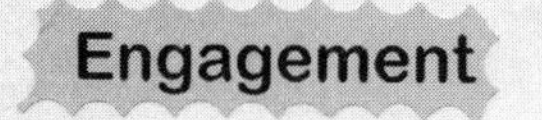

1. Graph: $y = x - 2$
2. $(-2)^4 = x + (-5)$
3. Find the Median: {-.3, -.03, -.4, -.1}

2) Review Homework: **(5 minutes)** *The homework was displayed on the overhead and I allowed my students to just check their own work today. Usually I ask volunteers to go to the board and write out their answers, but today I wanted to get through it quickly so I prepared the overhead in advance. I am finding more and more that preparing overheads saves time and makes my lessons run smoother.*

- Assignment: finish worksheet and do #'s 12 – 16, p. 610 in books.
- Put up transparencies with answers pre-written *(to save time).*
- **STRESS**: "Range" → we always look at the "category" – they thing that we surveyed about!

3) Worksheet: **(7 minutes)** *I could have done a better job explaining the "why" behind the calculations. Especially when it came to the median. Students understand the idea that the median is the middle number (it is a very visual concept), and they understand that the middle number is the (n/2 + ½) term (that is, if we have 10 terms, the median is the 10/2 + ½ = 5.5th term), but they did not really understand how to determine this from the line plots. If I had actually shown them what the line plots were, if I had drawn one out in a data set consisting of a list of numbers, I think that they would have understood better. Sometimes it is still hard for me to determine what is hard for learners to visualize!*

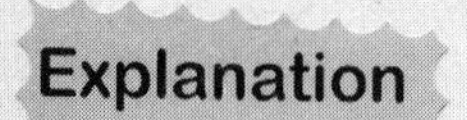

- We will complete the first side of the worksheet together
- I will model # 1
- A student will model on the overhead calculator.
- We will discuss what we are doing conceptually.
- They will try # 2, we will compare, and then repeat with #3

4) Dice Activity: **(10 minutes)** *I liked this activity because it not only led to a review of mean, median, and mode, but also, it built on the skill of addition (which is a weak point!). I had to be very watchful of the boys, though, some of whom were only able to role the dice 5 times because*

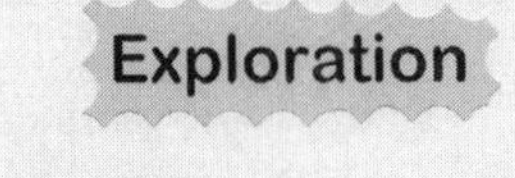

Source: Professional Portfolio of Tiffany Murphy

Accurate record keeping and communication with parents are demonstrated through this phone log.

Sample Phone Log

EBERWEIN; MOD
DATE; 3rd Quarter

Student Name	Person Contacted	Date Of Contact	Reason For Contact	Response
	Mom	2/24	failed to turn in permission slip	Good
	Mom	2/24	failed to turn in permission slip	message
	Dad	2/24	failed to turn in permission slip	Good
	Dad	2/24	failed to turn in permission slip	Message
	Dad	2/26	Constant disrespect	Uncooperative
	Mom	2/26	failed to turn in permission slip	So-So
	Relative	2/26	failed to turn in permission slip	Strange
	Mom	2/26	failed to turn in permission slip	Good
	Dad	2/26	failed to turn in permission slip	Good
	Dad	2/26	failed to turn in permission slip	Good.
	Grandmother	3/2	disrespectful behavior	Uncooperative
	Mom	3/3	improved behavior	Good
	Mom	3/3	disrespectful behavior	Good
	Mom	3/3	poor behavior	Good
	Mom	3/3	poor behavior	Good
	Mom	3/5	poor behavior	Good
	Mom	3/10	improved behavior	Good

This is the first page of my phone long from my internship at Martin Luther King Middle School. I have removed the student names. This artifact has been included here because I think that a huge part of professionalism is calling home to keep in touch with parents. Also, it is very important that teacher's keep a log of some sort for their own protection. That way if a parent falsely claims that they were never told about a particular situation, the teacher can simply point to the phone log as evidence.

Source: Professional Portfolio of Tiffany Murphy

These three electronic portfolio examples provide evidence in support of the Planning and Preparation standard. Each page contains hyperlinks that connect to further evidence.

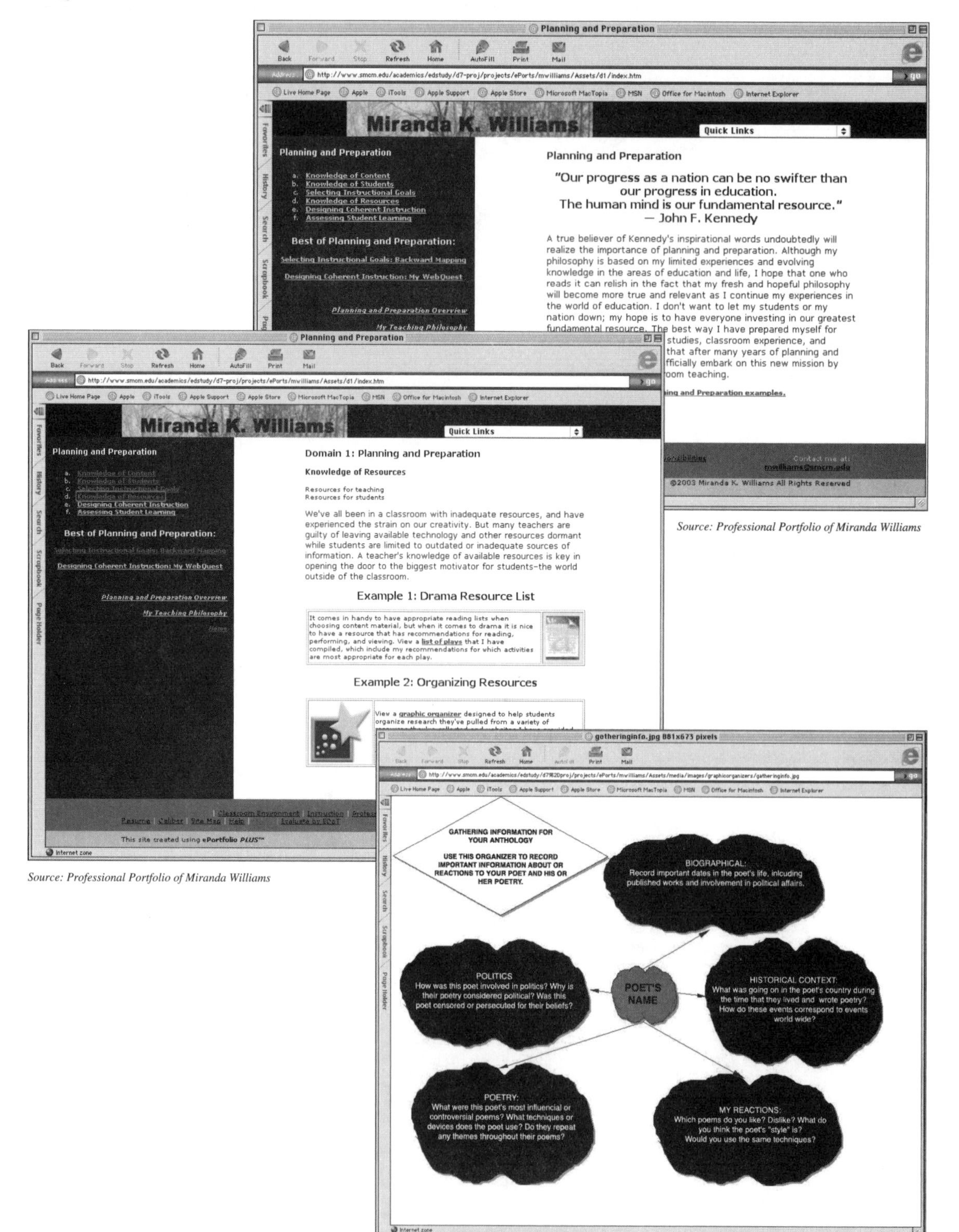

Source: Professional Portfolio of Miranda Williams

Source: Professional Portfolio of Miranda Williams

Source: Professional Portfolio of Miranda Williams

Source: Professional Portfolio of Rosanna Calabrese

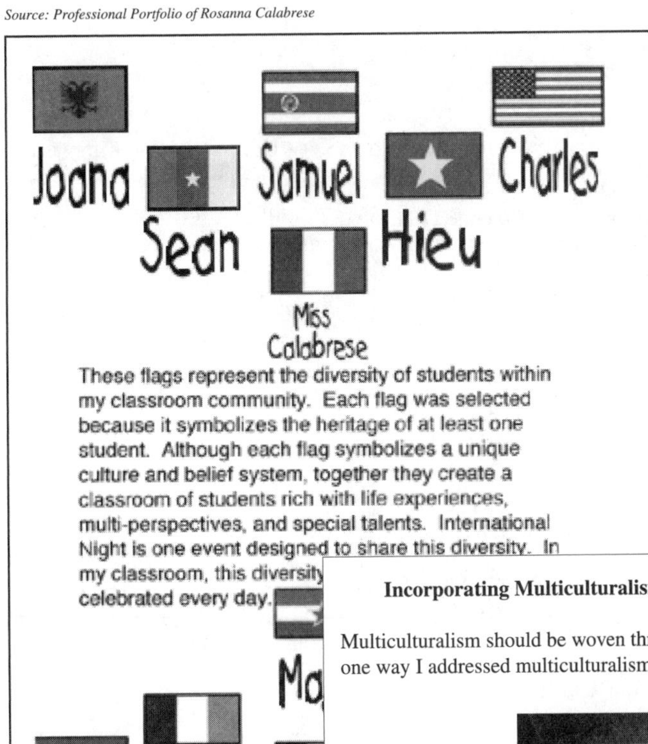

These flags represent the diversity of students within my classroom community. Each flag was selected because it symbolizes the heritage of at least one student. Although each flag symbolizes a unique culture and belief system, together they create a classroom of students rich with life experiences, multi-perspectives, and special talents. International Night is one event designed to share this diversity. In my classroom, this diversity celebrated every day.

Examples of activities and projects that show how you created a multicultural perspective in your classroom are important.

Incorporating Multiculturalism by Celebrating Woman's History Month

Multiculturalism should be woven through all curriculum via multiple forms. Here is one way I addressed multiculturalism in my classroom.

Above, you'll see a sample of books I used to integrate multicultural literature and information into the creation of our Woman's History Quilt. These books tell stories of women in many cultures: Hispanic, African American, Amish, etc. I enjoy books because they illustrate similarities among differing cultures. They were used to provide students with information and motivation for creating a quilt.

This is the quilt we created to celebrate famous women in history.

Each student created a square based on the woman he or she studied. Students researched women by reading and highlighting expository text. Some women we studied were Harriet Tubman, Helen Keller, and Susan B, Anthony etc.

Source: Professional Portfolio of Lauren T. Costas

Source: Professional Portfolio of Ryan Imbriale

Create Your Own Culture
Assignment Sheet

Project Description:
For the next few class periods, you and your "self-chosen" team (maximum 4 persons) will create your own culture. The goal for this project is (1) to introduce you to the sociological term "culture," (2) to enable you to demonstrate your understanding of different cultural attributes, and (3) to be creative while having fun. The project will concentrate on six main areas of sociology and culture. Each member of your team will be responsible for equal contributions to the project. Decide among yourselves who will be responsible for what areas. When you turn in your project, each member must submit a complete Rubric with an evaluation of your group's work as well as a self-evaluation of your contribution.

Written Components: In well-written, complete sentence paragraphs, write a description for each area of your created culture. The details of your culture should be created and discussed with your team members. Each member is responsible for writing up at least one component. The areas within your culture must include the following:

The Name of Your Culture: Be creative (but not silly)!

Family: Determine what the average family is like in the culture you created. Consider such possible areas as family size, income, divorce rate, social status, population, extended or n
what type of ceremonies th

Political Systems: Determ
Consider such possible are
of the people in the govern
and the government, how t
might deal with problems l
how are leaders determine

Economy: Determine the
areas as main products, ho
income is, is the economy
export, and is it an industri

Education: Consider poss
of people in schools, the ty
all the people, are there hig
most schooling done by te
they learn.

This double entry is a detailed explanation of a multicultural project with a tool for assessing this assignment. The photographs, not shown here, bring to life student involvement and project outcomes.

Create Your Own Culture
~Rubric~

		Student	Teacher
Written Components:			
The Name of Your Culture	2 pts.	______	______
Family	8 pts.	______	______
Political Systems	8 pts.	______	______
Economy	8 pts.	______	______
Education	8 pts.	______	______
Religion	8 pts.	______	______
Natural Features	8 pts.	______	______
Social Characteristics	8 pts.	______	______
Visual Component:	6 pts.	______	______
2-3 minute Presentation:	5 pts.	______	______
Individual Effort:	5 pts.	______	______
Team Efforts:	5 pts.	______	______
TOTAL POINTS	**75 pts.**	______	______

Student's Comments
(Use back if necessary.)

Teacher's Comments
(Use back if necessary.)

I taught Sociology to eleventh and twelfth graders. This is an example of a project students did to study the components of culture.

Source: Professional Portfolio of Ryan Imbriale

These electronic portfolio entries provide evidence of various methods for assessing student learning. By clicking on the hyperlinks, the reviewer can quickly assess rubrics and checklists that demonstrate the teacher's ability to design assessment instruments.

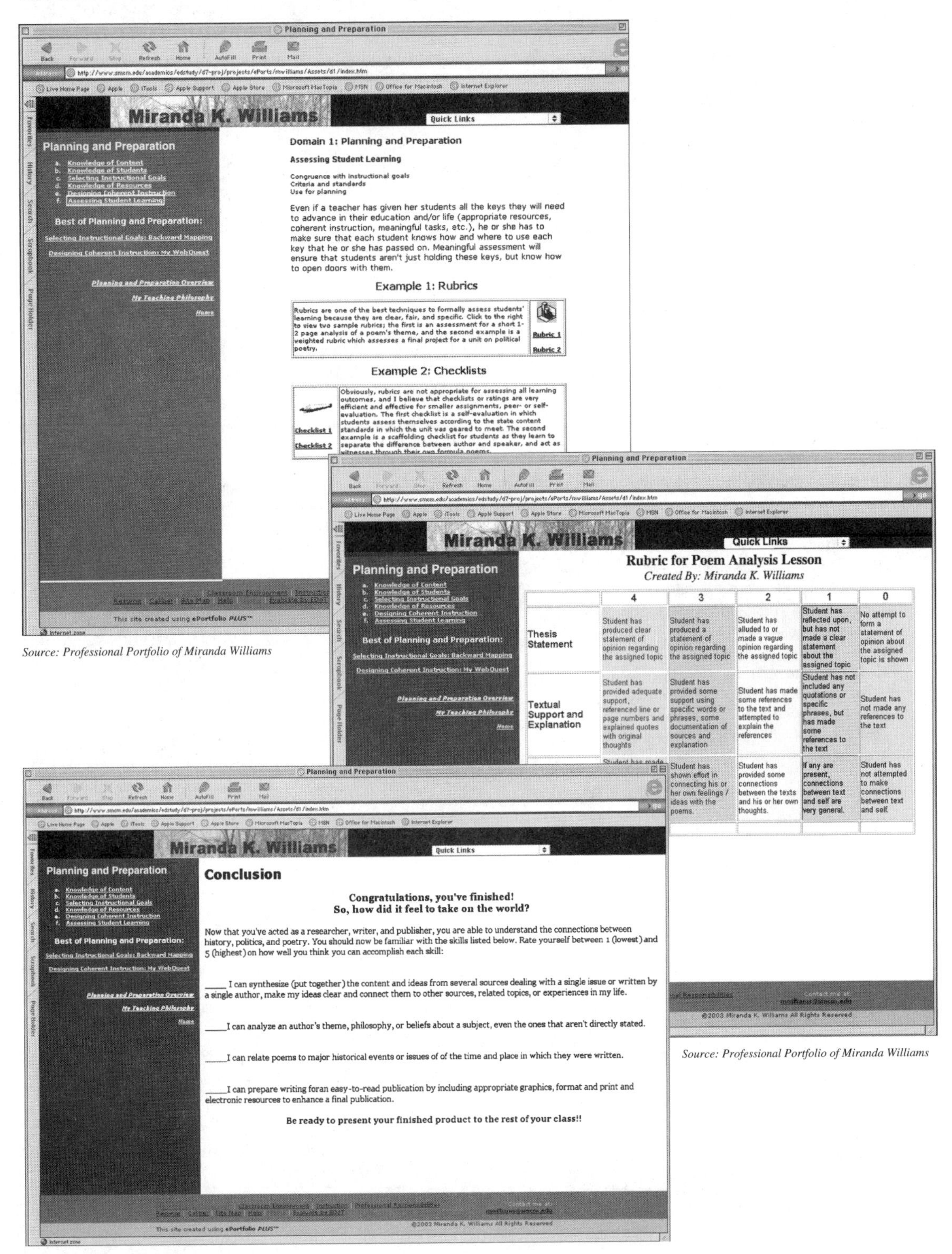

	4	3	2	1	0
Thesis Statement	Student has produced clear statement of opinion regarding the assigned topic	Student has produced a statement of opinion regarding the assigned topic	Student has alluded to or made a vague opinion regarding the assigned topic	Student has reflected upon, but has not made a clear statement about the assigned topic	No attempt to form a statement of opinion about the assigned topic is shown
Textual Support and Explanation	Student has provided adequate support, referenced line or page numbers and explained quotes with original thoughts	Student has provided some support using specific words or phrases, some documentation of sources and explanation	Student has made some references to the text and attempted to explain the references	Student has not included any quotations or specific phrases, but has made some references to the text	Student has not made any references to the text
	Student has made ...	Student has shown effort in connecting his or her own feelings / ideas with the poems.	Student has provided some connections between the texts and his or her own thoughts.	If any are present, connections between text and self are very general.	Student has not attempted to make connections between text and self.

Source: Professional Portfolio of Miranda Williams

Source: Professional Portfolio of Miranda Williams

Source: Professional Portfolio of Miranda Williams

SOCIAL CONTEXT

As each scrap of fabric in a patchwork quilt tells a unique story and comes together to create a unified work...

...the many dimensions of the student's life—home, school, and county—come together to create an educational community. The educational community as a whole permeates almost every aspect of society: families, students, school administrators, economics, politics, culture, etc. The classroom climate and the products of that environment therefore not only affect the students, but society as a whole as well. The individual learners come into the classroom with their own life experiences and values. This classroom community operates in the context of a school community that has its own characteristics, resources, and concerns.

It is my goal as a teacher to use these dimensions as resources to foster authentic, meaningful, and relevant learning experiences. By integrating school and home experiences, as well as demonstrating other community resources, I am able to create student-centered activities that motivate and invite the students to actively participate in their society.

I have chosen the following to documer
social experience to support their learning a

- **Montgomery County Recycling Cent** to be aware and experience the valuabl they live. In order to do that, I research that support the students' classroom le
- **Rumpus Party**—This was a celebrati our unit on Maurice Sendak. I invite excited to share their experiences wit and the families demonstrated their en
- **Newsletter**—This is another method I involved in classroom activities. I solic to reciprocate the sharing of informati
- **International Night**—This entry de community as well as the appreciatio community.
- **Collaboration with Specialists**—In experiences that demonstrate the interc as well as the various ways of knowin June Cayne, to design a learning activi my Maurice Sendak unit.

Source: Professional Portfolio of Rosanna Calabrese

These entries illustrate how a teacher bridges home, school, and community experiences to make learning more meaningful for the students.

INTEGRATING RECYCLING

The students used Kid Pix to create Earth Day posters. This activity integrated language arts, art, social studies, and technology.

This bulletin board displays student published work. The student wrote books about the many ways an object can be reused instead of thrown in the trash. The titles vary from the Six Lives of a Can to the Ten Lives of a Box.

This is one of the many literature theme baskets I have in the classroom. Students frequently read these to discover more about our subject of inquiry as well as to supplement their learning activities.

Source: Professional Portfolio of Rosanna Calabrese

This teacher has presented three examples of evidence that document her performance in designing coherent instruction. By clicking on any three examples, a larger image will appear.

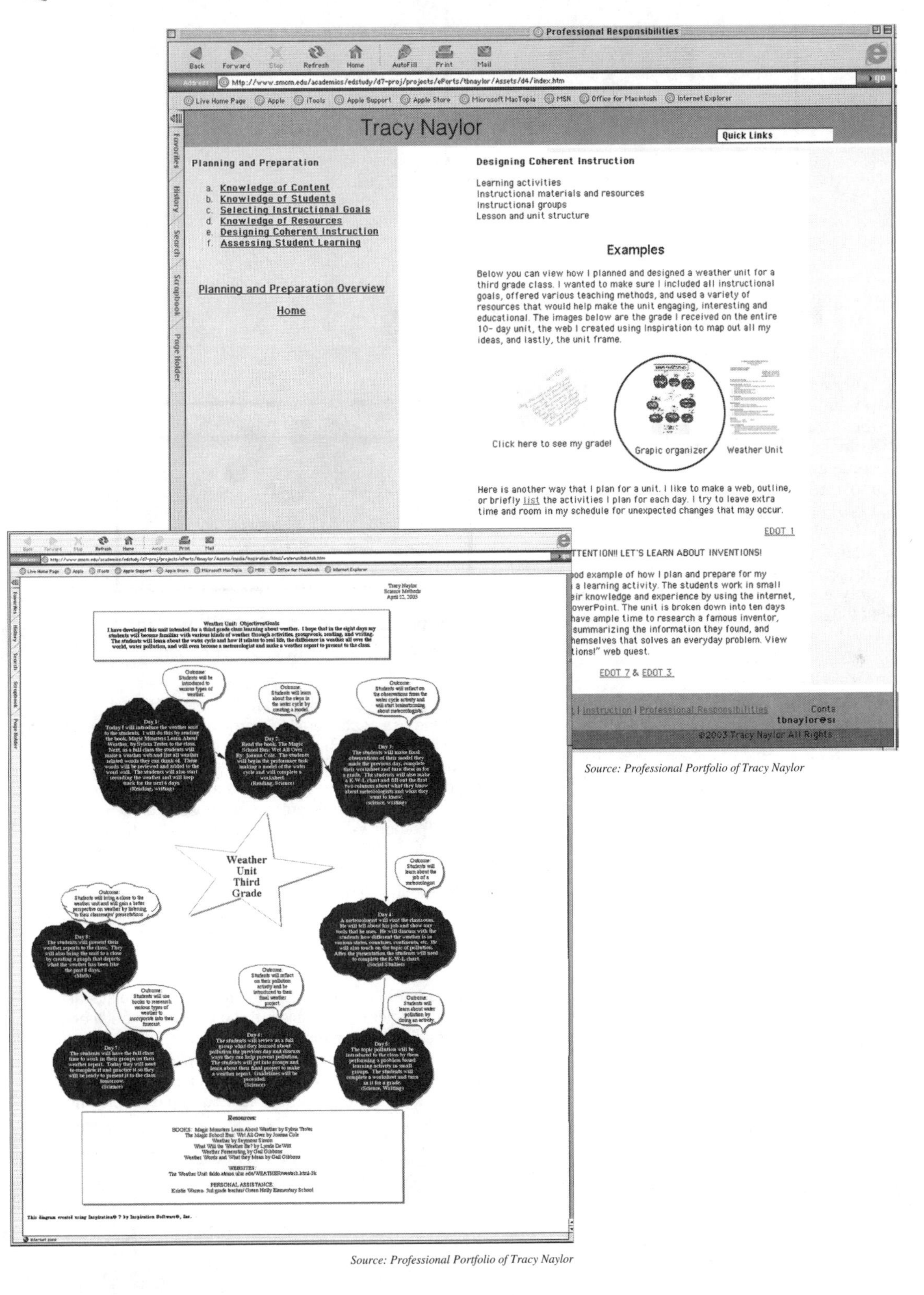

Source: Professional Portfolio of Tracy Naylor

Source: Professional Portfolio of Tracy Naylor

Didactic Teaching

Although I strive to vary my instru
possible, it is sometimes necessary
the students in a more structured
vidual exploration may allow. Dir
some cases a limited discussion led
most efficient method for this diss
tion. Limiting the use of this meth
effectiveness. Students who are fo
after day, to teachers drone on are
in their own education. This loss
only to decreased student perform
management problems also.

Source: Professional Portfolio of Scott Mooney

These narrative entries describe two different types of instructional strategies with students. Both entries include a reflection on the effectiveness of the strategy.

Cooperative Learning and Jig Saw Teaching in the Secondary Classroom

Secondary students have the ability to become more familiar with their content through the use of cooperative learning and jig saw teaching. In this example I was interested in the students' becoming familiar with seven examples of slave revolt during the 19th century. Instead of giving the students notes to take and readings for the whole class to complete, I broke the class up into seven different groups based on where they sat in the room. Each group was given a reading on one of the slave revolts and instructed that they would be responsible for teaching the rest of the class the appropriate information to fill in the graphic organizer. I allowed the students to work on their own material for an entire class period (45 minutes) and instructed them that they would be teaching their material at the next class meeting.

Reflection

This activity could have worked even better than it did if the students had participated in something like this previously. I found out that middle school aged students are not skilled in pulling out the truly important material from the text in a manner that allows them to teach the class. I am positive that these students would have been able to master this process after a more structured modeling example and repeated application.

Source: Professional Portfolio of Scott Mooney

Letter of Complaint Project

This assignment will require you to write a letter of complaint to a business. You will choose one of four situations below and write a letter of complaint to someone in authority at that business. This letter is due at the end of class.

The situations are:

1.) You brought your car into the dealer where you bought it because it was making a funny noise. You are not a car expert so you did not know what was wrong. As you are talking to the service guy, you are getting more and more worried. He spent a half-hour telling you what may be wrong and how it could result in more and more damage to your car. Because you have no experience in fixing cars you are taking his word for it. You leave the car with him and give him permission to fix your car.

You go to work and at the end of the day you pick up your car. The cashier gives you the bill for $600 and you are very shocked that a small noise could be so costly. You look for someone to explain to you why it is so much but everyone but the cashier is gone for the day. You are told that if you don't pay for the car then you cannot take it home. You need the car for work the next day so you decide to pay the bill and find someone to complain to the next day. The next day you find time to call the dealership and talk to the service guy. He gave you a very technical explanation that you really didn't understand and he seems incapable or unwilling to explain it so that you can understand. You finally hang up the phone thoroughly confused, more than a little angry, and out $600!

2.) You are shopping for clothes for the next school year. You have a bunch of money that you earned from working over the summer and are ready to spend a lot on a new wardrobe. You know where the good clothes are and you can't wait to buy as much as you can. As you start looking at the clothes for a while, you notice that the service people are ignoring you and running to the older customers to see if they need help. You look around for someone to open a changing room for you to try on some clothes and after 20 minutes, you find someone. That person gives you an attitude that tells you that he or she does not have enough time to spend on you.

After you have tried on a bunch of clot[...]
sales person comes over and looks at w[...]
realize that the person is counting the[...]
bring them up to the register, you agai[...]
to ring your purchases.

Source: *Professional Portfolio of Scott Mooney*

These two entries provide the portfolio reviewer with evidence that shows how the teacher facilitated thinking and problem solving. The scoring rubric identifies each area of performance expected from the activity.

Student's Name: __________ Date:__________

Letter of Complaint Scoring Rubric

		Your Score	My Score
Format			
•Address in the correct places -	5 pts.	____	____
•Three full paragraphs written -	5 pts.	____	____
•Date and your name in the correct place -	5 pts.	____	____
Content			
Introduction Paragraph			
•Did you explain who you were? -	5 pts.	____	____
•Did you explain what happened to initiate this letter? - 5 pts.			
Problem Paragraph			
•Did you explain what action the store took?-	5 pts.	____	____
•Did you explain why this action was not satisfactory?-	5 pts.	____	____
Resolution Paragraph			
•Did you explain what you want done?-	5 pts.	____	____
•Did you explain why you thought that this resolution was acceptable or reasonable?-	5 pts.	____	____
Accuracy			
•Did you correctly use one of the situations outlined in the assignment?-	10 pts.	____	____
•Did you address the letter to a reasonable person?	10 pts	____	____
•Did you use words that sounded respectful, full sentences, correct spelling, proper grammar?-	10 pts.	____	____
Total Points	**75 pts.**	____	____

Source: *Professional Portfolio of Scott Mooney*

Urban, Suburban, and Rural Unit

This unit started with a general overview and introduction to the terms: urban, suburban, and rural. Students were read storybooks that illustrated each type of community and then were asked to search the stories for comparisons and contrasts between the different communities. Graphic Organizers were used to demonstrate their understandings. Each student filled out his or her own diagram. Furthermore, the students wrote poetry, conducted informational interviews, conducted research of a community by examining textbook materials, and created murals.

As a class, we created a visual representation of their individual work. Below is a picture of the beginning of the bulletin board that acted as a constant source of learning during this unit. The students in this picture are working collaboratively to represent the common elements shared by urban, suburban, and rural communities. They brainstormed a variety of residential, recreational, and commercial attributes characteristic of these communities. I wrote their suggestions on cards and the students illustrated the text. When they came back to the floor, students placed the objects on the diagram and explained their reasoning. The students then gave a thumbs up or thumbs down to demonstrate their agreement or disagreement. If a student disagreed, he or she would argue his or her case, and the students together voted on where the card should be placed.

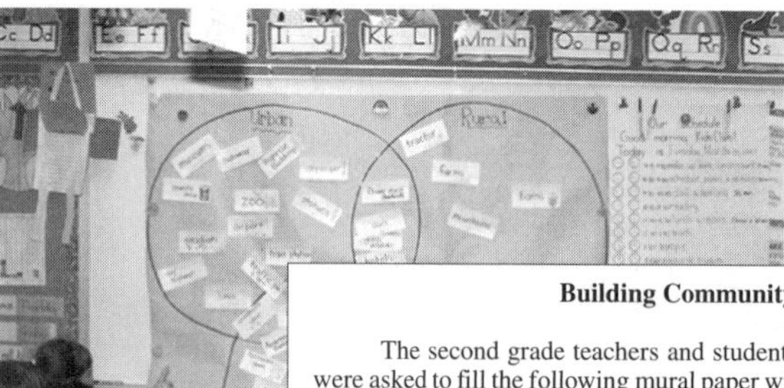

The following documents represent a few
on the big concept of many types of comm
kinds of urban communities. Third, we st
of a suburban community. Lastly, we
communities. Specifically, we stu

Source: Professional Portfolio of Rosanna Calabrese

The entry on the left describes the introductory lesson to a social studies unit. The use of photographs enhances the detailed explanation.

Building Community by Representing a Community

The second grade teachers and student teachers presented their classes with a task. They were asked to fill the following mural paper with their own representation of an Amish community. Creating this mural was an activity set up to promote community building with the classroom, as well as to give the students an opportunity to showcase their new knowledge about one type of rural community.

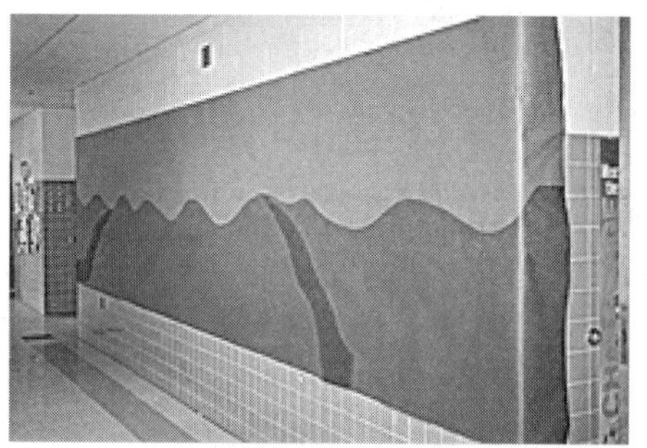

The Final Product

Here is the final product in all its splendor. As you can see, the whole second grade contributed to this colorful representation of an Amish community. The students made all the decisions regarding the mural and were just as proud of their working together as they were of the actual finished product.

Source: Professional Portfolio of Lauren T. Costas

Products such as the before and after mural related to the Urban, Suburban, and Rural Unit illustrate how the students contributed to a group activity.

A Reflection About Journal Writing

Reflecting upon my own education experiences, I remember one teacher who really motivated me and got me excited about learning. He integrated the subject, made science hands-on, and gave us a lot of autonomy. I felt that he appreciated each one of us. One of the methods he used was also one of my favorite, journal writing. The journal writing took place at the beginning and end of every day. We would write anything in the journal from poetry to complaints about the bully on the playground, to jokes or ongoing stories. I really looked forward to that time, especially because I knew that my teacher was going to read it and write something back. He would always write funny or caring comments that valued my perspective and encouraged me to think.

To this day I always valued that teaching strategy. I intend to use it in my own classroom. It offers the students the chance to reflect, release, read, and relate. It also offers the teacher a world of knowledge. It provides the tea
daily lives, creativity, sense of hu
concerns which can be utilized for
Journals allow students to ex
encouraging them to use their wr

Source: Professional Portfolio of Lauren T. Costas

This reflective entry emphasizes the power of using journaling as an ongoing part of the instructional day to gain knowledge about students, build communication between teacher and student, and plan for instruction.

Journal Assessment

Objective: This method of informal assessment allows me to evaluate individual student comprehension during instruction while reinforcing independent practice.

Fractions ar what's divided into fair Shares or equal parts.
yes
no

Description: This is a sample from a student's math journal. This entry was an independent practice activity that followed an initiatory concept attainment lesson about fractions. The students used their journals to write the "fraction rule" across their journal pages and to document their analysis of wholes to determine whether they were divided into equal parts. This student's work demonstrates that she has an accurate comprehension of equal parts or fair shares. She is able to discriminate which wholes are fractions and which do not fit the rule. While she was working independently, I asked her a few questions to evaluate her ability to articulate her thought process and defend her judgments. She modeled her thoughts by folding the shapes to demonstrate the equivalent of the parts. It was my assessment that this student was developmentally ready to progress to the next level of mathematical learning, generalization, and representation.

Source: Professional Portfolio of Rosanna Calabrese

This entry shows how journals may be used as a method for assessing learning in mathematics.

Survey of Student Experience

This worksheet requires students to make connections between literature and their own lives. As an educator it allows me to gain insight about a student's life experiences and integrate that information into instruction.

Matthew's Tantrum Name_______________

Remember a time that you were upset like Matthew in the book in the book Matthew's Tantrum by Jan Hill.

Write three adjectives that describe how you felt when you were upset.

___________ ___________ ___________

Draw a picture of what you looked like when you were upset.

What made you upset?

What did you or someone else do to make you fee
better?

How is this the same or different than the wa
Matthew's tantrum was solved?

Outcome: As a result of this connection between life and literature, the students were very eager to share their experiences. The students articulated their thoughts very clearly and were excited to discuss their tantrums in the small group setting. While it may not be "acceptable" to admit crying to second grade peers, my students were elated to find commonalities among their diverse home experiences.

Source: Professional Portfolio of Rosanna Calabrese

These examples show how a teacher uses knowledge of the learner to plan instruction. Each of these items provides introductions, explanations, and the outcomes of the activity.

K-W-L-S

K (What I Know Now)-W (What I Want to Know)-
L (What I Learned)-S (What I Still Want to Know)

Objective: The K-W-L-S chart strategy allows me to assess student background knowledge, identify misconceptions, develop student-directed inquiry lessons, plan lessons that integrate their interest and questions, as well as document student development and growth.

Description: Prior to initiating an interdisciplinary thematic unit on recycling, I took an inventory of student background knowledge. I asked students to think about their forthcoming field trip to the Recycling Center. I asked "What do you already know about recycling?" Student responses varied from "My family composts!" to "I can make stuff out of trash."

After discussing our experience with recycling, I posed another question to my students. "When we go on the field trip, what will you want to know about recycling?" The students used their personal interests to generate a list of questions. My students used these to focus their inquiry at the Recycling Center.

As a result of this survey of student knowledge and interest, I was able to design a unit that attended to their concerns. I developed activities that meet the needs and interests of the learners within my classroom community.

Source: Professional Portfolio of Rosanna Calabrese

Objective: I wanted my students to experience the differences between urban, rural, and suburban communities. I did this by changing the classroom layout to simulate the spatial relationships among these three communities.

Describing methods you use for experiential learning—such as this simulation activity—demonstrates your creativity in instruction.

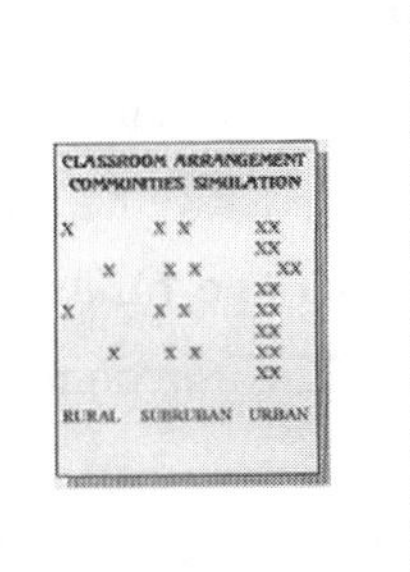

What happened here?!

Students express surprise o

Description: The students entered th find the desks rearranged. In one cor side. In the middle of the room eight d four desks were completely removed fr This rearrangement was to demonstr communities.

The students predicted why the r what each area of the room represente observations about the traffic, noise le classroom. The day concluded wi commonalities, their differences, and w

Source: Professional Portfolio of Rosanna Calabrese

Formal Assessment

I designed this formal assessment to elicit a variety of higher order thinking skills, as well as to provide a context for the students to apply their concepts of rural, urban, and suburban communities. I consulted Bloom's Taxonomy of Learning to target the types of thinking skills that would incorporate concrete and abstract thinking. This type of assessment provides me with concrete documentation of the students' ability to use a variety of higher order thinking skills to apply their knowledge. Here are three of the questions from this assessment.

In what type of community do you think the boy in Sun Up lives and why do you think this?

Look at the map and label each community.

Use this Venn diagram to compare and contrast rural and urban communities

Source: Professional Portfolio of Rosanna Calabrese

Include documents that show how you assess student learning.

The following four examples describe a teacher candidate's methods for assessing student learning and using assessment data to modify and plan instruction.

Assessment and Scoring

This quiz was created to assess students' understanding of function operations, compositions and inverses, various forms of notation, and realistic applications. Since the class is 45 minutes in length, the quiz must be short enough for students to finish while still addressing the necessary concepts. Each concept is addressed via three or four questions to give students an opportunity to show their understanding of the various concepts and notations. The functions are similar to those used in class and thus familiar to the students.

The quizzes were graded based on the following rubric. Each problem is worth 10 points. Students will receive two points for attempting the problem. Students will receive progressively more points for greater depths of understanding and correct computations. Students will be deducted only a few points for arithmetic errors in order to give students points based on their understanding of concepts. In addition to point markings, students will receive descriptive feedback on their quizzes, detailing their mistakes, giving suggestions, and encouraging their understanding of various concepts.

Questions	2	4	6	8	10
Function Operations	Attempted the problem, but shows no understanding of the concept.	Operations are attempted, but incorrect calculations or solutions are given.	Operations are attempted, but like terms are combined incorrectly or student tried to solve for x.	Operations are mostly correct but with 2 or 3 errors. Includes not using parentheses.	Accurate operations, correct answers. -1 for minor error.
Composition of Functions	Attempted the problem, but shows no understanding of the concept.	Does not use a composition- uses only one function or computes function values separately.	Uses first function correctly but not second or uses wrong function first.	Composition is mostly correct but with 2 or 3 errors.	Accurate composition, correct answers. -1 for minor error.
Inverse Functions	Attempted the problem, but shows no understanding of the concept.	Does not correctly create inverse, but shows slight understanding of the concept.	Does not interchange x and y, but computes inverse correctly otherwise.	Creates inverse using correct format but with 2 or 3 errors.	Created accurate inverse. -1 for minor error.

Source: Professional Portfolio of Julianne Cochran

This is an example of a rubric that was created to assess student performance from a short mathematics quiz.

Source: Professional Portfolio of Julianne Cochran

Informal Assessment: Student Cards

During warm-up and question and answer times I often used note cards with student names to remind me to focus on a select few students during the class period. I rotated these names daily so that I focus on different students each day and am not distracted by students who are more vocal or students who may be causing problems. At times I would keep notes on the students' card to remind me of their behavior or understanding during a particular class period.

Student Name

- struggles with inte
- works well in gro
- lots of pressure at

- ESL Student (level 2)
- can't count down from 10
- needs constant attention

Informal Assessment: Anecdotal Notes

During class work and throughout lessons, I used a notepad to keep track of student work and classroom management. This allowed me to focus on particular students and specific aspects of student understanding. I was able to use these notes to reflect on skills and concepts that should be reviewed and students who need specific attention. I have found it helpful to take notes when something comes to my attention rather than try to remember the class at the end of the day or at the end of the week.

Phillip was quiet and on task today, during warm-up.
James is struggling with the combinations.
Maresha is not paying attention again.
Boris shouldn't sit in the back of the room.
Still having trouble w/ experimental prob.
Maresha & Keisha talked all the way through 2nd mod.

Mod 3
Worked well on homework last night (except ESOL)
Luz talked through warm-up and classwork.
Simuel's phone went off during lecture.
Delante is attentive and inquisitive.
Worked better with calculators than the other class.

February 6, 2006 Review chapter 9
Mod 2
Tiffany was in a much better mood.
Front table is still talking too much.
Danny came in late - no pass.

Source: Professional Portfolio of Julianne Cochran

Including actual examples of what you have written in your anecdotal notes and note cards enhances the reviewer's understanding of the use of these assessment strategies.

Formal and Informal Assessment Reflection

The various assessments I created and implemented during my student teaching experience informed my instruction in a number of ways. Each assessment gave me the opportunity to think critically about my students on either an individual or class level. This in turn allowed me to alter instruction in an effort to teach my students according to their abilities and interests.

Formal assessments such as projects, quizzes, and tests were used during the semester to gauge students' understanding of various mathematical concepts and their applications, and students' problem solving abilities. The projects I implemented aided me in determining which concepts might need more attention. These assessments also identified students who are able to apply concepts to real-world situations and those who are unable to do so. The quizzes and tests I implemented were created based on the concepts taught in class. Additionally, I created these assessments to be direct and easy to understand. This allowed me to assess student understanding based strictly on their mathematical abilities and not their ability to read English. I found this to be necessary for ESL students as well as students with lower reading levels. While grading quizzes and tests, I was able to give students descriptive feedback about their work, reminders, and helpful suggestions. Once a quiz or test was graded, I was able to find the average grade for a particular class and identify the most commonly missed problems or common errors. I was then able to give this information to students and take the necessary time to address particular issues or concepts.

Informal assessments, such as student note cards and anecdotal notes informed my instruction by helping me keep track of particular students or classes on a daily basis. Using student note cards allowed me to focus on specific students each day and assess their understanding of mathematics as well as their needs or abilities. I was then able to alter instruction to meet these needs by creating particular lessons or spending more time with the student during class. Anecdotal notes were often useful in reflecting upon a certain class period. During the day I am often too busy to pay attention to various instances that occur during class. These notes allowed me to reflect upon the class and think about ways to handle certain issues that occurred. Each assessment was an excellent guide in determining various forms of instruction to use, concepts to be revisited, and ways to address the needs or abilities of particular students or classes.

Source: Professional Portfolio of Julianne Cochran

This reflection captures the teacher's thinking about the methods and results.

This entry includes a short description of an overnight camping trip. It emphasizes special activities beyond the classroom. It helps the portfolio reviewer to understand the importance of this event and the meaning it had for the teacher and students.

Learning Happens Outside of the Classroom

The following are documents of the overnight camping trip that I attended with a fifth grade class. This was an incredible experience for me as it added to my perspective of the many students I was working with in the classroom. I gained a lot of insight into the possible problems and benefits that come with a large scale trip that incorporates learning in many aspects. From this trip I learned many ways to extend learning experiences beyond those within the walls of the classroom. I observed students use their strengths and multiple intelligences as they were engaged in physical, social, and problem-solving activities.

To encourage students to interact with all different students, the teachers chose the students' daily activity groups. We then included students in the process of choosing their tent mates.

As a group leader on this trip, I was a silent member of the team. I facilitated a series of cooperative confidence building activities. It was important to me that the students come up with their own positive solutions to each given problem.

Here you see the Jaguars, our group's chosen name, working together through many different activities in which teamwork is a must! Before and after each activity, we processed as a group about how we could improve and use good cooperative group strategies.

I was excited to see some follow through with these strategies in class when we returned from the trip.

Source: Professional Portfolio of Lauren T. Costas

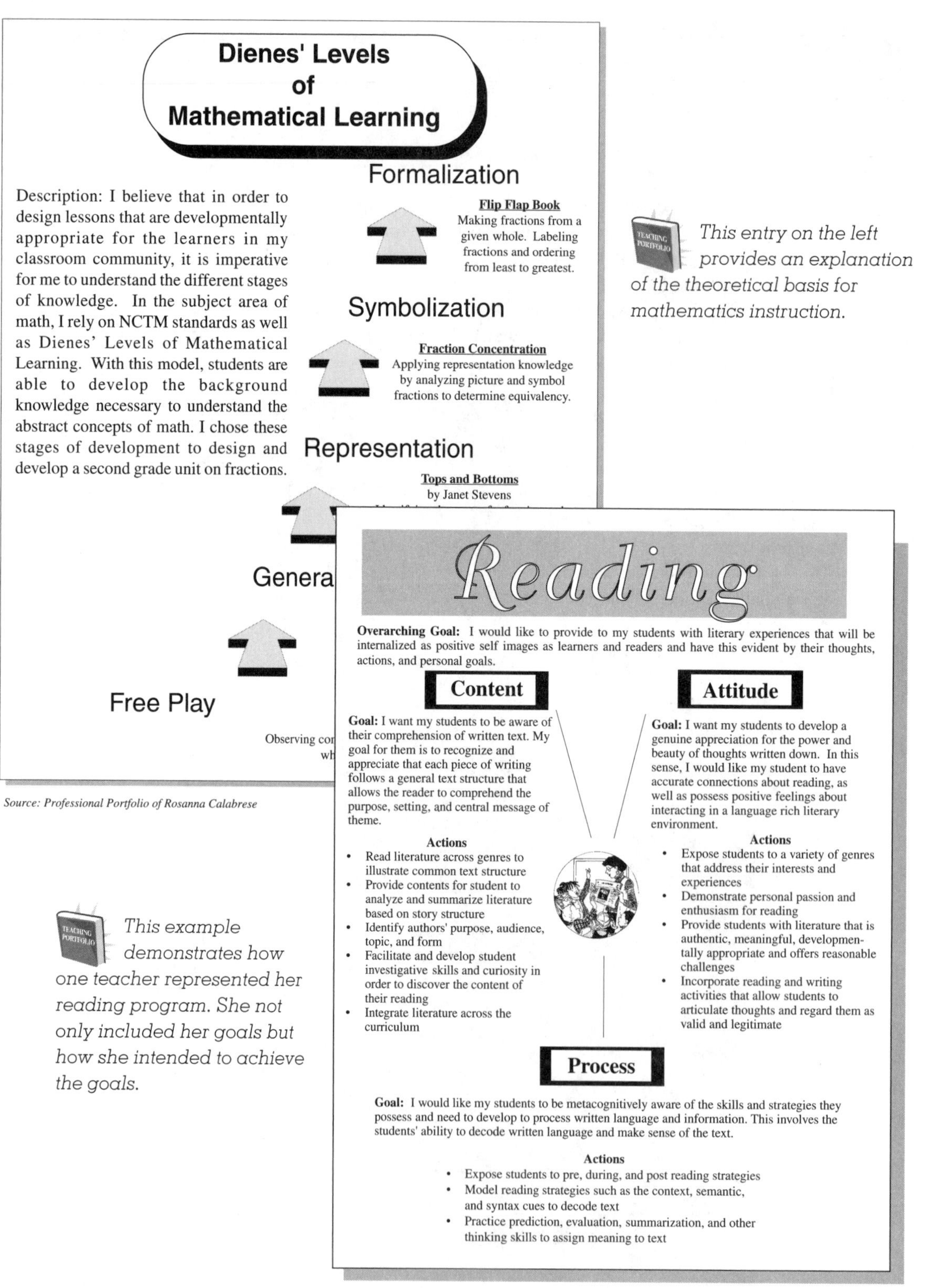

Dienes' Levels of Mathematical Learning

Description: I believe that in order to design lessons that are developmentally appropriate for the learners in my classroom community, it is imperative for me to understand the different stages of knowledge. In the subject area of math, I rely on NCTM standards as well as Dienes' Levels of Mathematical Learning. With this model, students are able to develop the background knowledge necessary to understand the abstract concepts of math. I chose these stages of development to design and develop a second grade unit on fractions.

Formalization

Flip Flap Book
Making fractions from a given whole. Labeling fractions and ordering from least to greatest.

Symbolization

Fraction Concentration
Applying representation knowledge by analyzing picture and symbol fractions to determine equivalency.

Representation

Tops and Bottoms
by Janet Stevens

Genera

Free Play

Observing co
wh

Source: Professional Portfolio of Rosanna Calabrese

This entry on the left provides an explanation of the theoretical basis for mathematics instruction.

Reading

Overarching Goal: I would like to provide to my students with literary experiences that will be internalized as positive self images as learners and readers and have this evident by their thoughts, actions, and personal goals.

Content

Goal: I want my students to be aware of their comprehension of written text. My goal for them is to recognize and appreciate that each piece of writing follows a general text structure that allows the reader to comprehend the purpose, setting, and central message of theme.

Actions

- Read literature across genres to illustrate common text structure
- Provide contents for student to analyze and summarize literature based on story structure
- Identify authors' purpose, audience, topic, and form
- Facilitate and develop student investigative skills and curiosity in order to discover the content of their reading
- Integrate literature across the curriculum

Attitude

Goal: I want my students to develop a genuine appreciation for the power and beauty of thoughts written down. In this sense, I would like my student to have accurate connections about reading, as well as possess positive feelings about interacting in a language rich literary environment.

Actions

- Expose students to a variety of genres that address their interests and experiences
- Demonstrate personal passion and enthusiasm for reading
- Provide students with literature that is authentic, meaningful, developmentally appropriate and offers reasonable challenges
- Incorporate reading and writing activities that allow students to articulate thoughts and regard them as valid and legitimate

Process

Goal: I would like my students to be metacognitively aware of the skills and strategies they possess and need to develop to process written language and information. This involves the students' ability to decode written language and make sense of the text.

Actions

- Expose students to pre, during, and post reading strategies
- Model reading strategies such as the context, semantic, and syntax cues to decode text
- Practice prediction, evaluation, summarization, and other thinking skills to assign meaning to text

This example demonstrates how one teacher represented her reading program. She not only included her goals but how she intended to achieve the goals.

Source: Professional Portfolio of Rosanna Calabrese

Source: Professional Portfolio of Scott Mooney

Using Computers as a Mode for Instructional Delivery

The use of technology in the classroom has been gaining momentum for many years. I feel fortunate that I am entering the field at this time due to the fact that I can utilize my expertise with computers to assist my students' gaining as much as possible out of various electronic learning aids. Weekly trips to the computer lab as well as daily use of a computer in the classroom can aid the students in their preparation for life in the "real world." Having students use as many programs as possible, such as the Internet, word processing applications, and even learning HTML, will prove to them that they are capable of the successful use of a sometimes scary medium.

Teachers know that using the Internet in class is a daunting challenge in that the students have the opportunity to work on projects that would not be approved of by the teacher or school administration. I understand the risks involved with using technology in the classroom and advocate the close supervision of students at all times when they are using computers in any capacity. The risk of having one bad apple spoil the bunch is too great to allow for anything less than full cooperation by the students with all appropriate rules and regulations rega

Provide information about your repertoire of skills in the use of technology. Here are three ways of representing your competencies and use of technology in the classroom.

Using a Survey to Determine Computer Usage

Students who are required to complete essays or other assignments on a word processing machine tend to receive higher grades. This correlation may result from the ease with which the teacher can read students are required to type out their as writing while they type. For most student lag time allows students to think through

To determine if I can expect my class to b year I will administer this questionnaire. much as possible about the students' prev their daily usage. If a majority of my stu count on being able to attempt more comp class of novice computer users. I will also students are capable of finding access to assignments. This will be extremely impor weekend.

Name:

Address:

Phone #:

Mother's Name:

Father's Name:

Do you have a computer in your home?

If not, do you have easy access to a compu

How much have you used a computer in the

How much have you used a computer in the

If you were given an assignment that calle you be able to find an instrument to fulfil

If no, why not?

Source: Professional Portfolio of Scott Mooney

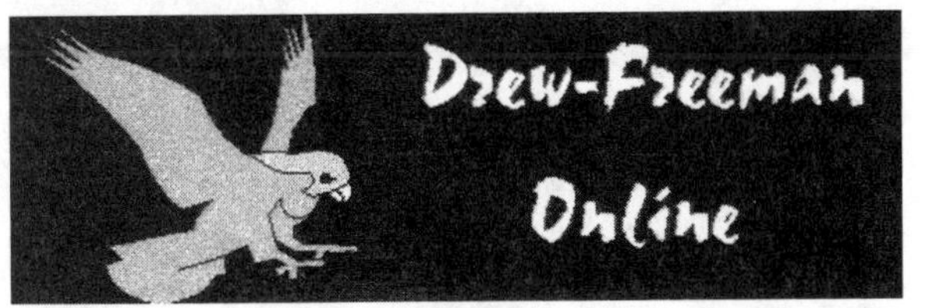

Internet and Computer Skills

Web Author:
- *Created Drew-Freeman Middle School's World Wide Web site*
- *Responsible for maintaining World Wide Web site*
- *http://www.radix.net~drewfreeman/*

Internet Instructor:
- *Introduction to the Internet course for teachers in Prince George's County Public Schools accreditation program*

Computer Proficiency:
- *Windows 3.1 - 95*
- *HTML3.0*
- *Java*
- *DOS*
- *Unix*
- *Mac*
- *IBM*

Source: Professional Portfolio of Ryan Imbriale

Student Evaluations

a) Ms. Murphey really helped me when...

she gave examples of how to solve problems. When you see this, then you should do this.

she worked out the problems on the overhead

These are just some clips of what other students said about me. Most of the kids said things like, "Ms. Murphey helped me when she told me how to solve a homework problem." But I cut these out because I liked their specificity. I was very pleased to see that a student liked my use of the overhead. I prefer that to the board because I feel like I am closer to the students when I am sitting there than I am with my back turned to them when I am at the board. Also, I was happy to see that a student liked my "When you see this, you should do this" technique for teaching. Both of these comments have encouraged me!

b) I get upset when Ms. Murphey...

Isn't Happy

asks us to raise our hand when we have a question.

Most students wrote "N/A" or "Ms. Murphey has never made me upset" for this question. I thought it was really cute that a student said they were upset when I am not happy! And I know that students get upset when I make them raise their hands. But to that I say, "tough!" I have been focusing on that from day one! I do not like students calling out! For now I can just say that I know it may be annoying, but I think it's detrimental to the class to have calling out.

c) One thing that I wish Ms. Murphey would change is...

The One, Two, three hand count she makes us think were in 1st grade

to talk slower

her teaching lesson to make it more fun like doing math games.

I took this section really seriously. I want to know what students do not like about me because maybe changing that will make me a more effective teacher. One student doesn't like my "quiet signal." Unfortunately, that was the only method that I was consistent about enforcing. I will work on developing another one in the future. Also, I can easily work on "talking slower" which I know is a weakness of mine. I am not sure how to incorporate games in to my lessons. This student is right. I just have to be more creative.

Source: Professional Portfolio of Tiffany Murphy

This entry is a creative way of displaying the teacher's reflections about student feedback.

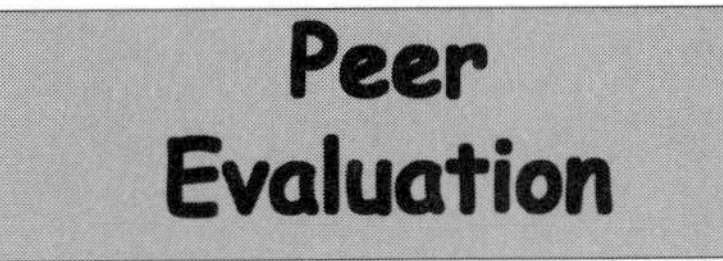

Objective: Peer and self-assessments allow students to develop their evaluative skills. They become responsible for determining the quality of their work. This empowers the students, as well as provides me with a framework to collaboratively evaluate students.

Author's Name: ____________________ Story ____________

The author identified the characters in the story.	☺	😐	☹
The author told where the story took place.	☺	😐	☹
The author mentioned the story's problem and how it was resolved.	☺	😐	☹
The author told the main idea in the first sentence.	☺	😐	☹
The author stuck to the topic of the paragraph.	☺	😐	☹

Description: One of my reading groups re recognized that the tale was a reflection of the author, not an original work. I asked the stude in the form of a paragraph. We discussed th paragraph structure and decided what would be I created this evaluation sheet based on their sug read their summary paragraphs to each other with this form and then discussed their react utilized constructive criticism and the rubric to

Source: Professional Portfolio of Rosanna Calabrese

Include unique methods for evaluation such as this peer evaluation example.

How Am I Doing?

Hey, class!!! Remember me? I actually want your opinion about my teaching. Please complete the following evaluation. Be fair in your assessment, but most of all—be honest!!

Please circle the number that rates my performance.

(1: very poor . . . . 5: excellent)

1. *Enthusiasm*	1	2	3	4	5
2. *Attitude*	1	2	3	4	5
3. *Fairness*	1	2	3	4	5
4. *Knowledge*	1	2	3	4	5
5. *Creativity*	1	2	3	4	5
6. *Interest*	1	2	3	4	5

Comments:

Source: Professional Portfolio of Jeff Maher

Be sure to include documents that provide information about your effectiveness as a teacher. Evidence can be notes or letters from students, parents, administrators, and supervisors as well as solicited feedback received from a survey such as the one shown here.

Friday Folders and Anecdotal Records

One of the routines that my cooperating teacher and I established from the first week of school was the use of Friday Folders. During each week all morning work, class work, and handwriting papers are filed in each student's Friday Folder. The folders are kept in the students' desks and it is their responsibility to keep track of their folder and its contents. On Thursday, my cooperating teacher and I take the folders home to check. While checking, I kept detailed anecdotal records of each student's progress in the units we were studying. The records also kept track of missing and incomplete work. On Friday, the students took their folders home to share their work with their families. On Monday, the folders return to school empty and ready for the next week. The process of keeping anecdotal records of student progress had both given me practice in record keeping, and taught me to give attention to EVERY child's progress EVERY week. I was able to see patterns in missing assignments and note which students did not understand which concepts. This insight gave me the information needed to provide additional assistance to the students based on their individual needs. The following is a sample of my anecdotal records.

Source: Professional Portfolio of Emily Anne Cosden

TEACHING PORTFOLIO *Include examples of how you monitor and assess your students' progress.*

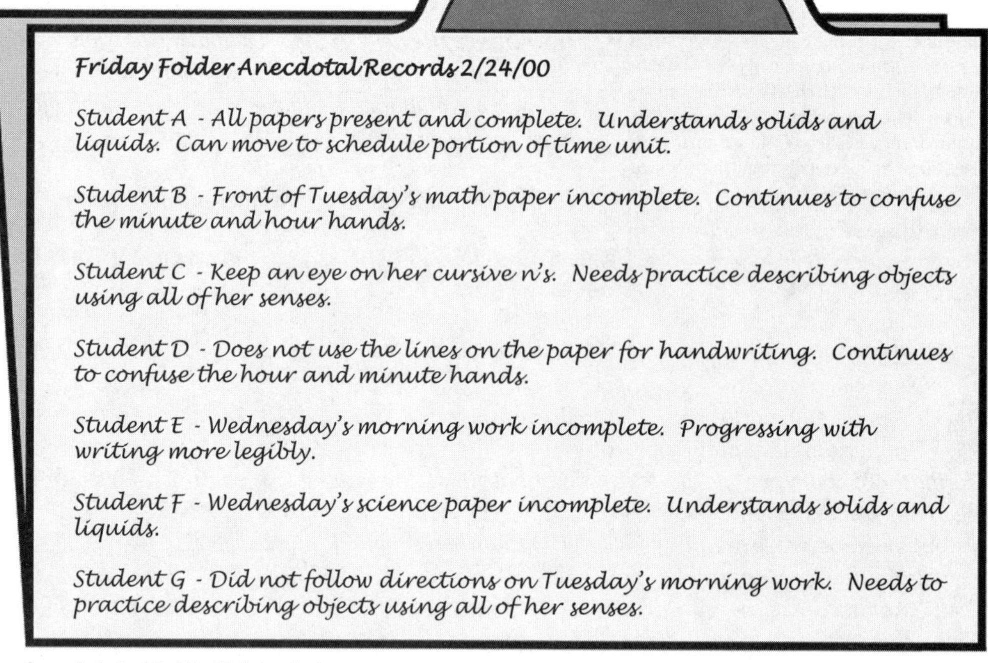

Friday Folder Anecdotal Records 2/24/00

Student A - All papers present and complete. Understands solids and liquids. Can move to schedule portion of time unit.

Student B - Front of Tuesday's math paper incomplete. Continues to confuse the minute and hour hands.

Student C - Keep an eye on her cursive n's. Needs practice describing objects using all of her senses.

Student D - Does not use the lines on the paper for handwriting. Continues to confuse the hour and minute hands.

Student E - Wednesday's morning work incomplete. Progressing with writing more legibly.

Student F - Wednesday's science paper incomplete. Understands solids and liquids.

Student G - Did not follow directions on Tuesday's morning work. Needs to practice describing objects using all of her senses.

Source: Professional Portfolio of Emily Anne Cosden

Bibliography of Special Education Related Topics

Harris, K. R., Graham, S., & Deshler, D. (Eds.). (1998). Teaching every child every day: Learning in diverse schools and classrooms. Cambridge, MA: Brookline Books.

*Hart, E. R., & Speece, D. L. (1998). Reciprocal teaching goes to college: Effects for postsecondary students at risk for academic failure. Journal of Educational Psychology, 90, 670-68.

Lieber, J., Schwartz, I. S., Sandall, S., Horn E., & Wolery, R. A. (1999). Curricular considerations for young children in inclusive settings. In C. Seefeldt (Ed.). Early childhood curriculum: A review of the research (pp. 243-264). New York: Teachers College Press.

Mamlin, N., & Harris, K.R. (1998). Elementary teacher's referral to special education in light of inclusion and prereferral: "Every child is here to learn...but some of these children are in real trouble." Journal of Educational Psychology, 90 (3), 385-396.

Sexton, M., Harris, K.R., & Graham, S. (1998). Self-regulated strategy development and the writing process: Effects on essay writing and attributions. Exceptional Children, 64, 3, 295-311.

Speece, D. L., MacDonald, V., Kilsheimer, L., & Krist, J. (1997). Research to practice: Pr
&

In order to individualize instruction for all students, I have independently researched strategies and theories related to special education. As a regular education classroom teacher, my current interests focus on ways I can help and improve instruction for included students faced with motivation, attention, and learning challenges. The sources listed above are among those resources that I have consulted and studied. I plan to earn a Master's Degree in Special Education.

After student teaching, I was hired as a long-term substitute social studies teacher for the remainder of the school year. I taught two ninth grade inclusion classes and three self-contained special education classes for eighth, tenth, and eleventh grades.

Source: Professional Portfolio of Merritt Imbriale

Transcripts, descriptions of courses or workshops attended, test scores, honors, or awards will validate your academic accomplishments. However, there are other ways to document your ongoing pursuit of knowledge. The above entry includes a short bibliography of articles read with a brief explanation of how this information is intended to be used. It also contains plans for future professional growth.

This electronic portfolio page represents an efficient way to access non-instructional documents such as a resume, letters of recommendation, transcripts, and test scores.

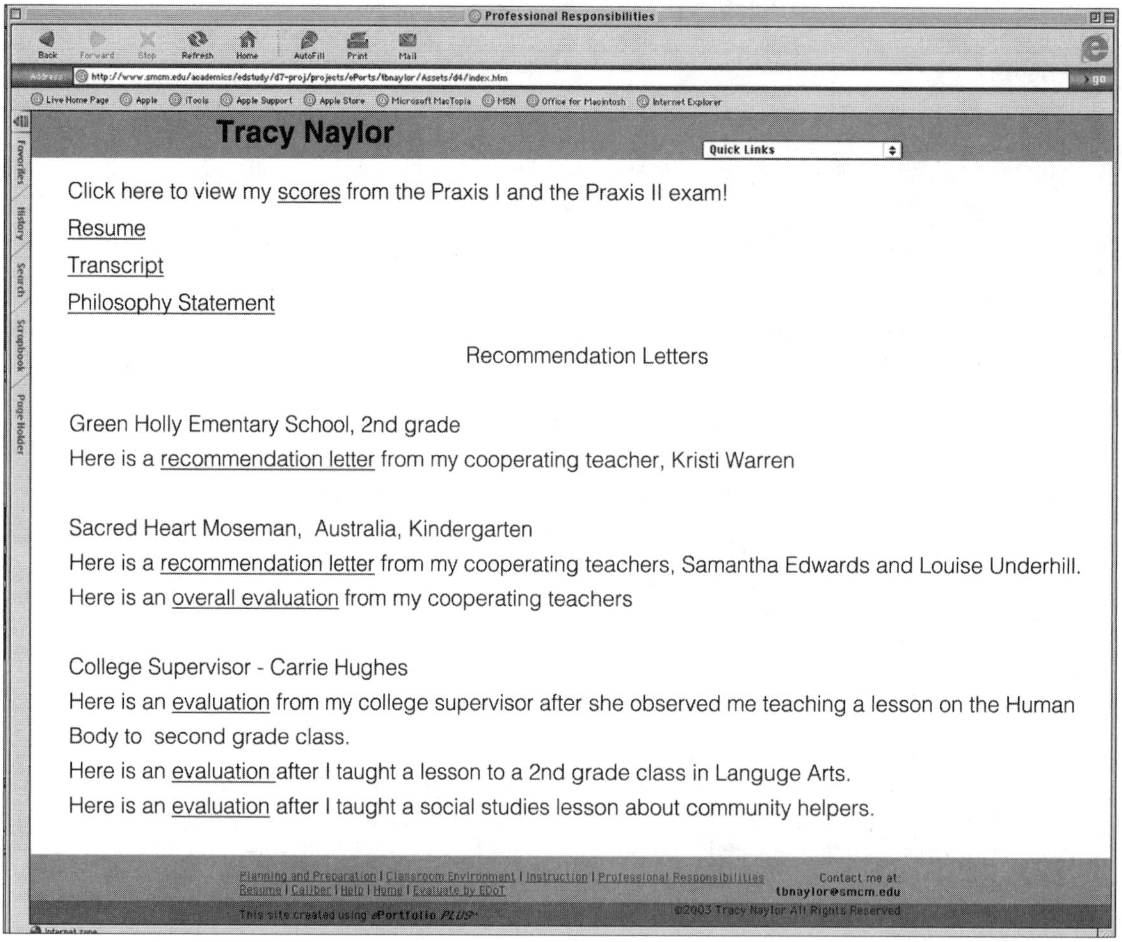
Professional Responsibilities
Back Forward Stop Refresh Home AutoFill Print Mail
http://www.smcm.edu/academics/edstudy/d7-proj/projects/ePorts/tbnaylor/Assets/d4/index.htm
Tracy Naylor
Quick Links
Click here to view my scores from the Praxis I and the Praxis II exam!
Resume
Transcript
Philosophy Statement
Recommendation Letters
Green Holly Ementary School, 2nd grade
Here is a recommendation letter from my cooperating teacher, Kristi Warren
Sacred Heart Moseman, Australia, Kindergarten
Here is a recommendation letter from my cooperating teachers, Samantha Edwards and Louise Underhill.
Here is an overall evaluation from my cooperating teachers
College Supervisor - Carrie Hughes
Here is an evaluation from my college supervisor after she observed me teaching a lesson on the Human Body to second grade class.
Here is an evaluation after I taught a lesson to a 2nd grade class in Languge Arts.
Here is an evaluation after I taught a social studies lesson about community helpers.
Planning and Preparation | Classroom Environment | Instruction | Professional Responsibilities
Resume | Caliber | Help | Home | Evaluate by EDoT
Contact me at:
tbnaylor@smcm.edu
This site created using ePortfolio PLUS
©2003 Tracy Naylor All Rights Reserved

Source: Professional Portfolio of Tracy Naylor

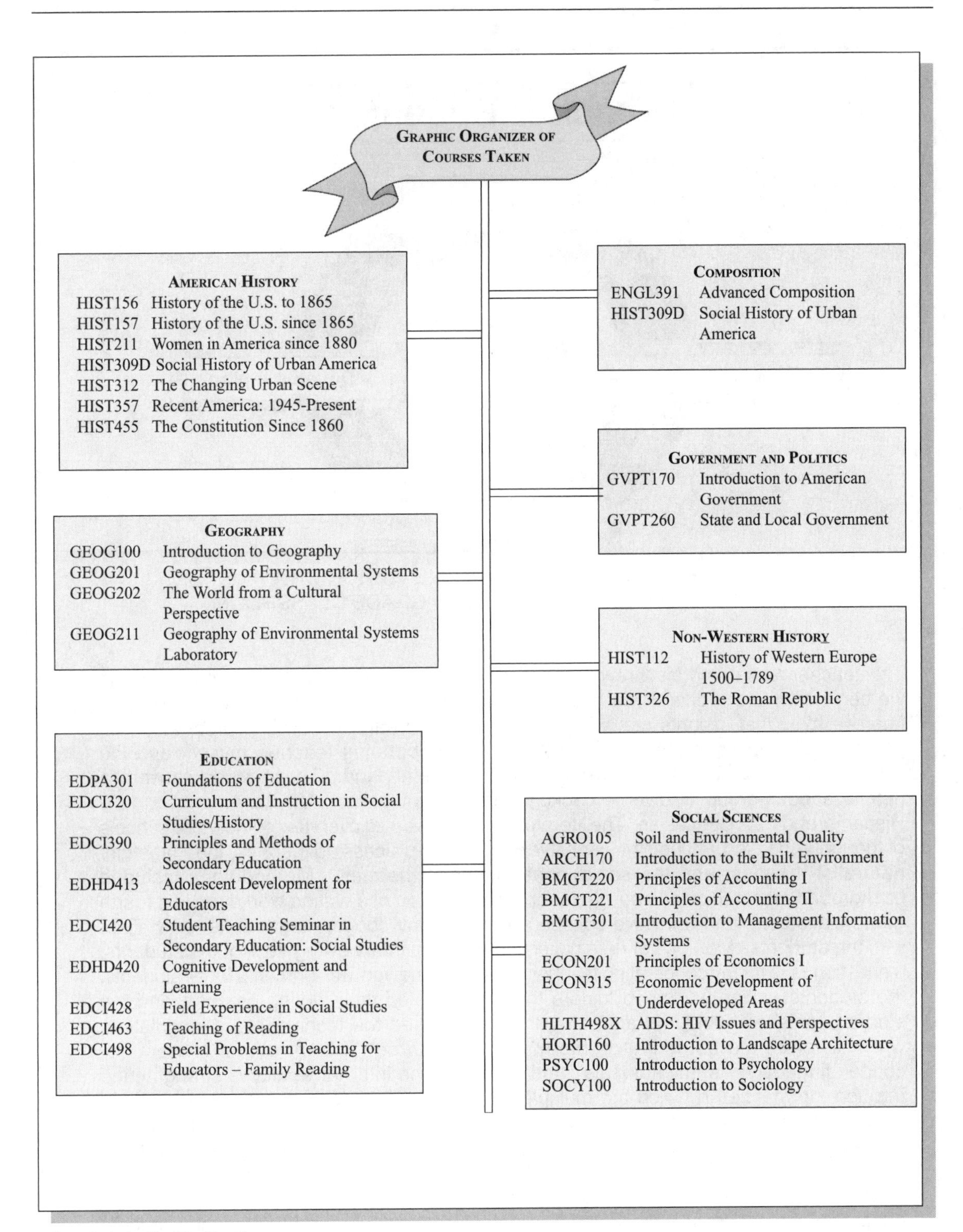

Graphic Organizer of
Courses Taken
American History
HIST156 History of the U.S. to 1865
HIST157 History of the U.S. since 1865
HIST211 Women in America since 1880
HIST309D Social History of Urban America
HIST312 The Changing Urban Scene
HIST357 Recent America: 1945-Present
HIST455 The Constitution Since 1860
Composition
ENGL391 Advanced Composition
HIST309D Social History of Urban America
Government and Politics
GVPT170 Introduction to American Government
GVPT260 State and Local Government
Geography
GEOG100 Introduction to Geography
GEOG201 Geography of Environmental Systems
GEOG202 The World from a Cultural Perspective
GEOG211 Geography of Environmental Systems Laboratory
Non-Western History
HIST112 History of Western Europe 1500–1789
HIST326 The Roman Republic
Education
EDPA301 Foundations of Education
EDCI320 Curriculum and Instruction in Social Studies/History
EDCI390 Principles and Methods of Secondary Education
EDHD413 Adolescent Development for Educators
EDCI420 Student Teaching Seminar in Secondary Education: Social Studies
EDHD420 Cognitive Development and Learning
EDCI428 Field Experience in Social Studies
EDCI463 Teaching of Reading
EDCI498 Special Problems in Teaching for Educators – Family Reading
Social Sciences
AGRO105 Soil and Environmental Quality
ARCH170 Introduction to the Built Environment
BMGT220 Principles of Accounting I
BMGT221 Principles of Accounting II
BMGT301 Introduction to Management Information Systems
ECON201 Principles of Economics I
ECON315 Economic Development of Underdeveloped Areas
HLTH498X AIDS: HIV Issues and Perspectives
HORT160 Introduction to Landscape Architecture
PSYC100 Introduction to Psychology
SOCY100 Introduction to Sociology

Source: Professional Portfolio of Scott Mooney

This graphic organizer is a creative way to highlight the courses most relevant to your area of certification. It can be an impressive supplement to your transcript.

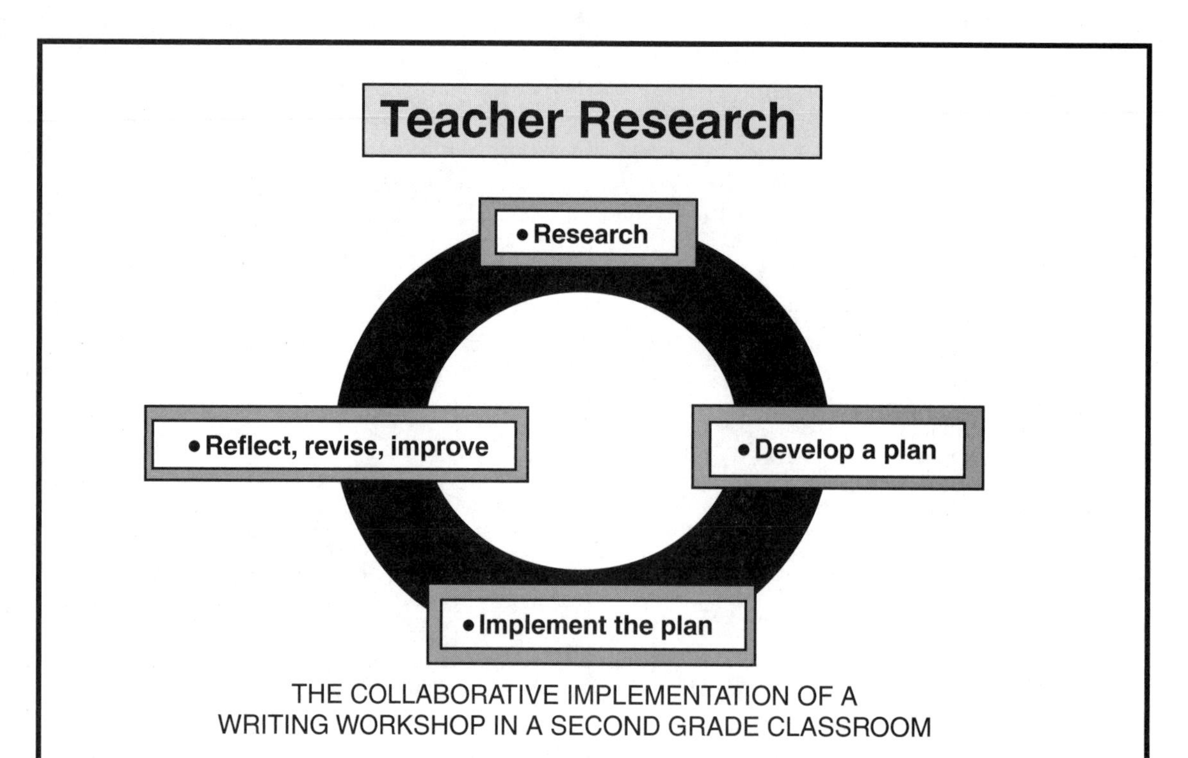

THE COLLABORATIVE IMPLEMENTATION OF A
WRITING WORKSHOP IN A SECOND GRADE CLASSROOM

Abstract

This teacher research project revolved around the following research questions: How do we begin a writers' workshop in this second grade classroom? How do we continually improve it? What insights can we gain about children and the writing process? The process encompassed the collaboration of my cooperating teacher, myself, and the students in a suburban to rural area of southern Maryland. These students were a heterogeneous group of diverse backgrounds, including 21% African American, 12% Hispanic, and 67% Caucasian. The literature review gives an overview of the three schools of thought regarding writing: the cognitive information processing theories, the Piagetian/ naturalist theories, and the social-constructionist theories. Methodology included background research on writing workshops, observation of a writing workshop in a fourth grade classroom, and reflective collaborations with my cooperating teacher as well as with the students. Methods of data collection included interviewing 46% of the students, a questionnaire for my cooperating teacher and me, homework assignments for all students, the students' writing workshop folders that documented their writing process, and the students' finished books. In analyzing the data, I used the technique of triangulation, which involves the gathering of information from three different points of view: my cooperating teacher's, my students', and my own. The internal validity is strengthened through the manner in which the multiple methods of data collection complement and check each other. The findings included a high percentage (73% of those interviewed) speaking of writing as something that helps them to learn. The majority (82% of those interviewed) cited that the act of writing itself helped them to become better writers. The study revealed that creative freedom motivated most of the students, that a special education student could be included in a meaningful manner, and that second graders can see themselves as authors.

Source: Professional Portfolio of Carol Dungan

This portfolio entry shows how one teacher conducted research to improve classroom instruction and increase student learning.

Source: Professional Portfolio of Denise Logsdon

Introduction to Video

A video was made of an introductory lesson on patterning. The students had previously done work with patterning two objects, but this was their first opportunity to pattern three different objects.

This video first includes an example of guided practice on patterning being done by the teacher. Then viewers can see the individual students as they are engaged in making patterns of three objects.
of instr

Here are two ways that teachers have provided information about video lessons included in their portfolio.

My Journey in Pictures:
Video Critique
(Approx. 1 hour)

Clip #1: Who's in the Shed?
Strategies Seen in This Clip:
-The flashlight in this lesson was used as a motivational tool for this lesson. Notice how focused the children are during the reading and how the flashlight enables them to easily follow along.
-As I read the story, several times I asked students to share their predictions. Not only did this give students practice in using this skill, but it also kept them involved with the story and allowed them to share their individual ideas with the whole group.
-A management strategy that I used with the children during this lesson was allowing them to pat their heads when they had the same prediction as another student. This prevented other children from calling out "Yeah, I was going to say that." In addition, the strategy also encouraged students to really listen to each other's ideas as they spoke.
-A final strategy that I used was a reminder to students to "think in their head" and not call out/raise their hands. I used this because I wanted each child to have enough wait time to think of his or her own prediction without the influence of others.

Clip #2: Big Hungry Bear
Strategies Seen in This Clip:
-Interactive chalkboard writing: Students used inventive spelling by sounding out words and writing them on their own individual chalkboards. This technique kept all students involved throughout the lesson. The chalkboards also allowed me to informally assess student participation and abilities.
-I used the "stop and listen" technique to gain students' attention before giving directions.

Source: Professional Portfolio of Kate Maczis

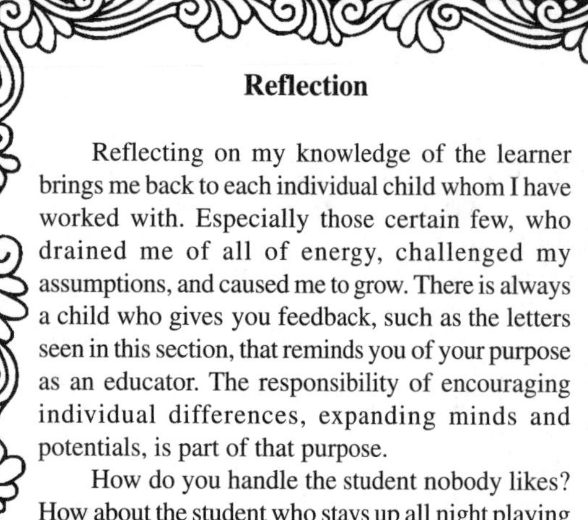

Reflection

Reflecting on my knowledge of the learner brings me back to each individual child whom I have worked with. Especially those certain few, who drained me of all of energy, challenged my assumptions, and caused me to grow. There is always a child who gives you feedback, such as the letters seen in this section, that reminds you of your purpose as an educator. The responsibility of encouraging individual differences, expanding minds and potentials, is part of that purpose.

How do you handle the student nobody likes? How about the student who stays up all night playing Nintendo? What about the students who get all of the support in the world, and then those who get none? It is a challenging dilemma, and one a teacher faces every day because inevitably all of these factors affect a child's school perfo[illegible] cannot be ignored.

Students have different needs. As [illegible] and more about each student, I learn m[illegible] about how to become a better teacher [illegible] those differences in my classroom. I fe[illegible] that my compassion for children an[illegible] development will always motivate me [illegible] meet children at their individual levels[illegible]

Source: Professional Portfolio of Lauren T. Costas

These examples of reflective entries represent teachers' thoughts, feelings, and insights about their teaching experience.

REFLECTIONS ON TEACHING

Many students have trouble acknowledging that they need help in art. Perhaps this is because what they produce is clearly visible to their peers. Understanding the nature and fragility of the young ego, I try and scout for students showing signs of confusion or trouble. Instead of putting them on the spot and embarrassing them, I make suggestions and try to help them to solve the problems for themselves. I have noticed that this can allow the student to take full credit for having overcome an obstacle and adds to his or her positive self-concept.

Source: Professional Portfolio of Mat DeMunbrun

News from Mrs. D's 4th Grade Class
January, 2001

Special Events:
The students from Mrs. D's 4th grade class will be participating in the following events:

- Art Show: February 5
- Field trip to Museum: March 20
- Science Fair: April 10
- School Play: May 9
- Physical Fitness Day: June 8

Keep your eyes open for flyers that explain the details of each of these special events.

Reminders:
- PTA meeting for February 10 will be at 7:00 p.m. in the multi-purpose room.
- Please remember to bring your canned food donation. Our class is in second place for the school-wide drive.

Start saving your used books for our March 22nd book sale. Mark your calendar NOW!

Three Cheers for the Readers of the Week!!!!

Congratulations to:
Cindy L.
Maleka E.
Greg G.
Michael F.
Takita M.
Tyrone P.

These students have read 10 or more books in the past month.

Classroom Highlights:
- We will begin our new science unit on preserving the environment next week.
- We are progressing rapidly in our higher level understanding of the use of fractions and decimals.
- The election was the best

These two examples relate to developing productive relationships with parents. This entry is a newsletter that keeps parents informed about classroom events.

Dealing with a Difficult Parent

One of the most significant learning experiences that I had during my student teaching involved interacting with a very difficult parent. The first week of school this parent began expressing displeasure with her son's education. She articulated disapproval of everything from his reading materials to the presence of a student teacher in his classroom. These and other concerns continued to present themselves throughout the year. From this experience I learned many strategies for handling this type of parent without placing any additional stress on anyone. During the second week of school, we began a communication log between my cooperating teacher, myself, and the parent. This log was taken home every night and returned the next day. In the log, the parent was able to express any of her concerns about her son or his education. We were able to easily address all of her concerns without taking away from class or planning time to speak on the phone. Another advantage of the communication log was that there was a record of every concern and all of our attempts to address the concerns. We also kept precise records of all telephone conversations. We were able to refer back to the communication log and the telephone records during conferences with the parent. Our extensive attention and detailed records gave the parent the feeling that she was being listened to and her concerns were considered valid. Gradually, the parent grew to trust us and, consequently, her concerns lessened. We were able to give this parent the attention and validation that she needed without putting her or ourselves in an uncomfortable position.

Source: Professional Portfolio of Emily T. Cosden

The entry above describes a strategy that was implemented to work more effectively with a parent.

REFLECTION
. . . is a KEY to professional and personal growth.

What Is the Relationship
Between Teaching and Learning?

For me, teaching and learning are inseparable. I believe that for true teaching to take place, learning must accompany it. And for learning to take place, teaching must be present in some form. Learning is to be valued more than teaching, for it is the reason teaching exists. This topic is a deep and involved one that cannot possibly be covered in this essay, but I will comment on some thoughts I have begun to form in this area.

First of all, I would like to say that I now understand that there is much more involved in learning to teach than I initially anticipated. I realize now that there is no recipe for being the perfect teacher. It is an art and a skill that will be continually built upon all of my life. One of the greatest gifts that this program has given to me is the opportunity to be reflective. This has encouraged me to "stimulate and facilitate significant and self-reliant learning" (Rogers, 1969). I cannot think of anything more important in my beginning and refining as a teacher than that of taking charge of my own learning process. It will be a worthy lifelong endeavor.

If somehow my own love for learning could be passed on to my students, it would begin to make a difference in their lives. I am in agreement with Suzanne Wilson (1990) when . . .

Source: Professional Portfolio of Carol Dungan

In order for the reviewer to have a more in-depth perspective of you as a reflective practitioner and problem solver, it is important to include your thoughts, feelings, and learnings that provide insight about your growth as a professional teacher. Keep in mind that reflections can be integrated throughout the entire portfolio in context with the artifact or can be used as an introduction or conclusion to a portfolio section.

APPENDIX A

Examples of Standards

Interstate New Teacher Assessment and Support Consortium (INTASC) Standards

The ten statements presented here are the basic principles underlying the knowledge, dispositions, and performances deemed essential for all BEGINNING TEACHERS, regardless of their specialty areas. They are specifically intended to address behaviors that constitute what novice teachers need to practice responsibly when they enter the teaching profession. A complete copy of the standards, including knowledge, dispositions, and performances, can be obtained by contacting the Council of Chief State School Officers, One Massachusetts Avenue NW, Suite 700, Washington, DC 20001-1431.

Principle 1: The teacher understands the central concepts, tools of inquiry, and structures of the discipline(s) he or she teaches and can create learning experiences that make these aspects of subject matter meaningful for students.

Principle 2: The teacher understands how children learn and develop and can provide learning opportunities that support their intellectual, social, and personal development.

Principle 3: The teacher understands how students differ in their approaches to learning and creates instructional opportunities that are adapted to diverse learners.

Principle 4: The teacher understands and uses a variety of instructional strategies to encourage students' development of critical thinking, problem solving, and performance skills.

Principle 5: The teacher uses an understanding of individual and group motivation and behavior to create a learning environment that encourages positive social interaction, active engagement in learning, and self-motivation.

Principle 6: The teacher uses knowledge of effective verbal, nonverbal, and media communication techniques to foster active inquiry, collaboration, and supportive interaction in the classroom.

Principle 7: The teacher plans instruction based upon knowledge of subject matter, students, the community, and curriculum goals.

Principle 8: The teacher understands and uses formal and informal assessment strategies to evaluate and ensure the continuous intellectual, social, and physical development of the learner.

Principle 9: The teacher is a reflective practitioner who continually evaluates the effects of his or her choices and actions on others (students, parents, and other professionals in the learning community) and who actively seeks out opportunities to grow professionally.

Principle 10: The teacher fosters relationships with school colleagues, parents, and agencies in the larger community to support students' learning and well-being.

Source: Interstate New Teacher Assessment and Support Consortium (INTASC), Council of Chief State School Officer (CSSO).

NBPTS Early Childhood/Generalist Standards

Three- to Eight-Year-Olds

The requirements for certification as an Early Childhood/Generalist are organized around the following eight standards. These standards have been ordered as important facets of the art and science of teaching young children. In fact, in the course of excellent early childhood teaching, teachers often demonstrate several of these standards concurrently as they skillfully weave their knowledge, skills, and dispositions into a rich tapestry of exemplary practice.

I. ***Understanding Young Children*** Teachers use their knowledge of child development and their relationships with children and families to understand children as individuals and to plan in response to their unique needs and potentials.

II. ***Promoting Child Development and Learning*** Teachers promote children's physical, emotional, linguistic, creative, intellectual, social, and cognitive development by organizing the environment in ways that best facilitate the development and learning of young children.

III. ***Knowledge of Integrated Curriculum*** On the basis of their knowledge of academic subjects and how young children learn, teachers design and implement developmentally appropriate learning experiences within and across the disciplines.

IV. ***Multiple Teaching Strategies for Meaningful Learning*** Teachers use a variety of methods and materials to promote individual development, meaningful learning, and social cooperation.

V. ***Assessment*** Teachers know the strengths and weaknesses of various assessment methodologies, continually monitor children's activities and behavior, and analyze this information to improve their work with children and parents.

VI. ***Reflective Practice*** Teachers regularly analyze, evaluate, and strengthen the quality and effectiveness of their work.

VII. ***Family Partnerships*** Teachers work with and through parents and families to support children's learning and development.

VIII. ***Professional Partnerships*** Teachers work with colleagues to improve programs and practices for young children and their families.

Source: Reprinted with permission from the National Board for Professional Teaching Standards, Early Childhood Standards, 1998, all rights reserved.

Performance Standards: The Council for Exceptional Children

Special education professional standards are governed foremost by the CEC Code of Ethics and a common core of knowledge and skills. The information below represents the skills section from the document entitled *What Every Special Educator Must Know: International Standards for the Preparation and Certification of Special Education Teachers.* For a complete set of standards contact The Council for Exceptional Children, 11110 North Glebe Road, Suite 300, Arlington, VA 22201-5704.

1. Philosophical, Historical, and Legal Foundations of Special Education
   - Articulate personal philosophy of special education including its relationship to/with regular education.
   - Conduct instructional and other professional activities consistent with the requirements of law, rules and regulations, and local district policies and procedures.
2. Characteristics of Learners
   - Access information on various cognitive, communication, physical, cultural, social, and emotional conditions of individuals with exceptional learning needs.
3. Assessment, Diagnosis, and Evaluation
   - Collaborate with families and other professionals involved in the assessment of individuals with exceptional learning needs.
   - Create and maintain records.
   - Gather background information regarding academic, medical, and family history.
   - Use various types of assessment procedures appropriately.
   - Interpret information from formal and informal assessment instruments and procedures.
   - Report assessment results to individuals with exceptional learning needs, parents, administrators, and other professionals using appropriate communication skills.
   - Use performance data and information from teachers, other professionals, individuals with exceptionalities, and parents to make or suggest appropriate modification in learning environments.
   - Develop individualized assessment strategies for instruction.
   - Use assessment information in making instructional decisions and planning individual programs that result in appropriate placement and intervention for all individuals with exceptional learning needs, including those from culturally and/or linguistically diverse backgrounds.
   - Evaluate the results of instruction.
   - Evaluate supports needed for integration into various program placements.
4. Instructional Content and Practice
   - Interpret and use assessment data for instructional planning.
   - Develop and/or select instructional content, materials, resources, and strategies that respond to cultural, linguistic, and gender differences.

- Develop comprehensive, longitudinal individualized programs.
- Choose and use appropriate technologies to accomplish instructional objectives and to integrate them appropriately into the instructional process.
- Prepare appropriate lesson plans.
- Involve the individual and family in setting instructional goals and charting progress.
- Conduct and use task analysis.
- Select, adapt, and use instructional strategies and materials according to characteristics of the learner.
- Sequence, implement, and evaluate individual learning objectives.
- Integrate effective, social, and career/vocational skills with academic curricula.
- Use strategies for facilitating maintenance and generalization of skills across learning environments.
- Use instructional time properly.
- Teach individuals with exceptional learning needs to use thinking, problem solving, and other cognitive strategies to meet their individual needs.
- Choose and implement instructional techniques and strategies that promote successful transitions for individuals with exceptional learning needs.
- Establish and maintain rapport with learners.
- Use verbal and nonverbal communication techniques.
- Conduct self-evaluation of instruction.

5. Planning and Managing the Teaching and Learning Environment
   - Create a safe, positive, and supportive learning environment in which diversities are valued.
   - Use strategies and techniques for facilitating the functional integration of individuals with exceptional learning needs in various settings.
   - Prepare and organize materials to implement daily lesson plans.
   - Incorporate evaluation, planning, and management procedures that match learner needs with the instructional environment.
   - Design a learning environment that encourages active participation by learners in a variety of individual and group learning activities.
   - Design, structure, and manage daily routines, effectively including transition time, for students, other staff, and the instructional setting.
   - Direct the activities of a classroom paraprofessional, aide, volunteer, or peer tutor.
   - Create an environment that encourages self-advocacy and increased independence.
6. Managing Student Behavior and Social Interaction Skills
   - Demonstrate a variety of effective behavior management techniques appropriate to the needs of individuals with exceptional learning needs.
   - Implement the least intensive intervention consistent with the needs of the individuals with exceptionalities.

- Modify the learning environment (schedule and physical arrangement) to manage inappropriate behaviors.
- Identify realistic expectations for personal and social behavior in various settings.
- Integrate social skills into the curriculum.
- Use effective teaching procedures in social skills instruction.
- Demonstrate procedures to increase the individual's self-awareness, self-control, self-reliance, and self-esteem.
- Prepare individuals with exceptional learning needs to exhibit self-enhancing behavior in response to societal attitudes and actions.

7. Communication and Collaborative Partnerships
   - Use collaborative strategies in working with individuals with exceptional learning needs, parents, and school and community personnel in various learning environments.
   - Communicate and consult with individuals, parents, teachers, and other school and community personnel.
   - Foster respectful and beneficial relationships between families and professionals.
   - Encourage and assist families to become active participants in the educational team.
   - Plan and conduct collaborative conferences with families or primary caregivers.
   - Collaborate with regular classroom teachers and other school and community personnel in integrating individuals with exceptional learning needs into various learning environments.
   - Communicate with regular teachers, administrators, and other school personnel about the characteristics and needs of individuals with specific exceptional learning needs.
8. Professionalism and Ethical Practices
   - Demonstrate commitment to developing the highest educational and quality-of-life potential of individuals with exceptional learning needs.
   - Demonstrate positive regard for the culture, religion, gender, and sexual orientation of individual students.
   - Promote and maintain a high level of competence and integrity in the practice of the profession.
   - Exercise objective professional judgment in the practice of the profession.
   - Demonstrate proficiency in oral and written communication.
   - Engage in professional activities that may benefit individuals with exceptional learning needs, their families, and/or colleagues.
   - Comply with local, state, provincial, and federal monitoring and evaluation requirements.
   - Use copyrighted educational materials in an ethical manner.
   - Practice within the CEC Code of Ethics and other standards and policies of the profession.

APPENDIX B

Professional Organizations

American Alliance for Health, Physical Education, Recreation and Dance (AAHPERD) www.aahperd.org/index.cfm

American Association of Colleges for Teacher Education (AACTE) www.aacte.org

American Council on the Teaching of Foreign Languages (ACTFL) www.actfl.org

American Library Association (ALA) www.ala.org

Association for Childhood Education International (ACEI) www.acei.org

Association of Teacher Educators (ATE) www.ate1.org

Council of Chief State School Officers (CCSSO) www.ccsso.org

The Council for Exceptional Children (CEC) www.cec.sped.org

International Reading Association (IRA) www.reading.org

International Society for Technology in Education (ISTE) www.iste.org

The Interstate New Teacher Assessment and Support Consortium (INTASC) www.ccsso.org/projects/Interstate_New_Teacher_Assessment_and_Support_Consortium

National Art Education Association (NAEA) www.naea-reston.org

National Association of Biology Teachers (NABT) www.nabt.org

National Association for the Education of Young Children (NAEYC) www.naeyc.org

National Association for Music Education (MENC) www.menc.org

National Board for Professional Teaching Standards (NBPTS) www.nbpts.org

National Council for the Social Studies (NCSS) www.ncss.org

National Council of Teachers of English (NCTE) www.ncte.org

National Council of Teachers of Mathematics (NCTM) www.nctm.org

National Education Association (NEA) www.nea.org

National Science Teachers Association (NSTA) www.nsta.org

North American Association for Environmental Education (NAAEE) www.naaee.org

Teachers of English to Speakers of Other Languages (TESOL) www.tesol.org

APPENDIX C

Worksheet: Linking Coursework to Standards and Portfolio Artifacts

Linking Coursework to Standards and Portfolio Artifacts

Directions:

- Identify the course.
- List the assignments.
- Determine how the assignment contributed to your knowledge, disposition, and skills.
- Identify the performance standard this supports.
- Reflect in writing what you learned.
- Consider what could be placed in your portfolio to capture this experience.

Course	*Assignment*	*Knowledge*	*Dispositions*	*Skill*	*Standard(s)*

Reflection:

Possible Portfolio Artifacts:

Course	*Assignment*	*Knowledge*	*Dispositions*	*Skills*	*Standard(s)*

Reflection:

Possible Portfolio Artifacts:

APPENDIX D

Worksheet: Documenting Your Professional Development Plan

Documenting Your Professional Development Plan Worksheet

Step 1: Identify your professional goal.	Goal: Theme: Performance standard:
Step 2: Explore options that will facilitate meeting your goal.	Options:
Step 3: Select appropriate option(s) and design an action plan for accomplishing the goals.	Action plan:
Step 4: Implement the plan.	When and how:

Step 5: Select and develop evidence that illustrates implementation of the plan.	List materials to develop or collect:
Step 6: Collect evidence that verifies teaching competency and accomplishments as well as results of instruction and student learning.	List documents:
Step 7: Reflection	Write about your personal growth and learning:

APPENDIX E

Sample Permission Letter for Photographs and Videos

Date ________________

Dear Parent/Guardian,

I am a teacher candidate from (identify your university or teacher training program). Throughout the next (provide time span) weeks, I will be taking pictures and/or videos of a variety of classroom activities to represent teaching experiences during my internship. As part of my teacher education program requirements, I am expected to develop a professional teaching portfolio. I would like to be able to include these pictures and/or videos of classroom activities in my portfolio and I would appreciate your permission to use items that may have your child in them.

These pictures and/or videos are for the purpose of "bringing to life" the documents I present in my professional portfolio. They would remain my personal property and would only be used for educational purposes associated with my teacher education program and for sharing my portfolio during employment interviews.

Please check one of the two statements below, sign, and return this document

to ________________________________.

______ I grant permission for my child to be photographed and/or videotaped in an instructional setting for educational purposes and for the photographs to be included in the teacher candidate's professional portfolio.

______ I do not give permission for my child to be photographed and/or videotaped for any reason.

Student's Name ________________________________

School ________________________________

Teacher's name ________________________________

Signature of
parent/guardian ________________________________

Date ________________________________

Sincerely,

Teacher Candidate

cc: Principal

APPENDIX F

Worksheet: Making Decisions about Potential Portfolio Documents

Making Decisions about Potential Portfolio Documents Worksheet

	Documents and validation materials I currently have that support the purposes of my portfolio.	*Materials I need to create or obtain to enhance this area including introductions, explanations, and reflections.*	*Which performance standard, theme, or does this support?*
Educational philosophy			
Planning for instruction			
Instructional units I have developed and taught			
My repertoire of instructional strategies			
Example of data-driven instruction			

	Documents and validation materials I currently have that support the purposes of my portfolio.	*Materials I need to create or obtain to enhance this area including introductions, explanations, and reflections.*	*Which performance standard, theme, or does this support?*
Technological skills			
Evidence of a multicultural perspective			
Evidence of how I have included all students in my instruction			
Classroom management/ discipline			

	Documents and validation materials I currently have that support the purposes of my portfolio.	*Materials I need to create or obtain to enhance this area including introductions, explanations, and reflections.*	*Which performance standard, theme, or does this support?*
Parent, teacher, student conferences			
Professional development plan			
Subject matter competency			
Diagnosis and assessment of student learning			

	Documents and validation materials I currently have that support the purposes of my portfolio.	*Materials I need to create or obtain to enhance this area including introductions, explanations, and reflections.*	*Which performance standard, theme, or does this support?*
Professional development activities			
Community involvement			
Professionalism			
Letters, notes, recommendations, and evaluations			
Travel, hobbies, talents, skills, and other experiences that influence my teaching and enhance the educational program			

APPENDIX G

Sample Format for Introducing a Video into Your Portfolio

Some teachers choose to provide a video of their teaching as part of their portfolio documentation. This is an excellent idea; however, you will need to include some type of introduction of your video that will increase the viewer's understanding of the lesson. Remember to keep the video short, between ten and twenty minutes. Be sure that the video shows a balance of your teaching and student involvement. You can include an introduction to the lesson at the beginning of the video and your analysis of the lesson at the end.

Video Information

Teacher's Name ______________________ Grade Level ____________

Subject Area ____

Description of setting and class/group:

Title of Lesson ______________________ Viewing Time ____________

Lesson Objective and Rationale:

Description of the teaching episode (background information related to the lesson or portion of instruction taped):

Suggested focus areas when viewing the video:

Results of instruction and/or evidence of learning:

Personal reflections and analysis of teaching:

APPENDIX H

Worksheet: Writing Effective Reflections

Writing Effective Reflections

Reflections should provide evidence of your ability to think critically, problem solve, make decisions, relate theory to practice, learn from experience, and analyze your performance and growth.

IDENTIFICATION	Identify a teaching experience.
DESCRIPTION	Describe with factual statements what you did, how you did it, why you did it and the effect on student learning.
ANALYSIS	Write about your thoughts and feelings regarding the experience, your teaching decisions, and learner reactions.
GENERALIZATIONS	List your learnings and insights realized as a result of your thoughtful analysis of the experience.
ACTIONS	What will you do differently that leads to improved instruction and the increased probability of student learning?
REFLECTION After thoughtful consideration of the above information, write a reflection that includes components from this process and place this reflective entry with your artifacts related to the teaching episode.	

APPENDIX I

Worksheet: Evaluating Your Portfolio

Self-Evaluation Worksheet

Instructions: After considering the questions posed in each section, answer with a **yes** or **no**, then rate yourself with an ***E*** = *excellent*, ***S*** = *satisfactory*, ***NI*** = *needs improvement*. If you have rated any section of your portfolio with an *S* or *NI*, think about what you could do

	Introduction and Organization of Portfolio	*Performance Standards, Themes, or Goals*
Definition	The introduction sets the stage for the content of your portfolio. It is the opening statement that includes information regarding your philosophy of teaching, learning, or leadership, and may include your professional goals that relate to the purpose of your portfolio. Portfolio organization refers to the way the portfolio is assembled. It includes the housing of your assets and the manner in which they are displayed.	*Performance standards* identify the knowledge, dispositions, and skills that a teacher should know and be able to demonstrate. They provide the conceptual framework for portfolio development and documentation. *Goals* identify areas for professional development. They correlate with performance standards or themes. *Themes* are generic categories that are inherent throughout the performance standards.
Attributes That Promote Quality Portfolios	____ Is my introduction meaningful, informative, and related to the purpose of my portfolio? ____ Are my philosophical beliefs expressed clearly? ____ Are the contents housed appropriately? ____ Is the evidence organized effectively? ____ Are the documents easily accessible? ____ Does the overall appearance reflect a professional image? ____ Does my introduction demonstrate correct use of grammar, punctuation, word choice, spelling, and sentence formation?	____ Are performance-based standards, themes, or goals used as the foundation for my portfolio documentation? ____ How have you communicated the use of standards, goals, or themes and supporting evidence to the reviewer?
Action Plan for Polishing and Refining My Portfolio		

to give yourself a rating of excellent. Write your ideas for improving the quality of your portfolio in the action plan section. When you believe that you have represented yourself the best that you can, you are ready to present your portfolio.

Documentation	*Introductions, Explanations, and Reflections*
Documentation refers to the evidence selected to support your professional competencies. It may be a combination of teacher-made materials, student work, evaluation documents completed by others that validate your professional performance, and additional materials as appropriate to the purpose of the portfolio.	Narrative entries that provide information about specific documents and insight about the portfolio developer's thoughts related to teaching and learning.
____ Is my evidence relevant to the purpose? ____ Are my documents directly related to a standard(s), theme(s) or goal(s)? ____ Do the documents provide substantial evidence in support of my competency and growth toward that standard(s), theme(s) or goal(s)? ____ Do I have a variety of assets organized thoughtfully and displayed effectively? ____ Are my assets accompanied by introductions, explanations, and reflections? ____ Are my evaluative documents current and completed by professionals who have first hand knowledge of my performance? ____ Do my documents show significant evidence to support student learning and the results of my instruction?	____ Are my introductions at the beginning of each section clearly articulated, do they provide a rationale for inclusion of the forthcoming documents, linkage to my philosophical beliefs, and comments about how the documents support the standard, theme, or goal? ____ Do my explanations provide significant information to help the reviewer understand the relevance of this evidence and how it supports my ability to teach, impact student learning, or demonstrate leadership? ____ Do my reflections provide evidence of my ability to think critically, problem solve, make decisions, relate theory to practice, learn from experience, and analyze my performance and growth? ____ Do my introductions, explanations, and reflections consistently demonstrate correct use of grammar, punctuation, word choice, spelling, and sentence formation?

APPENDIX J

Worksheet: Overall Portfolio Assessment Instrument

Overall Portfolio Assessment Instrument

Directions: Place an X on the continuum that reflects your evaluation of each of the following portfolio aspects. Use the Comments section to provide feedback regarding your assessment.

1. Introduction to Portfolio

1	2	3	4	5
Provides little or no information about the purpose, organization, and rationale for selection of documents				Provides significant information about the purpose, organization, and rationale for the selection of documents

Comments:

2. Philosophy Statement

1	2	3	4	5
Lacks personalization and not educationally sound				Personalized and educationally sound

Comments:

3. Standards, Themes, Goals

1	2	3	4	5
No obvious evidence that performance standards, themes, or goals have been considered				Clearly evident that performance standards, themes, or goals have been considered

Comments:

4. Documentation

1	2	3	4	5
Limited documents that lack substance, have little meaning, and do not provide adequate evidence in support of performance standards, themes, or goals				Variety of documents that have significant substance and meaning and provide irrefutable evidence in support of performance standards, or goals themes, or goals

Comments:

5. Introductions and Explanations Accompanying Artifacts

1	2	3	4	5

Narratives lack clarity and do not provide enough information related to the artifacts and their relevance to the performance standards, themes, or goals

Clearly articulated narratives that provide substantial information related to the artifacts and their relevance to the performance standards, themes, or goals.

Comments:

6. Reflective Entries

1	2	3	4	5

Narratives unclear, lacking insight, critical thinking, and problem solving, and show no evidence of commitment to growth and learning

Narratives are very clear, reveal significant insight, critical thinking, problem solving, and serious commitment to growth and learning

Comments:

7. Professional Development Plan

1	2	3	4	5

Plan is not appropriate to the professional needs of the individual and does not identify goals for a higher level of performance

Plan is most appropriate in meeting the professional needs of the individual and identifies goals for a significantly higher level of performance

Comments:

8. Writing Mechanics

1	2	3	4	5

Narratives unclear, with many errors in grammar, spelling, and punctuation

Narratives clearly articulated, with no errors in grammar, spelling, or punctuation

Comments:

9. Organization and Appearance of Portfolio

1	2	3	4	5
Messy, unprofessional appearance, unorganized, and difficult to locate documents				Neat, professional appearance, logical organization, and easy access to documents

Comments:

10. Overall Rating

1	2	3	4	5
Unsatisfactory portfolio that does not support teaching competencies		Satisfactory portfolio that adequately supports teaching competencies		Outstanding portfolio that irrefutably supports teaching competencies

Comments:

Overall Comments and Recommendations:

APPENDIX K

Examples of Portfolio Guidelines and Assessment Tools

Villa Julie College, Stevenson, Maryland

Portfolio preparation is seen as a process and takes place over the course of three years of pre-service teaching experience. Although the nature of portfolios is that each student's work is unique, there are certain characteristics common to most portfolios at each stage. The following contents are required for the exit portfolio, graduation, and completion of the student teaching internship.

Contents for Exit Portfolio

Credentials

- Resume
- References
- Transcripts
- NTE scores
- GPA
- Final evaluations from supervising teachers and college supervisor

Professional Development

- Professional development plans
- Short- and long-term teaching goals
- Self-assessment of goals set and goals achieved
- Specific data about the schools assigned: name of schools, addresses, phone numbers, names of supervising teacher(s), principal, and university supervisor
- List of pertinent activities, responsibilities, and observations regarding the above named schools
- Summary of professional growth workshops given or attended
- Evaluation/reflection of other professional development efforts
- Professional organizations and responsibilities
- Honors and awards

Philosophy and Reflection

- Reflective responses that provide the insight into the student's knowledge, skills, philosophy, or professional perceptions as a teacher
- Personal logs or weekly self-assessments from field placements

Teaching Strategies and Methodology/Planning, Implementation, and Evaluation of Instruction

- Samples of written lesson plans
- Methods and strategies used to integrate
  - — multicultural perspectives
  - — inclusion
  - — learning disabilities
  - — varying learning styles and modalities
  - — classroom management and behavioral problems
  - — application of technology
- Samples of assignments and projects developed for children
- Products/samples of students' (children's) work
- Written evaluations from the supervising teacher, college supervisor, peer coach, and others
- Interdisciplinary unit
- Photos of any special activities or projects including captions
- Samples of bulletin boards (include photos if available)
- Videotape of teaching a lesson with attached critiques

Communication and Human Relations Skills

- Samples of parental communications
- Parental involvement
- Peer coaching experiences
- Clippings and articles about field placement class, school, or self from school newsletter and local paper
- Letters of appreciation and commendation

Personal Skills

- Volunteerism
- Special talents and skills

Source: This material is reprinted by permission of Dr. Deborah Kraft, Villa Julie College.

VILLA JULIE COLLEGE * STEVENSON, MARYLAND 21153-0614

EDUCATION DEPARTMENT

SCORING RUBRIC FOR THE EXIT PORTFOLIO

A composite score of 3 or above for each Dimension of the rubric and each General Trait is required. *Students who receive any score of 1 or 2 will be given an opportunity to revise and resubmit their portfolio*

	DIMENSIONS OF TEACHING			GENERAL TRAITS		
Points	**Written Documentation**	**Reflections**	**Visuals**	**Language**	**Organization**	**Presentment**
	This trait refers to written content that includes lesson plans, narratives, course assignments, and tables used to document knowledge & skills in Dimension.	*This trait refers to expressed thoughts or opinions resulting from careful consideration of evidence used to document knowledge & skills in Dimension.*	*This trait refers to pictures, graphics, charts, or videos used to demonstrate knowledge & skills in Dimension.*	*This trait refers to the use of the conventions of standard written English; such as grammar, mechanics, word usage, and spelling.*	*This trait refers to the manner in which the contents of the portfolio are arranged to demonstrate student's unique skills and abilities.*	*This trait refers to the overall appearance of the portfolio and the manner in which the appearance of the portfolio orients the reader.*
5 Exceptional	•Demonstrates: -Critical thought & reasoning -Breadth and depth of understanding •Provides substantial description & explanation	•Demonstrates: -Critical thought & reasoning -Breadth and depth of understanding •Provides substantial description & explanation	•Extensive and outstanding use of visuals to demonstrate knowledge & skills in Dimension •Visuals of consistently high quality greatly enhance demonstration of knowledge & skills in Dimension	•Outstanding use of the conventions of standard written English.	•Follows a focused and logical organization •Clearly shows original thinking •Highly imaginative	•Professional quality •Impresses the reader •Outstandingly clear, bright, and colorful
4 Thorough	•Demonstrates: -Careful thought & reasoning -Clear understanding •Provides fair description	•Demonstrates: -Careful thought & reasoning -Clear understanding •Provides fair description	•Excellent use of visuals to demonstrate knowledge & skills in Dimension •Visuals enhance demonstration of knowledge & skills in Dimension	•Effective use of the conventions of standard written English	•Follows a logical organization •Demonstrates careful thought •Distinctive	•Distinctive appearance •Effectively orients reader •Consistently clear, bright, colorful
3 Adequate	•Demonstrates: -Superficial thought & reasoning -General understanding •Provides fair descriptions	•Demonstrates: -Superficial thought & reasoning. -General understanding •Provides fair descriptions	•Sufficient use of visuals to demonstrate knowledge & skills in Dimension •Visuals used •Average quality	•Minor errors in the use of the conventions of standard written English	•Fair organization •Demonstrates thought	•Acceptable appearance •Reader's orientation is generally maintained •Generally clear, bright, colorful
2 Inadequate	•Demonstrates: -Limited thought & reasoning -Incomplete understanding •Provides vague descriptions	•Demonstrates: -Limited thought & reasoning -Incomplete understanding •Provides vague descriptions	•Minimal use of visuals to demonstrate knowledge & skills in Dimension •Quality of visuals varies	•Several errors in the use of the conventions of standard written English	•Organization is confusing or hard to follow	• Inconsistent appearance •Confusing orientation for the reader •Inappropriate use of color
1 Unacceptable	•No evidence of: -Thought & reasoning -Understanding •No description or explanation	•No evidence of: -Thought & reasoning -Understanding •No description or explanation	•No visuals to demonstrate knowledge & skills in Dimension	•Extensive errors in the use of the conventions of standard written English	•No apparent organization	•Poor, sloppy appearance •Does not orient reader

Source: This material is reprinted by permission of Dr. Deborah Kraft, Villa Julie College.

VILLA JULIE COLLEGE * STEVENSON, MARYLAND 21153-0614

EDUCATION DEPARTMENT

SCORING FOR THE EXIT PORTFOLIO

A composite score of 3 or above for each Dimension of the rubric and each General Trait is required. *Students who receive any score of 1 or 2 will be given an opportunity to revise and resubmit their portfolio*

Student: Assessed by: Date:

Dimension	SCORE: Written Documentation	Reflections	Visuals	Composite Score
1. Demonstrate mastery of appropriate academic disciplines and teaching techniques.				
2. Demonstrate an understanding that knowledge of the learners' physical, cognitive, emotional, and socio-cultural development as the basis for effective teaching.				
3. Incorporate a multicultural perspective which integrates culturally diverse resources, including those from the learner's family and community.				
4. Demonstrate a knowledge of strategies for integrating students with special needs into the regular classroom.				
5. Use valid assessment approaches, both formal and informal, which are age appropriate and address a variety of developmental needs, conceptual abilities, curriculum outcomes, and school goals.				
6. Organize and manage a classroom using approaches supported by research, best practice, expert opinion, and student learning needs.				
7. Use computer and computer-related technology to meet student and professional needs.				
8. Demonstrate an understanding that classrooms and schools are sites of ethical, social, and civic activity.				
9. Collaborate with the broad educational community including parents, businesses, and social service agencies.				
10. Engage in careful analysis, problem-solving and reflection in all aspects of teaching.				

General Trait*	Score
Language	
Organization	
Presentment	

Additional required content: ***(refer to page 33 of the Education Handbook)***

Resume
Credentials
Evaluations
Professional Development Plan

Source: This material is reprinted by permission of Dr. Deborah Kraft, Villa Julie College.

George Mason University, Graduate School of Education

The Professional Development Portfolio: A Performance-Based Document

Introduction

The Professional Development Portfolio is a requirement for the successful completion of a licensure program but is only one of several factors considered in determining a pre-service teacher's readiness for teaching. The product is designed around university program goals and published professional standards that represent the professional consensus of what beginning teachers should know and be able to do. The Interstate New Teacher Assessment and Support Consortium (INTASC) articulated the ten standards incorporated into this document. The evaluation of the portfolio and its presentation will be integrated with the overall evaluation of the program work and internship. The Professional Development Portfolio may also be used during a job search.

Guidelines for Professional Development Portfolio

The following recommendations will be helpful to pre-service teachers preparing the portfolio:

- The portfolio is an evolving document and should be continually in a state of development.
- The portfolio should be comprised of pieces that the intern has selected because they are significant examples of growth. Faculty and teachers may suggest entries.
- The appearance of the portfolio should not overshadow its contents; however, an organized document demonstrates careful thought and preparation.
- Each section of the portfolio should include a reflective statement in which the intern examines the samples included and analyzes their significance.
- Reflections should not merely provide a description of the material included, but should tell why a particular item or strategy was chosen, what the student learned through an experience or what he or she would do differently/similarly the next time, and how the student might use this information in the future to improve his or her professional practice.

Portfolio Contents and Format

The Professional Development Portfolio, as an evolving, formative document, should be organized in a looseleaf binder to allow for good organization, easy access to materials, and frequent updating. The eight required sections provide the framework for the portfolio. Below are suggestions of sample products that could be included under each. All of these suggestions need not be included. Choose the piece of evidence that best illustrates each section. **Each section should contain a reflective statement.**

Source: This material is reprinted by permission of Rebecca K. Fox, George Mason University, Graduate School of Education.

Title Page

Table of Contents

I. **Professional Documentation**
Résumé
Philosophy of Education—provides information about the intern's educational beliefs and evolving philosophy of education. The essay should address the pre-service teacher's perceptions of him- or herself as a developing teacher and state the individual's philosophy of education.

II. **Content Pedagogy and Planning (INTASC Standards 1 and 7)**
Provides information and evidence about actual classroom instruction, lesson preparation, and class time management.
Possible Items for Inclusion:
Instructional unit and lesson plans—select examples of most growth or best work, with examples of work done by students (with appropriate permission) and planned forms of assessment for Unit/Daily Lesson Plans
Instructional materials developed by the intern
Evidence of adaptations or accommodation to these lesson plans for various learning styles, abilities, instructional levels, interests, and needs of students taught
Photographs of classroom activities

III. **Student Development and Learning (INTASC Standards 2, 3, and 4)**
Provides evidence that the teacher can evaluate student performance to design instruction appropriate for social, cognitive, and emotional development.
Possible Items for Inclusion:
Example(s) of instructional design appropriate to students' stages of development, learning styles, strengths, and needs (i.e., an example of a lesson resulting from an assessment)
Evidence of multiple teaching and learning strategies used to meet the needs of diverse learners (i.e., example of a single lesson using numerous teaching strategies)
Evidence of teacher knowledge of appropriate services or resources available/used to meet exceptional learning needs of students when needed (i.e., an interview with a reading specialist or resource teacher)

IV. **Motivation and Classroom Management (INTASC Standard 5)**
Captures how the teacher creates a rich classroom environment that is supportive of working in his or her setting with learners who have varied learning styles and needs.
Possible Items for Inclusion:
List of successful strategies used in the classroom
Description or diagram of classroom with explanation
Photographs of bulletin boards and learning environment

V. **Communication and Technology (INTASC Standard 6)**
Shows how the pre-service teacher models effective communication strategies in conveying ideas and information and uses a variety of media communication tools to enrich learning opportunities.

Possible Items for Inclusion:

Examples of different types of technology used in the classroom (i.e., WebQuests, lists of websites used, software programs, videos) to enrich learning opportunities
Student products—with appropriate permission
Compilation of websites used for professional research or class preparation
Example of a lesson plan that incorporates technology

VI. Assessment Strategies (INTASC Standard 8)

Possible Items for Inclusion:

Compilation of assessment techniques used for authentic and performance-based assessment
Case study of an individual, with summary of assessment strategies
Evidence of assessment strategies you have used in the classroom
(i.e., student examples, rubrics created and used)

VII. Reflective Practice: Professional Development (INTASC Standard 9)

Provides evidence that the teacher uses classroom observation, information about students, and research as sources for evaluating the outcomes of teaching and learning; uses professional literature, colleagues, and other resources to support self-development as a learner and as a teacher.

Possible Items for Inclusion:

Reflective statement (includes a portion that will be completed at the conclusion of the student teaching internship to respond to the following questions: How have your educational philosophy and goals changed as a result of your student teaching experience? What types of professional development do you now see as important? What are your goals as a professional educator?)
Documentation from the student teaching internship, which might include:
Observation reports completed by the university supervisor or mentor teacher
Bi-weekly progress reports
Evidence of the development of reflective practice—Journal entries or excerpts from a teaching journal, reflections of a lesson
Videotape and self-observation report of a lesson taught

VIII. School and Community Involvement (INTASC Standard 10)

Provides information about and evidence of communication/collaboration with parents and/or other professionals within the school and with parents/guardians.

Possible Items for Inclusion:

Evidence of communication with parents/guardians, school community, students and/or colleagues (letters to or other communication with parents/guardians and students, solicitation of their help in classroom or on other projects)
Evidence of attendance at and involvement in team or departmental meetings (i.e., notes taken)
Evidence of participation in collegial activities designed to promote a productive learning environment in the school community

Portfolio Evaluation

Student ______________________________ Date ______________

University Supervisor______________________________________

Evaluation by:

_____ University Supervisor _____ Student (Self) _____ Cooperating Teacher

Directions: Please evaluate each of the areas below using the following rating scale:

5 = Excellent, 4 = Good, 3 = Satisfactory, 2 = Marginal, 1 = Unsatisfactory

______ Philosophy of Education: Contains personal statement of philosophy of education; reflects evolution in beliefs about teaching/learning process; includes statement of professional goals

______ Résumé: Quality of copy; acceptable format; relevant professional experiences included

______ Content Pedagogy and Planning: Documentation entries demonstrate growth and careful choice. Integration evident through choices of unit and daily goals and objectives; planning includes assessment measures; examples include work done by the students and instructional materials developed by the intern; evidence provided for adaptations or accommodation for various learning styles and needs; plans reflect the intern's philosophy of education

______ Student Development and Learning: Provides example(s) of instructional design appropriate to students' stages of development, learning styles, strengths, and needs. Provides evidence of multiple teaching and learning strategies used to meet the needs of diverse learners (i.e., example of a single lesson using numerous teaching strategies included)

______ Motivation and Classroom Management: Presents an example of an environment supportive of working with learners of many styles and needs; careful thought evident; procedures carefully thought through. Includes successful strategies used in the classroom by intern and evidence of classroom management style. Strategies support intern's philosophy of education statement

______ Communication and Technology: Provides examples/evidence of use of technology in the classroom and evidence of student learning outcomes

______ Assessment Strategies: Provides several examples of assessment strategies and techniques used in the classroom; strategies support the intern's philosophy of education statement

______ Reflective Practice—Professional Development: Demonstrates careful thought and reflection as a teacher practitioner who evaluates his or her choices and actions; provides evidence of intern's ability to work toward goal of continuous reflective teaching; provides evidence of intern's awareness of strengths and growth during the student teaching internship. Shows support of intern's philosophy of education statement

______ Family and Community Involvement: Information provided about communication and/or collaboration with parents or guardians and/or other professionals in the school and surrounding community; includes evidence of communication with parents/families to support students' learning and well-being

______ Overall Organization and Appearance of Portfolio

______ Presentation by Intern

______ Overall Evaluation of the Professional Development Portfolio

ADDITIONAL COMMENTS:

Source: This material is reprinted by permission of Rebecca K. Fox, George Mason University, Graduate School of Education.

APPENDIX L

Worksheet: Evaluating the Technical Aspects of e-Portfolios

Evaluating the Technical Aspects of e-Portfolios

Directions: Review each question and provide formative feedback in the first column and your ideas for improvement in the second column.

Question	*Colleague Evaluation*	*Suggestions for Improvement*
Do the narratives demonstrate consistent, correct use of grammar, punctuation, word choice, spelling, and sentence formation?		
Is the content of the portfolio logically organized and the information meaningfully connected?		
Are there multilinked pages with all links clearly labeled and working, and an easy-to-use navigation system?		
Are the graphics and photographs clear, high quality, and relevant?		
Are the video clips short, meaningful, and audible?		
Does the visual display demonstrate effective use of quality design principles for the choice of background, size and style of lettering, color selection, and placement of text and graphics?		
Does the electronic portfolio work for viewers with various hardware and software configurations?		

Glossary

Accountability: Under the NCLB legislation, states implemented standardized testing of all children in grades 3 through 8, which served as the determinant of educational progress toward the goal of total proficiency in 2014.

Adequate Yearly Progress (AYP): Under NCLB, states established annual benchmarks to ensure student progress in the following subgroups: ethnicity, poverty status, disabilities, and English Language Learners. Schools that fail to demonstrate AYP in any of the subgroups for two consecutive years are identified as poor performing and in need of improvement.

Aggregated Data: Grade-level test scores analyzed as a whole for means, standard deviations, etc.

Artifacts, documents, entries, evidence, examples, items, and materials: Terms used interchangeably, referring to the contents of the portfolio.

Authoring tools: Software programs useful in developing digitally enhanced products.

CD: An optical disk that is physically the same as an audio CD, but contains computer data. Storage capacity is about 680 megabytes (MB). CDs are interchangeable between different types of computers.

Data analysis: An analysis of standardized or classroom-based data for trends, patterns, and evidence of differences among subgroups.

Data-driven instruction: Use of ongoing (authentic, work sampling, performance, standardized) assessment data as the means of planning and delivering instruction.

Digital assets: Electronic versions of examples that are digitized and then placed in the portfolio for later retrieval. They may be lesson plans, videos, graphics, etc.

Digital Asset Management (DAM): The collection, selection, and creation of documentation.

Disaggregated Data: Grade-level test scores analyzed for means, standard deviations, etc., for each of the subgroups established under NCLB.

Dispositions: The attitudes teachers develop to think and act in a manner that is professionally acceptable.

DVD (Digital Versatile Disc or Digital Video Disc): An optical storage medium that has greater capacity than a CD. DVDs can be used for multimedia and data storage. A DVD has the capacity to store a full-length film with up to 133 minutes of high-quality video in MPEG-2 format, plus audio. (From ComputerUser.com)

Electronic portfolio/e-portfolio (digital or computer-generated portfolio): The electronic/e-portfolio sometimes referred to as a digital portfolio or a computer generated portfolio, is a multimedia approach that is typically published on the World Wide Web (WWW), a DVD, or a CD. The electronic portfolio allows the teacher to present teaching, learning, and reflective artifacts or assets in a variety of digital media formats (audio, video, graphics, and text).

ELL: English Language Learners.

Entrance portfolio: A collection of specific materials required by a teacher education program as a component of the screening and admissions process.

ESOL: English as second or other language.

Exit portfolio: A final selection of specific documents that provide substantial evidence of a teacher candidate's knowledge, dispositions, and skills of teaching and/or fulfilling the requirements of the teacher education program. This portfolio may be required to successfully complete the teacher education or certification program.

Explanations: Narratives that provide information about the evidence presented. They provide a better understanding of the document that cannot be captured by the artifact alone.

FARMS: Free and Reduced-price Meals; a federal government indicator of poverty.

Holistic assessment: Evaluation that strives to assess many facets of the learner in many ways. Methods of assessment can include observations, role plays, portfolios, and oral and written questions.

Homepage: The first page that opens at any website, or a main branch at any website. The standard HTML for the file name is index.htm. The homepage is commonly referred to as the splash page because it should initially impress the visitor to the site.

HTML (HyperText Markup Language) A format that tells a computer how to display a web page. The documents themselves are plain text files (ASCII) with special *tags* or codes that a Web browser knows how to interpret and display on a computer screen.

Hyperlink: A connection (or link) in an HTML (HyperText Markup Language) document that leads to another World Wide Web site, or another page within the same document. Hyperlinks are usually underlined or shown in a different color from the surrounding text.

Hypermedia: Units of information that are interconnected by links.

Hypermedia "card" program: A software program that allows the integration of graphics, sound, and movies in a single file. Electronic cards or screens are linked together by developer-created buttons.

In-service teacher: An individual who is employed by the school or school system as a classroom teacher or specialist.

INTASC standards: A set of teaching performances which includes the knowledge, dispositions, and skills expected of the beginning teacher. The standards were established by the Interstate New Teacher Assessment and Support Consortium (INTASC).

Interview portfolio: A polished selection of exemplary documents and reflective entries that represent a teacher candidate's best work and accomplishments.

Introductions: Narratives that are usually found at the beginning of the portfolio or at the onset of each new section with the intent to provide an overview of the forthcoming material.

ISTE: The International Society for Technology in Education: A professional organization dedicated to providing leadership and service to improve teaching and learning by advancing the effective use of technology in K–12 education and teacher education.

Link: Words in an HTML document that lead to another World Wide Web site, or to another place within the same document (also called a hyperlink). Linked text is usually underlined or shown in a different color from the surrounding text. Sometimes graphics are links or contain links. A link is activated by clicking it.

Multimedia: The presentation of information in more than one format, e.g., video, audio graphics, or text.

Multimedia slideshow software: Multimedia slideshow software allows the portfolio developer to create electronic slides that incorporate sound and video in a linear sequence.

NBPTS standards: A set of high and rigorous performance standards that identify what accomplished teachers should know and be able to do. These standards were established by the National Board for Professional Teaching Standards (NBPTS).

No Child Left Behind (NCLB): Landmark educational legislation signed into law by President George W. Bush with the ultimate goal of eliminating the achievement gap in American schools. NCLB consists of four pillars: stronger accountability for results, more freedom for states, proven education methods, and more choice for parents.

PDF documents: A standard file format that preserves all of the fonts, formatting, colors, and graphics of any source document, regardless of the application and platform used to create it.

Performance-based assessment: Assessment that requires learners to provide an answer or create a product that demonstrates personal knowledge or skills, or a better understanding of what is learned and put into practice; otherwise known as assessment of performance-based learning.

Performance standards: Shared views within the education community of what constitutes professional teaching. Standards include the knowledge, dispositions, and skills of the effective teacher.

Phases of portfolio development: A step-by-step method for working through the entire portfolio development process

Platform: The computer operating system, such as Microsoft Windows or Apple OS X.

Portfolio assessment: An approach to measuring a collection of digital resources used to evaluate teaching performance. It may be a paper portfolio or an electronic portfolio.

Pre-service teacher: Individuals that are enrolled in a teacher education program or teacher certification program. They are also referred to as teacher candidates, student teachers, or teaching interns.

Professional development plan: A teacher's set of activities that are based on identified goals for professional growth.

Professional knowledge: A foundation of information about teaching, learning, and students that provides the basis for informed decision making.

Professional teaching portfolio: A selection of artifacts and reflective entries representing a teacher's professional experiences, teaching competencies, and growth over a period of time.

Reflection: A process that requires careful and analytical thinking about issues related to the teaching profession. Reflection is a highly complex thinking process that is cultivated over time.

Rubric: Established performance criteria to be measured (knowledge and skills) using a point scale that describes the level of performance.

Showcase portfolio: A polished collection of exemplary documents and reflective entries that highlight an in-service teacher's best work and accomplishments.

Skills: The ability to transfer knowledge of teaching and learning into behaviors necessary for effective teaching.

SPA: Specialized program associations such as the Council for Exceptional Children.

Storyboarding: Creating a rough outline of what the website will look like.

Template: A model to use as a guide in making other similar items (as a portfolio template).

Web-authoring software: Applications that translate text, graphics, and other digital media into a format that is displayed by a Web browser.

Working portfolio (in-service): A collection of teaching evidence and reflections displayed as paper or digital assets that provide ongoing documentation of a teacher's growth and accomplishments related to the teacher's goals for ongoing professional development.

Working portfolio (pre-service): A collection of teaching evidence and reflections displayed as paper or digital assets that provide ongoing documentation of a teacher candidate's growth at various benchmarks throughout the teacher education program.

References

Barrett, H. C. (1999). Electronic teaching portfolios. In SITE 99: *Society for Information Technology & Teacher Education International Conference* (ERIC Reproduction Service No. ED 432 265).

Barrett, H. C. (2000). Create your own electronic portfolio: Using off-the-shelf software to showcase your own or student work. *Learning and Leading with Technology, 27* (7), 14–21.

Barrett, H. C. (2005, May 13). "At-a-Glance Guides" common software tools for creating and publishing electronic portfolios. Retrieved October 17, 2007, from http://electronicportfolios.com/ALI/index.html.

Barrett, H. (2007). Dr. Helen Barrett's favorite links on alternative assessment and electronic portfolios. Retrieved October 17, 2007, from http://electronicportfolios.com/portfolios/bookmarks.html.

Barrett, H. (2007, September 24). Dr. Helen Barrett's electronic portfolios. Retrieved October 17, 2007, from http://helenbarrett.com.

Cambridge, B., Kahn, S., Tompkins, D., & Yancey, K. (Eds.). (2001). *Electronic portfolios: Emerging practices in student, faculty, and institutional learning.* Washington, DC: American Association for Higher Education.

Campbell, D., Cignetti, P., Melenyzer, B., Nettles, D., & Wyman, R. (2001). *How to develop a professional portfolio: A manual for teachers.* (2nd ed.). Boston: Allyn & Bacon.

Darling-Hammond, L., Wise, A., & Klein, S. (1995). *A license to teach: Building a profession for 21st century schools.* Boulder, CO: Westview Press.

Delandshere, G., & Arens, S. A. (2003, January/February). Examining the quality of the evidence in pre-service teacher portfolios. *Journal of Teacher Education, 54* (1).

Fiedler, R., & Pick, D. (2004, October). Adopting an electronic portfolio system: Key considerations for decision makers. *Association for Educational Communications and Technology, 27th.* Chicago, IL (ERIC Reproduction Service No. ED 485 082).

Gibson, D., & Barrett, H. (2003). Directions in electronic portfolio development. *IT Forum, Paper #66.* Retrieved July 22, 2004, from www.electronicportfolios.com/ITFORUM66.html.

Goldsby, D. S., & Fazal, M. B. (2000). Technologies answer to portfolios for teachers. *Kappa Delta Pi Record, 36* (3), 121–123.

Interstate New Teacher Support and Assessment Consortium. (1992). *Model standards for beginning teacher licensing and development: A resource for state dialogue.* Washington DC: Council of Chief State School Officers.

Kilbane, C., & Milman, N. (2003). *The digital teaching portfolio handbook: A how-to guide for educators.* Boston: Allyn & Bacon.

Martin-Kniep, G. O. (1999). *Capturing the wisdom of practice: Professional portfolios for educators.* Alexandria, VA: Association for Supervision and Curriculum Development.

National Commission on Teaching and America's Future. (2004). *Summary report: High quality teacher preparation–Higher education's crucial role.* New York: Author.

National Commission on Teaching and America's Future. (1997, 2004). *What matters most: Teaching for America's future.* New York: Author.

Strudler, N., & Wetzel, K. (2005). The diffusion of electronic portfolios in teacher education: Issues of initiation and implementation. *Journal of Research on Technology in Education, 37* (4), 411–433.

United States Department of Education. (2002). Four pillars of NCLB. Retrieved April 10, 2008, from www.ed.gov/nclb/overview/intro/4pillars.html.

Wallace, R. C., & Porter, R. (2004). A call to arms for school leaders: Can you assist student(s) market their skill(s) and competencies through electronic portfolios? Society for Information Technology for Teachers in Education. SITE Conference 2004, Atlanta, GA.

Wolfe, K., & Dietz, M. E. (1998). Teaching portfolios: Purposes and possibilities. *Teacher Education Quarterly, 25* (1), 9–22.

Index

D

E

F

R

S

NOTES

NOTES

NOTES

NOTES

NOTES

NOTES

NOTES

NOTES

NOTES

NOTES